Jomo Kenyatta

SUFFERING WITHOUT BITTERNESS

Jomo Kenyatta

SUFFERING WITHOUT BITTERNESS

The founding of the Kenya Nation

EAST AFRICAN PUBLISHING HOUSE

East African Publishing House
Uniafric House, Koinange Street, P.O. Box 30571
Nairobi, Kenya

First published in February 1968
Reprinted March 1968

Distributed in the Commonwealth by
Heinemann Educational Books Ltd., 48 Charles Street,
London W.1 and in U.S.A. by Northwestern University Press,
Evanston, Illinois

Printed in letterpress by afropress ltd.
Saldanha Lane, P.O. Box 30502, Nairobi, Kenya

Foreword

It has been my intention for some time to make known, as a broad and factual coverage, the background of events which preceded my arrest and imprisonment, and subsequent patterns which led to my release and assumption of leadership in the Government and public life of Kenya.

The purpose of the narrative section of this book has been to trace these principal events, bringing a number of factors and influences into the record, spanning a period between the end of the First World War and the attainment of internal self-government (which we call Madaraka) in Kenya in 1963. Thereafter, in the Appendix section, there is reproduced a collection of my speeches, which serve to tell something of the continuing story of the Republic of Kenya from 1963 until the celebration of Kenyatta Day in October 1967.

It is fitting in this Foreword, looking back over nearly half a century of challenge and effort in a vastly changing human scene, that I should advance some reflections. If asked to define what causes have inspired my life and striving, I would say that I have stood always for the purposes of human dignity in freedom, and for the values of tolerance and peace. Yet today, in our sophisticated world society, such simplicities are overwhelmed by complexities of ideology and power. I sometimes wonder who, among the humble men of great or struggling nations, can really benefit, when expediency obscures justice, or when cunning and force outweigh what is right.

Politics is an arena with formidable pitfalls for the man of ideals. Yet without the driving-force of some idealism, the politician is a sterile man. I have spent my entire adult life in the service of my people. Like many others, I have at times regarded and used politics as the weapon underlying both the language and the medium of public undertaking, in pursuit of such objectives here as meaningful independence, enduring stability, national unity, economic progress and social justice. Once or twice, in all this long period, the pendulum of political fortune has swung me towards some uncomfortable situations. There were evenings of bitterness. But I could never find solace in despair.

Kenya is a living entity. On our intensive farms and ranches and plantations, as well as in the wilderness of bush and plain, life is surrounded and influenced by natural phenomena. Although the Republic of Kenya, with its refineries and factories, its power projects and research institutions, its services as a hub of communications and a centre of business, is rapidly and desirably emerging as a modern State, yet still our real problems arise more from natural causes and effects than they do from the machines.

In a life of close association with the soil of Kenya, I have found joy and humility in the seasonal rhythms both of plant and of animal life, and in the crafts of careful husbandry. But I have seen drought and flood, hail and tempest. I have seen locusts come, and crops destroyed by virus or fungus, and livestock stricken by rinderpest or tick-borne disease. One must learn to suffer and endure, to replant or rebuild, to move on again. And as with farming, so in politics, the practitioner must never lose faith.

Later portions of the narrative section of this book and much of the Appendix material will illumine the task that we describe as nation building, the momentum of which is still growing with each passing day. But as these pages will also show, I have always been concerned, since before the days when there were organised movements or regional agencies of world bodies, with the dignity and progress of Africa as a whole, so that the strength and the influence of Pan-Africanism in world affairs could be the ultimate response of our peoples.

In such a context, I should say a little here about the situation in the Congo as it was in 1964, especially since in a recent book published by one of the United States Ambassadors to Kenya there was some travesty of fact.

In November of 1964, world attention was focussed once more on the Congo, attracted by the landings at Stanleyville (now Kisangani) of Belgian paratroops carried in American aircraft, the fate of white hostages in the Stanleyville area, and the increasing employment there of mercenaries in military units of the Leopoldville (now Kinshasha) Government.

As Chairman of the ad hoc Commission on the Congo established by the Organisation of African Unity, my intervention had formally been sought — at that time — on behalf of civil prisoners of many nationalities. I undertook to do whatever was possible to prevent loss of life, while making it very clear to appealing nations that my efforts would be wholly nullified if any kind of unilateral military action were taken.

It is poignant to recall now that, a few hours before a notorious "rescue operation" was launched by the United States and Belgium, imperilled hostages were still alive. I had been in touch by telegram with the Stanleyville authorities, and I was in active discussion in Nairobi with one of their personal representatives about the repatriation of civilians through the International Red Cross.

This accredited Stanleyville representative had arrived in Nairobi on November 22, and at once, in consultation with the United States Ambassador, I arranged for a tripartite meeting on November 23. As an outcome of far-ranging submissions advanced at this meeting, it was necessary to adjourn in order that the American Ambassador could seek fresh instructions from his Government. I had hoped that a further meeting could be held that night (November 23) or on the following day. In the event, appalling happenings in Stanleyville on November 24 were launched by the paratroop landings, and an unknown number of civilian hostages were killed.

I was neither consulted about nor advised of the decision, before the news came of paratroop landings in Stanleyville. This action was taken by the United States and Belgium, despite the fact that both Governments were in possession of my most earnest views and advice, and while an Ambassador of the United States was in consultation under my chairmanship in search of negotiated means for a peaceful resolution of the recurrent crisis. Such military adventurism, which in fact failed to prevent the murder of many hostages, completely disrupted the pattern of reconciliation which had been taking shape.

Turning over such sombre pages of history can have little point unless there is reflective outcome, and a moral for men of the future to retrieve. When first consenting to preside over an African Commission on the Congo, I had no illusions at all. This was a problem of almost infinite complexity: its elements were both obvious and tortuous, coldly brutal and swiftly passionate. In theory, a paramount need was to remove all outside influence or contribution from the scene. In harsh reality, then, this was impossible to achieve. But even had there been a way, what then? Few if any of the African States were in a position to pour in their physical forces, to restore and maintain law and order, to safeguard basic services, to enable the people through the ballot-box to choose for themselves a national Government of reconstruction.

It seemed to me that an attempt must be made to exert the moral force of continental unity and Pan-African concern. My Commission, as lawfully sponsored by the O.A.U., was widely representative; deeply anxious both to curtail tragedy and to do what was right. As authorised and supported by my colleagues, my intention was to assist and conciliate, to draw opposing factions together, to save human life, and to bring about the climate of peace in which negotiated stages for the political and physical rebuilding of the Congo as a nation could have meaning. In the event, lip-service trial was given to the moral strength of all this African endeavour, but then a new crisis cut through all the threads of reason, with the abortive coup of frightened and of foolish men.

The presence of United Nations forces and advisers in the Congo then was not of itself the right answer, and from this fact can emerge a proposition in more general terms. Whatever moral principles may be embraced within international diplomacy, and whatever welcome initiative may be shown in meeting challenges to codes of conduct or the causes of human misery, many problems can arise in which the gap between local diagnosis and world understanding is so wide that writing and applying the correct prescription becomes difficult in practice. At least initially, there must be exerted the influence, and perhaps at times the discipline, of local or regional agencies. This is the point that underlies the struggles for practical cohesion, with readiness to share both contribution and sacrifice in pursuit of principles, over such areas as Africa, and South East Asia, and the Caribbean.

Disruption, disunity, isolationism: these are prime causes of friction and exploitation, and of human indignity, against which I have always set my mind. These are narrow concepts, for objectives which are selfish or petty, in a world wherein the common interests and fundamental needs of humanity are so wide.

The most essential need which I have constantly sought to proclaim and to fulfil in Kenya has been that of national unity; nationhood and familyhood must and can be contrived out of our many tribes and cultures. Nationalism rooted in loyalty to Kenya must come first, and be made a living force that can impel and compel all men and women to defend their country against both aggression and subversion. The Constitution of the Kenya Republic, and perhaps above all the thesis of African Socialism, now enshrine an appropriate philosophy, and the principles of national planning which must guide our activities.

As one of the growing pains of any young country, there must be challenges to unity and progress. In Kenya just now we have a clique, which has freely been permitted to assume the guise of an opposition Party. Its ingredients comprise elements of internal selfishness and external disruption which I earlier described as prime causes of human exploitation. But this is not a matter for surprise. A nation as a whole must learn resilience, and be permitted to mature through freedom to weigh sincerity against dialectic, wisdom against polemic, effective policy against glib theory, integrity against betrayal, truth against lies. Victory for the causes of unity and progress cannot be laid upon a country, like spreading a cloth on a table. It can only be won when all the people understand the issues, and make possible what has to be accomplished.

In the beginning, of course, there were problems far more massive and intractable than could be provided by the diversion of a factional group, pursuing a routine strategy in an unimaginative manner. At conferences prior to independence, and even when Uhuru was achieved, there was the tremendous task of creating a stable and prosperous State, in what was still a post-Emergency atmosphere, with elements of fragmentation and many unresolved problems, and with a forceful Opposition (KADU) which served to split the country.

In certain of the advanced nations, as they are called, political campaigning and close contact with the people provides sporadic excitement, going through the well-worn motions, perhaps some half a dozen times in every generation. Far more genuinely in Africa, real contact with the grass-roots of the African society has to be and to remain close, since politics, as the stuff of argument and the channel of aspiration and the safety-valve of personality and of hope, is an integral part of the living tissue of each day.

My work and my beliefs have always had their roots in service to the people, fortified at all important times by their mandate and by mutual bonds of faith. This, it may be felt, is an almost obligatory submission for any statesman to advance. But I have had the good fortune, throughout my long life, for this always to be meaningful. Today, I go onto the farms or into the homes of the people, not as Royalty bestowing condescension, but unaffectedly, understanding and sharing the tempo and tribulations of their lives. I have never grown away from the people, and at massive public rallies we meet on common ground as fellow-men. They know me best as I have always been: as one of them.

No man has ever devised any wiser criterion, for the national direction of public affairs, than Government of the people, by the people and for the people. Distorted as this simple cause may be, in sundry blocs or regions, by ambition or autocracy, by fear disguised as freedom, it has always been the core of my political purpose. And there is more to this than just morality. The latent achievement and potential contribution of the people of Africa require foundations in basic freedoms of expression, in the sense both of participation and of influence, on the road to social justice.

When approaching such challenges in Kenya as national unity and effective nation-building, I have always told my people what I believed to be the simple truth, never employing tricks to win some cheap applause or to gloss over setbacks or reality. I have left the people in no doubt about my views and intentions, or about the national policies of the Kenya Republic. It has been my task to point the way, to encourage and measure advancement, to some extent perhaps to inspire our national progress. In all this, without rushing any individual or stampeding the community, the moral force reflected in the spirit of

'Harambee' — embracing the will and the sacrifices of the people — has, with gathering success, amassed new social services and economic patterns.

We have been creating throughout Kenya a family or community spirit that in Swahili is called "Ujamaa". And the ultimate ideal would be to extend this "Ujamaa" to all humanity, recognising that all men everywhere, although in their various ways, share the same basic wish to enjoy security, the fruits of endeavour and pursuit of contentment.

The smaller nations in the world today, confronted on many sides by the towering cumulus of financial might and nuclear prospect, can do little more than set an example in furtherance of such beliefs and ideals. Together with our brothers in Tanzania and Uganda, we in the Republic of Kenya have now allied ourselves within a new East African Treaty of co-operation. This instrument implicitly acknowledges that whether or not there might be political differences as between these three States, or distinct national interests springing from historical background or contemporary realities, yet there will always remain issues on which a common front can carry us most swiftly over common ground. Completion of this Treaty derives from the strength of our belief that human need must ultimately triumph over all else. And it was heartening to learn that, at the meeting between President Johnson and Prime Minister Kosygin in mid-1967, these two leaders did not concern themselves so much with the opposing arithmetic of missiles as with means of relieving tension and of sustaining basic human aspirations.

One of the great affronts to human dignity, which I have always opposed, is that of racialism. Never a rational attribute of mankind, this has become an engineered burden on the whole cause of humanity, inflicted by the weakness of arrogance, by opportunities for rewarding domination, and by its effectiveness as a tool of political intrigue. We still have, here in Africa, outposts of what may fairly be described as fascist dictatorship, in that both the will and the rights of the people are suppressed, and an artificial authority is uneasily maintained on the Herrenvolk concept of racial divinity.

South Africa is the most powerful example of a system that is morally wrong. This is why Kenya and many

allied countries have condemned the South African
regime, seeking both to join and to weld world opinion
into an effective instrument, not for revenge or punishment or disintegration of virile economic structures, but
for pursuit of the ideal of human dignity in freedom without which mankind has no purpose. The Republic of
Kenya has made many sacrifices in applying a trade
boycott to South Africa. It has not been easy to find
alternative markets for many of our products, so that
loss of revenue and increased unemployment have
resulted. Our people have not simply borne this with
stoicism; they have insisted on it, because the underlying
principle is so vital to all that we believe. Such a gesture,
even from a small country, can never be quite meaningless. But neither can it have great practical significance,
so long as many of the massive States — so fluent in
paying lip-service to principle in United Nations counsels
— continue to uphold South Africa, making blatant their
view that commercial advantage or strategic consideration underlie a real indifference to morality.

Rhodesia is another issue, and here I wish to offer only
brief remark. In Rhodesia there has not simply been a
manoeuvre in politics. There has occurred and been upheld, quite openly, by a comparative handful of arrogant
men, a revolution against the Queen and against the
British Parliament and Judiciary. By their default, the
British Government and people have condoned treason,
and have become — in effect — accessories to the offence
of the overthrow of law which is described as revolution.
In this, they have countenanced a mortal thrust at the
very concept of a multi-racial Commonwealth, and have
shrugged off the portents of racial explosion which
British inertia and indifference to principle might one
day make more bitter. Let me perhaps offer one word of
advice to the British people. This is not an issue based
on "kith and kin". There is no refuge to be found in
propaganda innuendo of sneaking sympathy for "a jolly
sporting effort". What is threatened here is no less than
the rule of law itself, the total jurisdiction of the Courts
of Britain. Should precedent be created, insofar as major
crime may pass without the lawful retribution defined
and established by society, then the law of the jungle
must lie on the outskirts of every city and every village
and every home. And it would indeed be poignant if
Britain, which has in the past bequeathed so much to

the world in all the institutions and scruples of law, were
to be the springboard of breakdown of this fundamental
basis of orderly social behaviour.

We live in a world of remarkably rapid scientific and
technological advances. Even the motor-car had not been
seen when I first walked across the hills of Kikuyu
country. Yet soon, there will be vehicles to carry men
through Outer Space and onto other planets. Much the
same principle of extraordinary progress could be marked
in almost any field: in biochemistry and medicine; in
techniques of agricultural production and food processing; in television engineering; in sources of industrial
power. All these things, of course, profoundly influence
the unfolding environment of humanity. At the same
time, they may be slow to influence some fundamental
tenets, governing the daily lives of individuals or particular communities.

I have always believed that the best way to achieve
worthwhile human ambitions is through hard work. To
me, 'Uhuru na Kazi' is a living reality. My day is taken
up with all the tasks that can beset a Head of Government who is also Head of State, although my diaries bear
witness to duties as well as a Party President and a
constituency Member of Parliament, as a host, and even
as a farmer! My home in Gatundu is open to and entered
by many groups and delegations, since the work I under-
take in every role would be of small account if I failed
to maintain contact with the people.

This outline is not plaintively put in; still less in search
of admiration. I believe in the fullest utilisation of each
fleeting day. Of all the deadly sins, that of sloth seems
to me the most contemptible, a flaunting of the very
purpose of Creation. There is so much, always, for the
wit and resourcefulness of man — driven by the will —
to conquer or contrive.

That my countrymen and colleagues have agreed with
me is plain. By all the unglamorous statistics and
symbols with which national temperatures and pressures
are portrayed, Kenya's march since 1963 towards
economic prosperity and underlying social adjustment
has been more than just gratifying. It has been described,
by competent assessors, as something of a phenomenon.
And the one certain thing is that no such progress could
have been achieved without the fervour and the hard

work of the people. On all our farms and ranches, in the factories and offices, at the docks and in the forests, in the hospitals and schools, on the railways and plantations, in the building industry and power stations, in the warehouses and shops, in the fishing fleets and out in the National Parks, it is the living spirit of a people that has been on the move to make this progress possible. In the vanguard always, their corporate efforts more measurable and more open to public scrutiny, have been the Civil Service and the Security Forces, whose dedication to challenge and to duty have set standards for everyone to match.

But as a path to the tempting goal of prosperous nationhood — which history has sometimes shown to be elusive — hard work by itself is not enough. There must be the guideline of principles. There must be exhaustive planning, and disciplined organisation, and a liberal besprinkling over the whole national structure of ordinary commonsense.

Students of politics in Kenya will recall the occasion known as the Limuru Conference, when KANU assembled in all its strength, in a sense to map out the whole future of the Party, and to temper conflicting ideas in the fire of reason and debate. This was the meeting that saw, not so much the final debunking of old furies, as their relegation to the sidelines, with the whole KANU leadership reinforced from the essential morality and rugged sense of the people, equipping our Government and Parliament by this new mandate to continue with the steady direction of Kenya's progress in modern world society.

Perhaps especially during the early years of any nation-building period, there are many temptations and dangers to which people are liable to succumb. One of the most critical is the tendency to hide behind slogans, allowing secondhand or external dogma to serve as substitute for original and painstaking thinking. Another is the readiness to permit emotions and passions to spread like a blanket of fog over all economic and social reality. There can be so many "isms", so many eccentric or injected or irrelevant ideas, so many young men — both within and outside Parliament — with burning convictions and boundless assurance. I welcome this youthful energy. But on reaching maturity they will realise what all their frantic efforts to condemn — and impulses to disrupt — have cost their countrymen. We leave them free. We remain as we must, tolerant. We draw upon resilience, to cushion their excesses, while the country still goes forward. These are simply the prices a society must pay, to build a nation that is truly rooted in its own faith.

In a speech reproduced in the Appendix section of this book, made when I was still Prime Minister on Kenyatta Day in 1964, I proclaimed to the people, and to all friends of this country, that the foundation of our future must lie in the theme: forgive and forget. There was no point then, and there is still less purpose today, in dwelling on the past, in stoking fires of revenge or animosity, in looking back on scenes of anguish. Uhuru for Kenya had to be joyful, not sombre; vigorous rather than brooding. National integrity and national dignity were the stuff of the future, and this was ours to create. And I have sometimes looked with wonder on the jargon of our times, wherein those whose minds reside in the past are called "progressive", while those whose minds are vital enough to challenge and to mould the future are dubbed "reactionary".

We have had a testing road to travel, to instal here a stable form of Government, under an acceptable Constitution, to weave and sustain new patterns of a thriving national fabric, and to take our place in international society. Large segments of the total challenge we confronted have not yet been overcome. Yet it remains true that we shall never find work for the unemployed by substituting empty slogans for national thought and concerted endeavour. We shall never bridge the gaps between our "haves" and "have-nots" here by weakening our African Socialism through motives springing from impatience or jealousy or intrigue, but only by faithfully exerting its nature and stipulations and strength.

So many things demanding priority have had to be tackled: the refashioning of the Public Service; the attraction and marshalling of capital; Africanisation of the economy; the organisation and structures of commerce; building and equipping the Armed Forces to safeguard national security; massive efforts in expanding education from primary to post-graduate stages; the countrywide provision of health services and improvement of housing; community development and domestic welfare undertakings; substantial measures of land reform through resettlement schemes and registration of titles; techniques for the rapid modernisation of agriculture; planning and enterprise for the swift ancillary development of industry and tourism; sustaining the National Youth Service and measures of unemployment relief; conservation and management of basic natural resources; apparatus and procedures in fields of local government and industrial relations; a whole programme of better road and air communications, and the launching of projects for hydro-electric power; support for the Organisation of African Unity, and for the United Nations, in pursuit of international security and confidence; and of course the hard reality of budgeting, to meet the burden of rising recurrent expenditure, to meet increasing proportions of our own development expenditure, to make possible all the things we had to do, and to bring ever closer the things that we wanted to do.

Much indeed has been achieved. There are some who proclaim that more might have been done, or things might somehow have been different. To them, and to all enjoined to feel despondent about the triumphs they have won, let me make this one remark: there has been no other way.

Finally, appreciation is due to my old friend and colleague, James Gichuru, who has kindly read the manuscript and made some constructive suggestions. His personal contribution, to the whole narrative of dignity and stability in Kenya, has been unexcelled.

So far as compilation of this volume is concerned, thanks are due to two members of my staff. Duncan Nderitu Ndegwa, now the Governor of the Central Bank of Kenya, was the first Permanent Secretary in my own office, and as such served with distinction, for nearly four years, as Head of the Civil Service and Secretary to the Cabinet. He has contributed much to this work, in all its stages, especially in spheres of judgment and of inspiration. The practical labour, in terms of research and presentation, has fallen on Anthony Cullen, who joined my personal staff in 1964 a few months before I became the President of the Kenya Republic. He has devoted many hours to this task, in the midst of a variety of other assignments and duties. Between them, these two have produced a book which — over its span of nearly fifty years — has painted in the past against the backcloth of today. Through revelations both of facts and of motives, I hope that it will shed some light on our road to nationhood within the brotherhood of man.

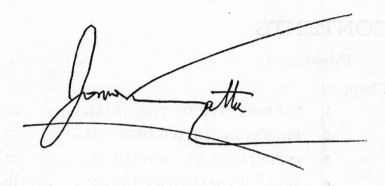

CONTENTS

Appendix of Speeches

Chapter 1

PERSPECTIVE OF THE TRIAL

ARENA OF EMERGENCY

His Excellency, Mzee Jomo Kenyatta, President of the Republic of Kenya, delivered in December 1964 the commemorative 'Celebration of Republic' — known as "Jamhuri" — speeches which appear in the Appendix section of this volume. Read in their setting of other speeches, before and since, these perhaps symbolise the philosophy and scruple, the physical and moral resilience, of the man.

His office in Harambee Avenue, Nairobi, before the move to State House was complete, was inundated at that time with cables and letters of tribute and congratulation: from Monarchs and Presidents and Prime Ministers; from writers and philosophers; from world industrialists and scientists; from politicians and Church leaders; from the great and the humble in all walks of life . . .

Yet in January 1953, this same man had stood in the dock — simply as the accused, Kenyatta — for one of the most notorious trials in all Commonwealth history. It was held at Kapenguria, an otherwise obscure African hamlet in the remote District of West Pokot, a few miles from Kenya's border with Uganda.

Kenyatta had been arrested when the Emergency was declared in Kenya on October 20, 1952. He stood trial thereafter — or what passed for trial — on the allegation that he had managed and was a member of the unlawful society of Mau Mau.

In purpose and implication, and through the weight of
the whole machinery of litigation that was brought to bear,
this was the trial of Kenyatta. But more than this, it was a
calculated enterprise, distorting all respectable trappings
of the rule of law so as to stifle and destroy this man.
There is no intention in this work to sponsor or reopen
bitterness. Mzee Kenyatta himself would not wish this.
The record now, however, must be made dispassionate,
objective. And Kapenguria made a mockery of that noble
concept, so ordinarily a property of British Justice, that
justice must perforce be done and seen.

Everything was planned and conducted with impeccable
showmanship. While principal instruments were *force
majeure* and ruthless preconception, these were most skil-
fully camouflaged beneath the emotional aura of the times.
And so powerful was the Administration that there was
every facility for officials to exploit the outcome with dis-
arming candour, as part of their outward fetish of doing
the right thing.

Even honourable men, in years thereafter, found their
doubts assuaged by the spate of suave reason from the lips
of their legal and executive advisers.

Any new or contemporary opinion on Kapenguria, when
once advanced, must have foundation on which to be
accepted. This volume in its entirety sets out the evidence.
In regard to the trial itself, there might perhaps be
protestation, that extracts — selected solely for their
relevance — may not always be objective. However,
research scholars seeking total objectivity may refresh
their memories by consulting the complete Court record.
Others with more limited opportunity may peruse newspaper files, or study one of the books which set out, as
thesis rather than narrative, to paraphrase the case. The
purpose here is not to trample over beaten paths, but point
the route to new enlightenment.

This now is the perspective of fifteen years (since
Kapenguria) of rapidly moving history. This perspective is

presented not in righteousness, but in the simpler cause of
ordinary justice, or of truth without attendant sting. For
too many years of this long time, only one side of the coin,
kept polished by the glib invective of men ensnared by
their own transaction, was presented for the world to
see . . .

A narrative must have a starting point. Here, this
documented narrative commences with the trial, principally because this is the event in respect of which the revelation of truth can take shape, and where fuller interpretation can begin.

There was, of course, feverish activity and contrivance
over the period between the arrest of Kenyatta (October
1962) and his appearance in his own defence in January
1953. This was a time of conditioning and preparation, and
of what in modern parlance might be known as "brain-
washing", on a massive local scale, and over all official
wires which reached from Nairobi to London.

It must simply be said, in terms — let it be stressed —
not of enduring bitterness but of unvarnished appraisal,
that Colonialism in the person of its servants became
committed to outrage. With every consequence of errors
and omissions dawning, the whole system, faithful to its
arrogance, felt bound to fight back. The record of the
build-up years is studded with instances of criminal
negligence, injustice, gross ineptitude, complacency,
treachery, dereliction of duty, betrayal of trust.

All these things now had (it was decreed) to be glossed
over, to be made to look respectable, to be given their
coating of official resilience. They must safely be drowned
beneath the flood of military assembly and deliberately-
distorted public opinion, which could reach such heights of
array and emotion, so quickly, that the past would be
forgotten in the present and presence of Emergency
powers, and power alone would be supreme.

The probing of future historians might discern that the
policy and understanding of the British Government may
have differed — both in intent and degree — from the policy
pursuit and attitudes of Colonial Office representatives

in Kenya, spurred on by those to whom the expression 'extremist white settlers' might justly apply. This was shrewdly recognized at the time, and was smoothly disposed of as awkwardness engulfed by heat of peril. It was held perhaps to be a trifling consequence — certainly no more — that any basically tolerant settlers on the farms, looking at Africa with realistic eyes, must be threatened by revolution after gearing themselves unfashionably to evolution. All must now be goaded by the huge fomented melodrama of brutality, the terrible tale of unprovoked rebellion, atrocities, civilisation suddenly threatened by barbarians, God by the godless, darkness versus light.

In absolute power, those in command in Kenya were corrupted absolutely. They placed many souls in purgatory. They sponsored acts beyond the comprehension of balanced minds, and remote from the reaches of pity.

And to make it all legal — this defence of their careers — they turned a Court of law into the perverted trappings of an amphitheatre. They brought Kenyatta there as a touch of brilliance which made their corruption currently impregnable. For all of truth — they thought — could be destroyed, by destroying the scapegoat at hand . . .

The principal examination of Jomo Kenyatta, as a witness in the Kapenguria trial, began on January 26, 1953. A Court transcript must necessarily note all interjections, repetitions and verbal stumbles. While these are here ignored, what follows — from this transcript — is an accurate reproduction, in condensed form, of Mzee's opening testimony on that day:

'The East African Association in 1921, with which I sympathised, opposed such things as forced labour of both African men and women, and the Registration Certificate introduced soon after the war. It was also concerned about land, and that people should have better wages, education, hospitals and roads. The Association worked by constitutional means, making representations to the Government in the most peaceful way we possibly could.

'The Kikuyu Central Association, from about 1925 onwards, pursued the same aims and objects, but by 1928 more grievances were added. Most of us had become aware of the Crown Lands Ordinance of 1915, which said something like: "all land previously occupied by native people becomes the property of the Crown, and the Africans or natives living thereon become tenants at the will of the Crown." When we realised this, we started a demand for its abolition, on the grounds that it was unfair for our people, because we were not informed of its enactment and had no say in its provisions.

'We were also protesting against the country's status being changed to that of a Colony, instead of a Protectorate. We knew the Africans would have less legal claim to their territory in a Colony than in a Protectorate, since the latter would be guided by the British Government until we could be left to our own affairs. We were told that everybody would have rights in a Colony, but Africans would have the least rights.

'If you woke up one morning and found that somebody had come to your house, and had declared that house belonged to him, you would naturally be surprised, and you would like to know by what arrangement. Many Africans at that time found that, on land which had been in the possession of their ancestors from time immemorial, they were now working as squatters or as labourers.

'I became a member of the Kikuyu Central Association in 1928, after the visit of the Hilton Young Commission which came to investigate land problems in Kenya. My people approached me saying they would like me to represent them, so I left Government service and joined the KCA. I immediately started a paper — the first newspaper in this part of the world published by Africans — called "Muigwithania".

'The KCA sought the redress of grievances through constitutional means: by making representations to the Government of Kenya, to various Commissions, and to the home Government in England.

'In 1929, I was asked if I could go to England to represent my people. By then our demands had increased, to include direct representation of the African people in Legislative Council. We were told when we approached the Government: "well, you know, we have no objection to you coming to Legislative Council or any other place of Government, providing you have education". We badly wanted to educate our children, so another reason why I went to Europe was to seek ways and means of establishing our schools.

'When I arrived in London, I prepared my case, sent a memorandum to the Secretary of State — then Lord Passfield — and made contact with Members of Parliament. There were many negotiations. A White Paper was then published saying, in essence, that the Government has decided no more African land would be taken away from them, and what was left to them would remain their land for ever. I think this reaffirmed as well another declaration — by the Duke of Devonshire in 1923 — to the effect that: "Kenya is an African territory and the African interest must be paramount, and whenever the interests of the African people and those of the immigrant races conflict, the African interests will always prevail".

'I think this 1930 White Paper was known as: "Native Policy in East Africa". But I have been placed at a great disadvantage because I cannot get my papers to present my case, so I have to rely on what I can remember. All my documents and files were taken away . . . (*Note: Mzee Kenyatta's personal files and documents were never returned to him by the Administration or the Police. An exhaustive search since Independence has proved fruitless, and the assumption can only be that they were destroyed.*)

'While in Europe, I had published the correspondence as between the KCA and the Secretary of State. I also had the opportunity of going to meet the Archbishop of Canterbury, and went to Edinburgh for an interview with the Moderator of the Church of Scotland.

'Speaking to a Committee of the House of Commons, I said we could take some of the good European and Indian customs, and those of our customs which were good, and see how we could build a new kind of society in Kenya.

'Whereas formerly it had been illegal for us to establish a school, we were now given permission by the Government to do so, if we could find land to build on, find the money to build, and find money to pay teachers. From about 1930, the Kikuyu Independent Schools Association and the Karinga ISA came into being. When I came back, I found they had over 300 schools educating more than 60,000 children, with no financial help at all from the Government.

'I went to Europe again in 1931 and stayed till 1946, when I found the KCA had been proscribed. I saw the Governor . . . (*Note: the late Sir Philip Mitchell*) . . . twice on this question, and had interviews with the Chief Native Commissioner several times to investigate the position. The Governor told me the matter would be reconsidered. He said he himself could see no reason why the Association should not start functioning, but he left the matter to his officials and to the Member of Legislative Council representing African interests. The Chief Native Commissioner said some people had behaved rashly and got themselves into trouble, so the matter was dropped.

'Our files show that the KCA was a constitutional organization, but the Police are keeping them.

'Early in 1947, when I was very busy in the activities of schools, I came to know about and joined the Kenya African Union. At the annual meeting in June, I was elected as President. The aims of KAU were to unite the African people of Kenya; to prepare the way for introduction of democracy in Kenya; to defend and promote the interests of the African people by organizing and educating them in the struggle for better working and social conditions; to fight for equal rights for all Africans and break down racial barriers; to strive for extension to all African adults of the right to vote and to be elected to parliamentary and other representative bodies; to publish a political newspaper; to fight for freedom of assembly, press and movement.

'To fight for equal rights does not mean fighting with fists or with a weapon, but to fight through negotiations and by constitutional means. We do not believe in violence at all, but in discussion and representation.

'We feel that the racial barrier is one of the most diabolical things that we have in the Colony, and we see no reason at all why all races in this country cannot work harmoniously together without any discrimination. If people of goodwill can come together, they can eliminate this evil. God put everybody into this world to live happily, and to enjoy the gifts of Nature that God bestowed upon mankind. During my stay in Europe — and especially in England — I lived very happily, and made thousands of good friends. I do not see why people in this country cannot do the same thing. To my mind, colour is irrelevant.

'Some time ago, I invited about 40 Europeans to meet me, and spent a whole day with them at our school at Githunguri. One of them said they expected to be chased away; then he apologised for the hatred that he had felt for us, and for believing that we hated the Europeans. That was a common attitude of many settlers who had never met me. I told him I was just an ordinary man, striving to fight for the rights of my people, and to better their conditions, without hating anybody.'

That was Jomo Kenyatta's own verbal outline, in January 1953 at Kapenguria, of his beliefs and attitudes and activities over the thirty years prior to the Emergency.

During this same month — in Legislative Council on January 15, 1953 — two of the Members nominated to represent African interests delivered to the House their views on the underlying causes of an Emergency condition. They made reference to grievances unheeded, African opinion discounted, piled-up economic pressures, and justice constantly denied. These are the most relevant extracts, taken from the Hansard record:

Finance for the Emergency which we have been asked to sanction would have been better spent on social services . . . The Government should have realised some time ago that something was building up . . . For a long time the grievances of the Africans have been put before the Government, but no heed has been taken and they have not been redressed. Now, when it is too late, we are asked to spend a lot of money . . . Jesus Christ would not have accepted the colour bar. But here, with the colour bar and everything happening, we are told to follow the Christian way of life . . . Is the Government consulting African opinion, the African leaders, to help the Government in dealing with this present terrorism? When the Council adjourns, the first person I meet on this question will be an African. Yet if I bring his views to the Council, nobody will listen to them . . .

I would say that the question of land is the cause of the trouble, or the main cause of Mau Mau. I think that it is now time for the Government to try and employ positive measures. What is happening with the Kikuyu is that they are suffering from land hunger. If that can be satisfied, I am sure the situation will be eased . . It is very absurd to hear from responsible people — such as the Colonial Secretary — that Mau Mau is not a child of economic pressure. It is dreadful to hear responsible people saying that . . . We know very well that Mau Mau is due to outstanding grievances of the Kikuyu people, and also other Africans. How many requests have been advanced by the Africans — say on the question of representation in this Council — and have never been heeded by Government?

These were courageous speeches at that time by Members — speaking for the African people as a whole — presumably nominated by the Colonial Governor in recognition of their maturity, and the value of their judgment on issues and provisions raised in the House.

But their words made no impression on official ears. Like Kenyatta himself, they went unheeded.

The contemporary position was simply that for thirty years, as will be further shown, pressure had been building up. When at last the ignition was fired, those responsible for ignoring all the warning dials, and the promptings of technicians, would have found it intolerable to acknowledge their negligence, or affront their conceit, by attaching some blame to themselves.

Jomo Kenyatta was selected as their villain . . .

There is no intention in this work of trying to present Mzee Kenyatta, in any context of ingratiation, as some kind of saint. This he would despise. He is a man of immense physical and mental vigour and extraordinary force of personality, driven always by those elements of compassion and dedication in leadership that distinguish in each century perhaps a handful of legendary figures.

But two things must be, and will indeed become, absolutely clear.

By the very nature and consequence of the Kapenguria trial, Kenyatta was presented to the world as the classical figure of an odious revolutionary. Through his conviction there, masquerading as legal process, he was dubbed as guilty of subversion, rebellion, arson, mass murder, brigandage and fratricide.

All this at once compounded a lie. It subsequently lingered — in any dispassionate assessment — as one of the most brilliantly calculated, fomented and perpetuated lies in the whole history of Imperial intrigue.

In reality, this lie became attached to a man who, yielding nothing of his ultimate purpose, always understood the arts and nuances of statemanship. This was a man always anxious to negotiate, prepared to move in steps. And this was the man who constantly warned that, by placing blind barricades of rejection or indifference in front of every step, there must eventually arise resentments which even he could not hold back. These warnings were given in the knowledge — as he has amply demonstrated since — that a better life for Kenya's people could only be built in a climate of stability and peace.

The second point emerges from the first. Whether as the accused at Kapenguria, or as the lawful occupant a dozen years later of State House in Nairobi, his fundamental philosophies and ideals, his ambitions and purposes, while growing in maturity or finding new outlets or applications, have really undergone no change.

EARLY DAYS IN KENYA

In his opening statement at the Kapenguria trial, which was earlier quoted, Kenyatta gave a broad outline of his views and activities over preceding decades. Rights of documentary reference and submission were denied to him then. Research and affirmed recollection since have made it possible to fill in certain gaps, adding detail and character to *precis* presentation.

Mzee Kenyatta's political life before the Emergency had three distinct phases: the early days in Kenya; the struggles and travels in Europe; and the half-dozen years back in Kenya that led up to his arrest.

The problem of land in Kenya really became an issue, both practical and emotional, at the end of the 1914-18 war. It was made more acute, soon thereafter, by fresh demarcations and the building of new roads (Dagoretti to Chania being one example) making boundaries between Kikuyu land and the European settled zone.

The East African Association — mentioned at the trial — had members from among and sought to represent all tribes. The roots of this body go back to 1919-20, when Harry Thuku was Chairman, and its Headquarters were in a house below the present site of the Norfolk Hotel. Kenyatta at that time had quit employment as a Court interpreter to become Assistant Water Engineer. He was enrolled in this Association as its Propaganda Secretary, required to contact and explain events to workers in Nairobi, and to organize visits by other leaders and speakers to places like Nyeri and Fort Hall.

By 1921, the Colonial Government started getting worried, and . . . perhaps as a rash gesture . . . Harry Thuku and some others were placed under arrest. This promoted a reaction that could, in its effect, be described as a General Strike. As Mzee has described it: "A large crowd moved into the centre of Nairobi, and gathered in deep and growing ranks around the Police Headquarters, situated then where the University College is today."

Jomo Kenyatta, whose leadership was beginning to be recognized, urged the people to sit down and keep calm, while he accompanied a delegation to the Secretariat to discuss Thuku's arrest. There, the group was advised that, if they would persuade the crowd to disperse, the Government would consider whether Thuku could soon be released.

When they returned, the delegation found that both temperature and tempers had risen. The crowd began moving in closer to Police Headquarters, from whence a shot was fired. Pandemonium followed and heavy firing ensued, until the people eventually scattered. Officially it was admitted that 25 people were killed, but in reality the casualties were in excess of 100. That night, units of the King's African Rifles were out, looking for ringleaders and breaking up any gatherings of people. Thuku was afterwards sent to Kismayu, and others to Lamu or Kwale. A general wage cut was applied to all known participants in the sudden strike.

The Kikuyu Central Association was organized around 1925, with Kenyatta — then responsible for the Nairobi water supply system — giving spare time assistance by writing memoranda and addressing meetings. At this time as well, in Nyanza, the Kavirondo Taxpayers Welfare Association was organized by Archdeacon Owen. As retort to this dawning political organization, missionaries in the central area came out in support of the Colonial Government, persuading and enabling certain Chiefs to establish a body called the Loyal Kikuyu Association, ostensibly representing the people through traditional authority, but in reality the utensil of forces opposed to nationalist demands.

When Mzee Kenyatta was urged, in 1928, to come out openly as the leader and spokesman of Kenya's people, he agreed to do so despite the well-intentioned pleadings of the Nairobi Town Clerk and the Water Engineer. They parted in mutual esteem. Then in his newspaper — mentioned at the trial — Kenyatta quoted the Biblical passages about strangers having come, taking our land and making us slaves. He was sent for by the Provincial Commissioner (now in early 1929) and was instructed to declare, in the next issue, that such passages should not be deemed to have political implication. Kenyatta managed to stall any action on this one, and in the event — not without some drama in regard to custody of passport and letters of introduction — when the next issue appeared he was on his way to Britain, travelling aboard a French ship. Last-minute objections by missionaries and members of the then Legislature were of no avail.

THE STRUGGLES IN EUROPE

Jomo Kenyatta thereafter spent some sixteen years in Europe, and travelled widely. The objects of these journeyings were twofold. As a student of anthropology, and of economics, he wanted to broaden his experience, to see the structures and consequences of many kinds of political and technical organization, and utilise many introductions to satisfy his interest in people. But all the time as well he was concerned about and in touch with, by letters and telegrams and petitions from home, the needs of Kenya's people, and all his active efforts were devoted to breaking down the rigours of Colonialism, through propaganda and discussion and negotiation.

He toured Russia briefly in 1929, and went there again — this time across as far as Siberia — in 1932. Many people had tried to persuade Jomo Kenyatta that Russian techniques in dealing with backward areas could have useful application in Africa, and he wanted to see for himself.

He visited Italy and France, and spent some time as well in Germany, where he attended one of Hitler's earliest mass meetings in Luna Park, Berlin. In 1936, Kenyatta toured Denmark, Sweden and Norway, where he was so impressed by the farming co-operatives that he made special reference to them (more than a quarter of a century later) in an early Parliamentary speech.

But Kenyatta's headquarters were in Britain, where he spent nearly all of his time. From 1930 until the outbreak of war in 1939, he lived in London, first in Cambridge Street — behind Victoria Station — and then in the Euston area. In the war period, his home was at Storrington, but for much of the time he was on tour, lecturing under the auspices of Southampton University on economics, anthropology and colonial development. For this purpose, he travelled around to visit searchlight units and military camps of all kinds, before the final invasion of France. He was also on the panel of the London School of Oriental and African Studies, available for lecturing and for teaching Swahili. After the war, Kenyatta was moved north, and based himself in Manchester for a while, this time visiting military hospitals and rest camps over a wide area.

It was during this long episode in Europe — strictly, between 1930 and 1937 — that Mzee Kenyatta wrote *Facing Mount Kenya.* Whenever he could, he was collecting material, or attending to preparation and production. He typed the manuscript himself, and did much of the work on the book at a house in Bois de Boulogne, Paris.

One of his earliest and most valuable contacts in England was Scott of the *Manchester Guardian,* to whom he was introduced in 1929. Subsequently, Kenyatta became closely acquainted with many political leaders, including Ramsay Macdonald and Arthur Henderson. But Scott was certainly responsible for illustrating the value of Press persuasion, and for paving the way towards a medium of argument and representation at which Kenyatta became increasingly adept.

A letter from Jomo Kenyatta, as General Secretary of the Kikuyu Central Association, was published in the *Manchester Guardian* on March 18, 1930. In this letter, he was concerned to establish a foundation for future work, and was already (22 years before the Emergency in Kenya was proclaimed) calling on the forces of sanity to relieve the mounting weight of repressions which could only have one end. The letter is quoted verbatim here:

The Kikuyu Central Association is not a subversive organization. Its object is to help the Kikuyu to improve himself, not to "ape" the foreigner. Our aims may be briefly summarised as:

(1) To obtain a legal right, recognized by the local Government, to the tenure of the lands held by our tribe before the advent of the foreigner, and to prevent further encroachment by non-natives on the Native Reserves;

(2) To obtain educational facilities of a practical nature, to be financed from a portion of the taxes paid by us to the Government;

(3) To obtain the abolition of the "hut tax" on women, which leads to their being forced into work outside the Native Reserves, or into prostitution, for the purpose of obtaining money to pay this tax;

(4) To obtain the representation of native interests on the Legislative Council by native representatives elected by the natives themselves;

(5) To be permitted to retain our many good tribal customs, and by means of education to elevate the minds of our people to the willing rejection of the bad customs.

Evolving from these points, we hope to remove all lack of understanding between the various peoples which form the population.

I would like to ask if any fair-minded Briton considers the policy of the KCA as outlined above to savour in any way of sedition?

The repression of native views on subjects of such vital interest to my people, by means of legislative measures, can only be described as a shortsighted tightening-up of the safety valve of free speech, which must inevitably result in a dangerous explosion: the one thing all sane men wish to avoid.

On May 1, 1931, Kenyatta had another letter published in the *Manchester Guardian,* this time on the specific question of parliamentary representation. The contemporary position in Kenya was that the Legislative Council dated back to 1908, when it was an official instrument entirely; Europeans received the franchise in 1920, and the first elections were held; the franchise was extended to Asians in 1923; by the beginning of 1931, African interests were only represented through the person of one nominated non-African. Kenyatta now was concerned not solely with the unacceptable principle implicit in this state of affairs, but also to try and make people understand why in practice it was so unreal. He wrote:

It is reported from Kenya that provision has now been made by the Government of Kenya for the appointment of two nominated unofficial Members, instead of one, to represent native interests in the Legislature. The appointment seems to be limited to Europeans, of whom one is likely to be a missionary.

We have demanded not representation by white men, but the right to be represented in the Council by Africans. Until this representation of Africans by Africans is justly settled, there can be no peace or prosperity in Africa.

Obedience to laws can only be justly enforced when those who are called on to obey them have had — either personally or through their representatives — an opportunity to enact, amend or repeal them. So long as we are excluded from this share of political power, we feel that we have been unjustly included within the operation of the laws, which in our view are only enactments aimed at the taxation and subjection of our people.

The Europeans who are not subjected to the same laws
and regulations as those under which the Africans suffer,
who do not know the home conditions under which the
Africans are forced to live, who only know the Africans
superficially, cannot speak for them. They may say what
they think the African wants, or what they would like
him to want. They cannot voice the real wishes of the
people.

These last two letters were written from his London
address. In a shorter letter (postmarked Birmingham)
printed in the *Manchester Guardian* of March 31, 1932,
Jomo Kenyatta turned to the land issue, and commented
on a recent debate in the Lords:

> Lord Olivier in his courageous speech in the House of
> Lords on March 23, pointed to the real cause of native
> discontent in Africa, and especially in Kenya. Lord
> Olivier pointed out that one of the results of the recent
> Selected Committee is that we now have "very strong
> evidence fully supporting all the claims made since 1924
> of the stealing away of native lands and granting them
> to Europeans".
>
> This land was stolen from 1902 onwards from Africans,
> sometimes through ignorance and sometimes by trickery,
> without compensation and without considering what
> would become of the Africans so evicted.
>
> What Africans want now is not promises, but deeds
> which will prove the justice of British rule.

Two years later, in a letter which appeared in the *New
Statesman and Nation* of May 12, 1934, Kenyatta wrote
from a London base, briefly and almost despairingly, about
the attitude to African affairs as typified by the itinerary
of a recent august excursion:

> The Secretary of State for the Colonies (*then
> Sir P. Cunliffe-Lister*) . . . when he visited Kenya,
> refused to meet the Kavirondo people, as he refused to
> meet the Masai Association, the Kikuyu Central Associ-
> ation, and a Joint Select Committee representing the
> whole Kikuyu community.

These bodies were informed that a Secretary of State
— visiting a Colony of less than 20,000 Europeans and
over 3,000,000 Africans — could not see his way to meet
one African group, "owing to the shortage of time at his
disposal". These things the African has to bear. He has
no means of redress at his disposal.

The New Statesman and Nation published a further
letter from Jomo Kenyatta on June 27, 1936. This was a
much fuller argument, hinged to the critical issue of land.
The KCA Secretary — as he then was — dealt with proportions of land-holding, economic frustrations to land-use, and
what later became the bitter anachronism of the 'White
Highlands'. These were his words:

"The history of native policy in Kenya, especially in
regard to the land question, affords a classical example of
the general worsening of the economic, political and social
conditions of Kenya Africans.

"More than half of Kenya's 144,000,000 acres is made up
of arid desert or semi-desert tracts. Turkana and the
Northern Frontier Province support only a very scattered
nomadic population. Drought and famine are a regular
feature. It is noteworthy that it is these very areas that
are shown in the Morris Carter Land Commission report as
'D Areas (subject to Native Priority Interest),' i.e.
intended to meet the future needs of an expanding native
population.

"The 1935 African Handbook shows that 4,700 Europeans
are holding among them about 5,200,000 acres of the most
eligible land in the Colony, some of it originally granted
to them free of all cost, the bulk held on 999-year leases
on merely nominal terms. The natives, who were pushed
out of a large part of this alienated land to accommodate
the Europeans, are today crowded in Reserves with a
density ranging from 165 to 1,100 per square mile.

"The necessity to earn money is a corollary of the
whole land question, for being landless, natives are unable
to maintain an independent existence. They are therefore

forced to go and work in the mines and on farms owned by settlers and vested interests, in order to obtain money to pay their Hut, Head and other taxes, not only for themselves but also for their dependents. Even those Africans who can find a piece of land within the Native Reserves are not allowed to cultivate economic crops, such as coffee, which would enable them to find a ready market and thereby obtain their tax money. And owing to the difficulty of earning money otherwise, the natives are compelled to work at rates of wages which their masters decide.

"When in 1932 gold was discovered within the Native Reserves, all past solemn pledges were conveniently forgotten; the Kenya Government passed a Bill through the Legislative Council amending the Native Lands Trust Ordinance of 1930, and entitling them to alienate the lands, which have since been granted to mining Companies, to be exploited not in the interests of the African peoples, but of European capitalists.

"And now, to add insult to injury, the Government proposes to establish 'White Reserves,' the Highland regions occupied by Europeans will be closed for ever against Africans and other non-European races.

"We therefore hope that the British people, especially those who believe in justice and fair play, will raise their voice in protest against the repressive policy which the Imperial Government is applying in dealing with their African wards. Even the most elementary democratic rights are denied to native races."

At virtually the height of the Second World War — on August 26, 1943 — a letter from Jomo Kenyatta was published by *The Listener,* submitted from the Storrington address. In this letter, and especially in a penetrating second paragraph, Kenyatta examined some contemporary discussion about the fitness of Africans to have their own elected spokesmen in legislative bodies, and generally to play a full part in the exertions and motivations of modern society. He declared:

"It is said by the British in Kenya that there is no native-born African well enough educated to sit in the Legislative Council. As a matter of fact, although Africans in Kenya who want to obtain a higher education are faced with almost superhuman difficulties, there are a few who by initiative, persistence and good fortune have triumphed over these difficulties, and who are today even better educated than some of the Arab and Indian representatives whose competence is not called in question, and are not less learned than some of the most respected of the Europeans.

"But education is not the sole quality needed in a representative: it is essential that he should also command the confidence of the people whom he represents, and should express their needs. If any African does this, the Europeans brand him as 'an agitator'. On the other hand, if he conforms to the standard of complacency expected of him by the Europeans, he will hardly be doing his duty by his countrymen. The dilemma is inevitable, because the settlers regard Africans as a useful supply of cheap labour, and would not wish to see them prosperous and free enough to be potential competitors.

"Let the Africans have equal educational facilities with the Europeans, and leave them free to make the best use of them. Give them an equal chance of economic enterprise, equal opportunity in business and the professions, and a say in the Government of their country. If they then show themselves unequal to the strain of western civilisation, they will have no right to resent being treated as a backward race.

"Africans who want self-government are always put off with: 'Not yet. Not till you are fit for it.' Certainly we aspire to be fit for self-government. But we should like to know who is to be the judge of our fitness, and by what standards will his verdict be pronounced?"

For the record, it was in the following year — 1944 — that the first African to enter Legislative Council was in fact nominated by the Governor to represent African interests there.

On a number of occasions, during this period in Britain, Kenyatta assisted with the formation of other nationalist groups, representing such countries as South Africa, Cameroons, and the Sudan. He also had a hand in organising the Somali Youth League, at the request of a number of Somalis who were then living in such centres as Liverpool and Cardiff. He met many West Africans whose ships had docked at Liverpool, and was always the rallying-point for those concerned with early nationalist endeavours.

He was also closely connected with the establishment and management of the Pan African Federation, which was started in London in 1935 during the Italy-Abyssinia crisis. From this concept, the International African Service Bureau emerged, to serve as a central office and library, the latter containing a number of Kenyatta's pamphlets: *Kenya the land of conflict, Hands off the Protectorates, Memoranda to the Colonial Secretary from the Kikuyu Central Association.* Kenyatta then principally organized a Pan African Conference in Manchester, shortly before returning to Kenya in 1946.

This meeting in Manchester, before he left Europe, made some considerable impact on Kenyatta's thinking, in two principal ways.

First, be became convinced that it was no longer enough to struggle in piecemeal fashion for the removal of grievances, or to secure the separate — still less the tribal — ingredients of human and political justice. He firmly decided, therefore, even at this time, that the paramount design must be to unite all the people of Kenya, and that the purpose must be nothing short of independence.

Secondly, there had been much talk at Manchester on the necessity for violence as a tool in winning independence; on the use of militant Trade Unions as shock troops; and on the whole motif of an end justifying any means.

Jomo Kenyatta took into dispassionate account the possible effect of this attitude — and its application in Africa — on the progress of Kenya towards the kind of sovereignty that would be well-ordered, and that could be secured to the accompaniment of, rather than at the price of, gathering and widely-shared prosperity. Kenyatta himself could be obdurate, and did not underestimate the tactical worth of controlled gestures of some militancy. But basically, he found violence — the "solution" to many challenges so glibly advanced by more barren minds — to be personally and even intellectually repugnant. Above all, he believed that to sow the wind of crude and unalloyed violence at that time, in Kenya, would reap the whirlwind of crushing repression in riposte; that it would simply — apart from ethics and moralities — never work; that it would not just perpetuate but magnify the miseries of the people; and that in such a process even the spring-board of resolve, giving hard-won glimpses of Kenya's future, would be buried beneath debris which could not be cleared again for many years.

Mzee Kenyatta had travelled to Europe as an African delegate, with the gathering status of national leadership. He could return now, already with much of the grasp and purview of the world statesman which he was destined to become.

THE PRE-EMERGENCY PERIOD

The portrayal of Kenyatta's activities and interests over those 16 years in Europe is sufficiently adequate to answer such questions as: what did he think? what did he do? what were his objectives? And it all serves to illumine the account of his purposes and endeavours, as submitted in summary and recollection during the opening phase of the Kapenguria trial.

When Mzee Kenyatta arrived back in Kenya in 1946, he found — as explained in his statement at Kapenguria — that the Kikuyu Central Association had been proscribed. Nonetheless, he was met at the station by former KCA members and colleagues, and taken to a house at Dagoretti. He was told, by this welcoming committee, that the KCA spirit was still underlying the battle for human and political rights. Its activities could no longer be openly conducted, but were pursued in some clandestine ways.

Kenyatta now was armed with so much more experience, and with new and fresh convictions. He was no longer thinking in KCA terms as at one time defined. He explained this to his old associates, and persuaded them that what was at stake was no longer a Kikuyu battle, with limited objectives, but a national struggle for the independence of the country, involving the people of Kenya as a whole.

The contemporary advice and activity of James Gichuru — whose beliefs and aspirations ran parallel with those of Kenyatta — was a major factor at that time. In 1944, Gichuru had been the principal founder and first President of the Kenya African Study Union, which was renamed the Kenya African Union in 1945.

Gichuru also met Mzee Kenyatta at the station, on the arrival day in 1946, and over the following months the two men worked closely together. In June 1947, James Gichuru stepped down to allow Jomo Kenyatta to become President of KAU, which by then — after a further year of maturity — had become better organized. Kenyatta at once started to codify and expand the KAU as the instrument through which his aims — through which universal African objectives — could be pursued by wholly constitutional means.

It was not an easy time to assume responsibility. In a number of areas, there was sporadic unrest. Around the beginning of 1948, there was trouble in Murang'a, the Fort Hall District to the north of Nairobi. The responsible Official there was Coutts . . . (now in retirement as Sir Walter Coutts) . . . who called on Kenyatta for assistance. These two men toured the area together addressing barazas, and the situation at once quietened down. Over the ensuing decade — when Coutts was intimately involved in what

might objectively be called the strategic persecution of
Kenyatta — he never referred to this assistance.

Jomo Kenyatta made no lavish promises. Right from the
early days of his task as KAU President, with the clear
aim of strengthening national character, he spoke to the
people in terms of hard work and the rule of law. For
example, during the annual conference of KAU in Nairobi
on July 6, 1948, he said this:

> Africans want freedom to govern themselves. But if
> we want freedom, we must eschew idleness. Freedom
> will not come falling from Heaven. We must work, and
> work hard, particularly on our shambas and on soil con-
> servation. We must build ourselves clean houses, which
> comply with the laws of health. We must eat only clean
> food, which has been properly cooked. If we use our
> hands, we shall be men. Otherwise, we shall be worth-
> less.

> After getting rid of idleness, we must get rid of our
> reputation for robbery and theft. There is no need to be
> a thief — if you have no other work, you can obtain all
> you need by getting hold of a jembe. I do not want to
> see any able-bodied man loafing around without work.

Still as President of KAU, Kenyatta then visited Meru
on August 18, 1948, and delivered a similar message:

> God has given us a good fertile country, and we can
> grow good crops. We used to say that the Europeans got
> rich by planting coffee. But when I was in Europe, I
> heard that some parts of our country had been opened
> for the planting of coffee by Africans. Then I came and
> saw that very fine coffee had been planted in Embu and
> Meru. Here you can work day and night to grow the
> best coffee possible. Where do you think all the fine
> things owned by Indians and Europeans come from?
> They do not come down from Heaven, I can tell you.

> If you want to be respected by others, you must be-
> have well and with restraint. You must tell the truth

at all times, and avoid idleness. Have nothing to do with thieves, who — not working themselves — live on other people's property.

In respect of the next three years, many more illustrations could be given of strictures or recommendations in similar vein. But the purposes of this treatise do not really require a catalogue of Kenyatta's every word.

Suffice it to say that, in the period 1948 to 1951, the KAU President devoted himself to dogged work and planning, with pauses for consolidation. First and foremost, perhaps, he was concerned with the welding and improving of the Kenya African Union as an effective constitutional machine. This involved the patient assembly and the gathering pattern, over an ever-wider radius, of political structure and discipline, the appointment of office-bearers, the decentralization of authority and effort to proven colleagues. Interwoven into all this were the time-absorbing processes — frequently frustrating — of education and the management of schools, adult literacy, and the raising of finance.

Perhaps especially, throughout this period, Jomo Kenyatta set out to build solid bridges of thought and activity across to all districts of Kenya. Arrangements were made at an early stage for Kenyatta to address public meetings in Meru and Embu, and to attend a public rally in Kitui. Later he went on tour throughout Nyanza. Other links were sought, and duly developed, with the people of Western Kenya and the Coast.

Over this vital span of years — 1948 to 1951 — there was the first emergence of a feeling in Kenya that "we are all in this together". This might be regarded as Mzee Kenyatta's supreme achievement at that time, springing from his tremendous personality and gift of leadership, always exerted in such a way as to co-ordinate with — rather than to dwarf — the efforts of such men as Gichuru and Koinange, who in the countrywide sense were (to begin with) better known.

Kenyatta seized every opportunity, as in the fight against the *kipande* (identity card) system, to promote or place emphasis upon issues on which the Africans felt strongly, so that national unity would be strengthened both consciously and subconsciously through themes and struggles which could bind all the people together. He used the Kenya Teachers College at Githunguri to bring representatives of many tribes together, and thus to ramify educated leadership. He worked with and through the Chiefs everywhere, who gladly provided him with lodging and paid heed to his words.

In 1951 itself, the Colonial Secretary in the then Labour Government . . . (*Mr. James Griffiths*) . . . visited Kenya to see things for himself. As an outcome of his deliberations in Nairobi, the composition of the Legislative Council saw a change. On the Official side, there now appeared eight ex-officio and 18 Nominated Members, all subject to the Government Whip. Ranged against them (technically) on the Unofficial side of the Council were now 14 Europeans, six Asian and two Arab Members, all elected. There was still no elected African, but the number of Nominated African Members — located on the Unofficial side — was increased to six.

Then came the year of the Emergency: 1952.

In respect of this critical year, it will be necessary — whatever the risks of repetition — to trace Kenyatta's journeys and utterances in some detail, with the latter verbatim. As President of the Kenya African Union, and now with undisputed national stature, he travelled widely in Central Province and the Rift Valley, delivering a series of speeches.

The record of evidence at this point illustrates beyond rational doubt that, far from being a catalyst of disaster, Kenyatta was an implacable opponent of lawlessness and violence. By all his words, and by his very presence, he stood unyieldingly for nationalist demands, to be secured by the forces of peace.

He risked his life, before he was arrested, to strengthen his national Party. His principles, rooted in personal philosophy tempered by wide experience, were those of constitutional means. Beyond this, he could envisage how terrorism must provoke such reprisals, and permit such propaganda, as to undo — or set right back — the effect of solid preparation and persuasion over thirty years.

It seems remarkable in retrospect that, in 1952, men of ingrained honesty, and often of undoubted brilliance, should have stifled or have found themselves deserted by such attributes. Some were inexperienced in Africa. Others were too experienced in the evasive inertia, followed inevitably by the face-saving measures, of paternalism. Some were swept along in the stream of a kind of witch-hunt, following the killing of a Police Officer and defiance of authority by a semi-religious organization. All were caught up in a monstrous lie.

The national Swahili newspaper *Baraza* — one of the *East African Standard* group of publications — covered a meeting at Muguga, about fifteen miles from Nairobi, in its issue of April 12, 1952. This account was quoted in evidence, incidentally, during the Kapenguria trial.

Baraza was staffed by professional journalists, who reported that: "Mr. Jomo Kenyatta, the President of the KAU, said last Saturday that, because of the rumours that had spread everywhere that KAU is connected with an Association which was proscribed — that is, Mau Mau — there should be no other meetings after the close of KAU meetings".

According to this entirely independent newspaper, the following announcement was then made at the Muguga meeting: "Let the people disperse after the KAU meeting has finished. Mr. Kenyatta does not like the name of KAU to be mixed up with Mau Mau".

Also quoted in the Court records was a report in the newspaper *Sauti ya Mwafrika* of June 20, 1952, in refer-

ence to a speech by Jomo Kenyatta at Naivasha at that
time. In this speech, he emphasised that demands must be
pursued peacefully, and warned against racial intolerance.
This — be it noted — was not a subtle or strategic address
to a select group of intelligentsia, but one of a series of
orations to the ordinary people who gathered in thousands
to hear him, standing in groups or perched in trees or seated
on the ground. The report of this Naivasha meeting read:

> When Mr. Kenyatta started to speak, he took a long
> time explaining the aims and objects of the Kenya
> African Union. He said that every member of the KAU
> must follow these aims and objects, which were to make
> demands to the Government in a peaceful way and
> through agreement. Mr. Kenyatta explained the benefit
> of getting our freedom in a peaceful way. He said some
> people think that when the KAU demands freedom, it
> intends to oust the other races when it achieves free-
> dom. But he said this was not the aim of KAU. When
> freedom was achieved, Africans would safeguard the
> foreign races who were in Kenya. He went on to say
> that KAU was an African organisation, agitating for
> education, business, social services, better wages, land,
> and African freedom to rule himself in a peaceful way.
> All these things will be achieved by the hard work of
> Africans. If we want our freedom we must set aside
> laziness, because laziness brings theft and robbery. We
> must be faithful and responsible Africans. We must love
> each other, and love other races as well. He ended his
> speech saying: I beseech you to become members and
> work hard.

The people at these meetings knew that Jomo Kenyatta
had been in England for a long time, and was therefore
familiar with the British people and their strength and
their ideas. It was noted that — against this background
— Kenyatta was fully prepared to speak out for the rights
of the Africans, and for the emergence of Kenya, and
against the Colonialism practised by Britain. This carried
great conviction among the African people. No other

leader, with or without such roots in experience and calcu-
lation, had seemed so undismayed by British power, or had
offered the real gleam of an alternative to the tradition of
Colonial omnipotence.

Then came two enormous mass meetings, of the greatest
possible significance to any appraisal of Mzee Kenyatta's
activities and objectives over this period. The first of these
was a KAU meeting at Nyeri on July 26, 1952, with an
attendance of at least 50,000 people.

There is an official record of his words at this meeting.
As an orator on such occasions, Kenyatta had — and indeed
still has — a magic touch and a capability without peer.
He could have inflamed this crowd and turned the country
onto any chosen path, bending the future to his will. In
the event, this was the occasion when he called for national
unity rather than subversion, and for the faithful pursuit of
democratic principles. He proclaimed that violence and
thuggery could only delay Kenya's independence. Denouncing Mau Mau and lawlessness, he urged this vast
assembly, and through them the millions to whom his
words would gradually seep, to renounce force and rely
instead on the supreme power of justice and brains.

It must, in all rationality, be accepted that the official
record of this speech was not kept hidden at the time from
the Governor, and from his principal executive and legal
advisers. If it was, such an eventuality seems too bizarre
for ordinary comment. But the presumption that it cannot
have been lends weight to the belief that Kenyatta's
arrest not only began the compounding of a lie, but also
symbolised an official environment composed — in whatever dismal proportion — of the elements of guilt and
panic.

What follows now is a quotation from the official record
of this Nyeri speech, abridged only for the purpose of
excluding repetition, humorous asides, parochial comment
or traffic-control strictures to the crowd:

4 Kenyatta, Nation

"*Jomo Kenyatta* . . . I want you to know the purpose of
KAU. It is the biggest purpose the African has. It involves
every African in Kenya, and it is their mouthpiece which
asks for freedom. If we unite now, each and every one of
us, and each tribe to another, we will cause the implementation in this country of that which the European calls
democracy. True democracy has no colour distinction; it
does not choose between black and white. We are here in
this tremendous gathering under the KAU flag to find
which road leads us from darkness into democracy. In order
to find it, we Africans must first achieve the right to elect
our own representatives. That is surely the first principle of
democracy. We are the only race in Kenya which does not
elect its own representatives in the Legislature, and we are
going to set about rectifying this situation. We are not
worried that other races are here with us in our country,
but we insist that we are the leaders here. We want our
cattle to get fat on our land, so that our children grow up
in prosperity; we do not want that fat removed to feed
others. KAU speaks in daylight. He who calls us the Mau
Mau is not truthful. We do not know this thing Mau
Mau . . . (*Note: this means, in the idiom, that we do not
"want" or "recognize" or "approve" Mau Mau*) . . . We
want to prosper as a nation, and as a nation we demand
equality, that is equal pay for equal work. Whether you
consider a chief, a headman or a labourer, he needs in these
days increased salary. He needs the salary that compares
with that of a European who does equal work. We shall
never get our freedom unless we succeed in this issue.
Those who profess to be just must realize that this is the
foundation of justice. It has never been known in history
that a country prospers without equality. We despise
bribery and corruption, those two words that the European
repeatedly refers to. Bribery and corruption are prevalent
in this country, but I am not surprised. As long as a people
are held down, corruption is sure to arise, and the only
answer to this is a policy of equality. If we work together
as one, we must succeed. Our country today is in a bad
state for its land is full of fools, and fools in a country

delay the independence of its people. KAU seeks to remedy this situation, and I tell you now it despises thieving, robbery and murder, for these practices ruin our country. Those people are wrecking our chances of advancement. They will prevent us getting freedom. We want a Commission in this country, a Royal Commission to inquire into the land problem. I think the Europeans here realise in their heart of hearts that our grievance is true. I will never ask you to be subversive, but I ask you to be united, for the day of Independence is the day of complete unity; if we unite completely tomorrow, our independence will come tomorrow. This is the day for you to work hard for your country. If there are two different types amongst a single people, we separate unity. KAU is a good Union, and we do not want divided people. I think Mau Mau is a new word. Elders do not know it. KAU is not a fighting Union that uses fists and weapons. If any of you here think that force is good, I do not agree with you. Remember the old saying that he who is hit with a club returns, but he who is hit with justice never comes back. I do not want people to accuse us falsely, that we steal and that we are Mau Mau. I pray to you that we join hands for freedom, and freedom means abolishing criminality. Whatever grievances we have, let us air them here in the open. The criminal does not want freedom and land; he wants to line his own pocket. Let us therefore demand our rights justly. When the Royal Commission comes, let us show it that we are a good and peaceful people, and not thieves and robbers. There are more than 100,000 people in the United Kingdom who have supported our Land Petition. The weapons with which we will fight are justice and brains.'

In the brooding and ominous atmosphere of that time, there could hardly have been a more courageous and a more pertinent speech. Leaving justice out of reckoning, it would have been possible then for the Colonial system to co-operate with Kenyatta, to stamp out the embers of terrorism before these were flared into holocaust, and allow him to split the incoming tide of nationalism into its com-

4*

ponent constitutional waves. But a few weeks later, Kenyatta was arrested, and an awful perfidy began.

The second of these equally large mass meetings was held at Kiambu on August 24, 1952. Using at times a different idiom, and often in more forthright phrases, Jomo Kenyatta here covered much the same ground. There is again an official record of the speech, and in this case there is no room for doubt that it was at once made available to the highest authorities, although no reference to the content of this speech was made by the Prosecution at Kapenguria. The following extracts are from the official record:

> Jomo Kenyatta started his speech with these words — "Many people were asked what this meeting is about and who the organizers are. The meeting is of the Kikuyu elders and leaders, who have decided to address a public meeting and see what the disease in Kikuyuland is, and how this disease can be cured. We are being harmed by a thing which some people seem to call Mau Mau".

> Kenyatta went on to ask all those who were against Mau Mau to raise their hands. Response was immediate and unanimous. He then went on to talk about the objects of the KAU, and to disclaim any association between the Union and Mau Mau activities. He ended his speech with these words — "Let us agree not to engage in crime. We have pleaded for more land for many years. A Commission will soon be coming out to look into the land question. If you do not stop crime, those people who come out on the Land Commission will be told that we are thieves, that we are this, that we are that, which would do us immeasurable harm. We must now work together".

The newspaper *Baraza* covered this Kiambu mass meeting quite independently of the official recorders representing the Administration and the Police. The report from *Baraza* which follows was eventually introduced — by the Defence — in evidence at the trial:

Amid cheers and applause, Mr. Kenyatta told his listeners that they would hear things that will put their country right; things which will bring peace and prosperity. Quoting Kikuyu proverbs, he said the sickness of the soul cannot be cured by the knife but by debate; discussion brings agreement, but silence brings suspicion and hatred.

He went on: "Mau Mau has spoiled the country. Let Mau Mau perish for ever. All people should search for Mau Mau and kill it. We want the Government to give us freedom to rule our own country, so we may live in happiness in this country which we were given by God. We do not want to oust the European from this country. But what we demand is to be treated like the white races. If we are to live here in peace and happiness, racial discrimination must be abolished. Our children require good education; we do not want them to be fools. We want higher education subsidised by Government, because we pay taxes to help our children. Workers should have their own organizations, just as in other countries of the world. Successful farmers should be given loans by the Government, to enable them to buy agricultural machinery and improve their farming, in the same way as the European farmers. KAU had requested the Government to allow Africans to convene meetings, to make their demands known peacefully, and if this was agreed there will be no trouble in the country".

He encouraged people to work hard on their farms and in business. Drunkenness was the root of much evil, and had turned many men into thieves.

Only 57 days elapsed after these declarations before Kenyatta was arrested. It is possible to ascribe motivation, not with the assurance of testimony, but at least with the confidence that has to emerge from the absence of alternative assumption. It must have been thought, by those responsible, that here was a man drawing inconveniently near to the attainment of at least some legitimate demands, by lawful means. It must have been thought that here was the one mature and powerful leader, in whose absence ambition — or even rebellion — could speedily be crushed. But whatever the composite of motives and emotions, Kenya was plunged into disaster. And those annals of justice to which the British people cling, with such modest and seemingly-casual devotion, were made to look shoddy, by the work of frightened servants of the Crown.

A few days after the Kiambu mass meeting of August 24, the Member for Law and Order in the Colonial Government of Kenya addressed a letter to the Colonial Office in London. Enclosing some draft legislation, he remarked at one stage: "Last Sunday, Jomo Kenyatta himself publicly condemned Mau Mau at a meeting of 30,000 Kikuyu, all of whom held up their hands at his request to signify that they approved his denunciation of Mau Mau. If this resistance movement gathers strength, then I think we shall succeed in rolling back the Mau Mau movement before too long. For the time being, it looks as if the thugs, who are the militant element in Mau Mau, have got their heads down."

There is no subsequent record of demur by the Member for Law and Order when Kenyatta was arrested. No more than imaginative theory could be devised, after this lapse of time, how his voice was silenced.

After Jomo Kenyatta was arrested, the reaction among all his people can hardly — looking back on it — be captured in words that are remote from criticism on grounds of seeming precious and melodramatic. But to serve the purpose of this volume, an attempt at explanatory description must clearly be made.

Profound shock is too ordinary a phrase. It was as though a cold, soughing wind from the deep blue ice of Arctic despair blew through the city streets and the townships, out into the villages, over the shambas, into the huts of the people. They were numbed by the cold and the cruelty, which tore their roots away, and their shelter, and their hopes of any future, and left them as orphans, bereft.

Kenyatta is gone . . . They have seized Kenyatta . . . Kenyatta is lost to us . . .

This was the message, carried by the growing gale of anguish. But not just a man had been taken away. Kenyatta was the living symbol, of aspiration, of self-respect, of yearnings, of the dawn of justice, of relief of hopelessness, of expression of all their resentments, of a glimpse of new life. He had stood amongst them like a mighty tree, their strength and their shelter against all the powers of exploitation, of rejection, patronage, neglect, discrimination. He was their champion, their statesman, their undisputed leader. He was their courage and their confidence, in face of frustrations set afire in virile men who are treated with contempt.

And when Mzee was lost to them, when the Old Man was taken away, the gale was whipped up into a hurricane. Men in their loneliness, and in their anguished fury, robbed of their hope and their inspiration and their discipline, set out to rend and tear. If the bulwark of hope was taken from them, then let there be catastrophe. If the web of peace was torn aside so brutally, then let there be war. If justice was denied to them, then let there be anarchy. If constitutional enlightenment was trampled underfoot, then let there be steel and fire. If compassion were dead, let there be cruelty. If the light had gone out of the world they knew and hoped for, let all be dragged down into the same darkness.

This in verity was the spark which plunged Kenya into such disaster. Brooding as had been the urge to rebel against repression, against privilege and denial, this one vicious stroke of Kenyatta's arrest unleashed the flames of unbridled revolution. There were sporadic and horrifying crimes before October 1952. But men did not take to the forests — en masse — before the Emergency. This is the truth, that must gnaw at the conscience of still-living men.

This last point is important, and worthy of emphasis. Those who built up an organisation of unbridled violence in Kenya were never the political associates or executive colleagues of Kenyatta. And while oathing of a general "binding" or "obedience" character could be traced back for some years, the so-called "killing oath" and some extremes of obscenity only developed after Mzee Kenyatta — the Old Man — was taken away.

In Britain at the time, there was at least one protesting voice. Speaking in the House of Lords on October 29, 1952, Lord Strabolgi declared: "That brings me to the arrest of the leader of the Kenya African Union, Mr. Kenyatta, who I am informed by those who know him and know his work has had no connection whatsoever with Mau Mau outrages, and is in fact one of the most farsighted Africans, who could be a great leader."

Lord Strabolgi's perception did him credit. But by then, several thousand miles away from Westminster, the die had been cast.

TRAVERSTY OF JUSTICE

Preceding sections giving some glimpse of early days in Kenya, the struggles in Europe, and the vital pre-Emergency years, comprise the setting against which Mzee Kenyatta's opening statement at Kapenguria may be recalled.

Such passages serve as well to illumine some important remarks he made a fortnight afterwards — on February 9, 1953 — during his re-examination as a witness by leading Defence Counsel, Mr. D. N. Pritt Q.C., Kenyatta said then:

'I blame the Government because — knowing that the Africans have grievances — they did not go into these grievances: shortage of houses in places like Nairobi, land shortage, and poverty of the African people both in the towns and in the Reserves. I believe if the Government had looked into the economic and social conditions of the people, they could have done much good.

'And instead of joining with us to fight Mau Mau, the Government arrested all the leading members of the Kenya African Union, accusing them of being Mau Mau. It should have been the Government's duty to co-operate with KAU to stamp out anything that was bad, such as Mau Mau. Instead of doing that, they have arrested thousands and thousands of people who would have been useful in helping to put things right in this country. It is on these points that I blame the Government; they did not tackle the business in the right way.

'They wanted — I think — not to eliminate Mau Mau, but to eliminate the only political organization, the KAU, which fights constitutionally for the rights of the African people, just as the Electors Union fights for the rights of the Europeans and the Indian National Congress for the rights of the Asians. I think and believe that the activity of Government in arresting all the leading members of KAU, who are innocent people engaged in ordinary business, is not the right way of combatting Mau Mau. Most of the people behind bars today are people who would be helping to adjust things and eliminate Mau Mau from the country.

'We know pretty well that the reason for our arrest was not Mau Mau, but because we were going ahead uniting our people to demand our rights. The Government arrested us simply because, when they saw we could have an organization of 30,000 or 40,000 or more Africans demanding their rights here, they said: we have an excuse to stop this — Mau Mau.'

This clearly went to the root of the matter, and the presentation of this truth has been curiously hushed up — or simply unseen by superficial observers of Africa — in almost all subsequent literature and discussion.

But what of the trial itself? How was this conducted, and what was the calculated arrangement of the Prosecution case?

This may be gauged from Mr. Pritt's final address, spread over two days beginning on March 2, 1953. Here again, any uneasiness about objectivity may be sensibly dispelled. Full transcripts, and other documentary testaments of almost equal weight, exist today. Every point may be checked and affirmed. And beyond this, while the whole tone and substance of the final Prosecution address — analogous in length and erudition — was spotlighted and paraded *ad nauseam,* few opportunities have existed until now to bring into the light of day the nature and manoeuvres of this litigation. It must be flatly stated that the rigged trial at Kapenguria — clinging to the skirts of the law as its facade — brought British justice, unknowingly to the mass of the British people, into sorry disrepute.

There is a matter that should be disposed of at this point. During the trial, and in later years, much play was made of the alleged political affiliations and international contacts of the leading Defence Counsel, Mr. Pritt. Insofar as any such allegations may have held any substance, and even then assuming that opinions based thereon could be of worth, all such issues are considered for the purpose of this volume to be totally irrelevant. It is nowhere in dispute that as Counsel for the Defence at this trial — the only capacity in which Mr. Pritt figures in this narrative — his legal performance, despite many imposed and mechanical handicaps, was masterly.

It is impractical to reproduce Mr. Pritt's final address in full, since in the Court record this occupies 76 foolscap pages of type, often single-spaced. It is inevitable in this that there should have been some repetition, some clipped comment, some pouncing between arguments or from note to note, some purely legal submission with references, some exchanges of acid courtesy when the Prosecution objected to a point; and at no time did a learned Counsel so calculate his style of delivery as to make this well amenable to the different medium of print. But what follows now is an accurate precis, employing a selection of Mr. Pritt's unaltered words, of the case as he saw it at that stage:

'The prosecution case in this very serious litigation was scarcely properly prepared at any stage, either in the weeks or months preceding the charges, or in the weeks or months when the accused were already in detention, or during the period of the case itself.

'It does not seem that the prosecution has ever made up its mind on what is the essence of its case against the accused.

'I could understand the prosecution attitude if some political or other pressure had brought about the launching of a case that never should have been launched, but in no other way can I understand it.

'Some of the witnesses we wanted to call were in England, and the Government of Kenya refused to give us any safe conduct for them to come here.

'I have constantly wondered why so much of the prosecution evidence, and so much of their examination of the accused and witnesses, has seemed so remote from the allegations contained in the charges, which relate to management and membership of Mau Mau.

'Managing Mau Mau? Well, where? In what fashion, with what assistance, in what office, with what policy, with what documents? There was never anything.

'In order to convict Mr. Kenyatta of managing, the evidence would have to show that he is the manager, that is to say the one person who is at the head of the management, and not just one of a number of persons taking part in management. Therefore I would submit that Mr. Kenyatta not only cannot be convicted of being a manager, as a matter of law, because there is no evidence of his management in that sense of the word, but that he cannot be convicted of assisting in the management, since he is not charged with assisting in the management.

'The prosecution's case is sought to be built up out of all sorts of little bits and pieces, and little items on the periphery, and never any real evidence of anything seriously connected with Mau Mau.

'The charge against Kenyatta is that — from August 1950 onwards — he was managing Mau Mau. It is suggested there is some evidence to prove this because he drafted a letter in 1948, which was never sent, addressed to former members of the Kikuyu Central Association, asking them — in effect — to come and see him.

'It is of course perfectly true and obvious that, in this world of scapegoats, whenever you do something that somebody does not like, you are called Mau Mau in some parts of the world and Communist in others. In the United States, General Marshall has even been called a Communist.

'You have to prove something grave and terrible, that the accused participated in a terrorist organization, whereas there is very substantial evidence that the body in which they are most prominent — the Kenya African Union — is a plain and outspoken enemy of that organization.

'It is obvious that if Mau Mau is anything like it is shown to be, then it must be bitterly hostile to the one great African organization with a large membership, and capable — as the evidence showed — of recruiting in broad daylight at one single meeting 4,000 new members putting down their subscriptions in hard cash. The Kenya African Union is seeking to travel constitutionally some way down the road along which Mau Mau wants to travel by terrorism, and every time the KAU can enlist a new member, Mau Mau loses the possibility of enlisting a member.

'There was not one syllable of anything that Mr. Kenyatta had ever said or written, that could be put to him by the prosecution, that contradicted in any form his statement of his moderate and constitutional policy.

'The prosecution case at one point could be put like this — because a man is aware that someone is publishing a song book, he becomes criminally liable as a manager of an illegal organization which is not mentioned in the song book, since some of the songs in the book advocate a policy which is also advocated by the illegal organization in question. This is the sort of nonsense that develops in modern political repression. You might as well find a subversive political organization demanding equal pay for equal work, and try and link this with some responsible organization having similar demands, such as the Liberal Party in England. In this case, there is no evidence whatsoever of any sale of these books, or of any songs being sung from these books; they were only published three or four months before the Emergency.

'We have the Rawson Macharia incident resting on one weak witness countered by ten good witnesses, and I submit this incident is now completely dead . . . (*Note*: The Macharia "evidence" was seized upon as a factor upholding the conviction of Kenyatta at this trial. Later in this volume it will be shown that Macharia was carefully instructed, bribed and duly rewarded, for committing perjury at Kapenguria) . . . If the prosecution so behaved over this incident, that one cannot have any confidence that they even verified that they had a reliable story, we may think equally badly of the rest of their case.

'Again, in respect of the Muthondu incident, the prosecution put a solitary witness into the box, but failed to make such enquiries among other witnesses as must have led them to drop this allegation.

'They decided not to call this woman because they formed the view that she was unreliable and untruthful. I think this is the most magnificent example of sheer impudence I have ever heard in a Court in my life. The people who called Rawson Macharia, the people who also called Njui, the people who also called Waweru, the people who called Munyi, start suddenly becoming, if you please, fastidious about their witnesses. I leave this to the amazement of the multitude.

'The prosecution line, in respect of utterances at meetings, seems to be — if you don't at any time denounce Mau Mau, that is very wicked of you, and when you do denounce Mau Mau you don't mean it. Such a case is a fake.

'The prosecution is brought on behalf of the Government. The Government would presumably have their own intelligence reports of various meetings. These would presumably convey to the Government the exact extent to which Kenyatta had denounced Mau Mau. Given these reasonable assumptions, the Government and prosecution would surely have said to themselves — well, whatever else we can do, we can never make out a case that he failed to denounce Mau Mau at such-and-such a meeting, because it is obvious that he did denounce it.

'The prosecution conducted this case for many weeks as though there had never been a Kiambu meeting last August, and never saying a word about it. In due course — although we lacked the facilities to prepare as we would have wished — we proved that the meeting was held, that it was attended by 30,000 people, that it was considered by the Press and the public as a huge success, that it was accepted at its face value to be a genuine and important step in the fight against Mau Mau, and that it was broadcast. Then, of course, the prosecution found themselves in the pit — I will not say the pit which they dug for themselves, because that would imply some form of active thought — but the pit which they must have known was there, and into which they must have known they would fall if they did not take some precautions. Now they cannot answer, because even if there were any evidence by which they could answer, it is too late for them to call it.'

That devastating indictment of the case as brought might conceivably have had greater effect under the salutary glare of worldwide publicity media. In fact, the address was perforce delivered in a situation so remote from Nairobi, and so bare of amenities, that — as one journalist put it thereafter — it might as well have been Tibet. And even Nairobi in those days lacked the equipment and facilities that are commonplace today. The whole intrigue was nourished on such careful advantages . . .

On April 8, 1953, the 58th day of the Kapenguria trial, judgment was delivered by the magistrate, Mr. R. S. Thacker, Q.C. The record shows that Kenyatta was convicted on both counts, sentenced to seven years imprisonment, with a recommendation that he be confined thereafter.

In all the history of legal process, there can hardly have been a more astounding verdict as an outcome of trial proceedings. It caricatured — rather than echoed — those farcial performances of law in Police States which, before and since, have been widely condemned by humanists and liberal-minded men.

Almost at once after the trial, the magistrate left by air for Britain. Some time afterwards, it was reported in Kenya that he had been admitted to the Bar in Southern Rhodesia. These facts, too, could lend some substance to suspicion, which must now be felt by the most credulous of mortals, that the issue and the conduct of this trial involved more than jurisprudence.

Another lawyer on the Defence side at Kapenguria, speaking in Legislative Council in May 1961, made further revealing comment on this whole litigation, and on the circumstances in which it was conducted. In the interests of chronology, these revelations will be introduced at their appropriate place in the narrative.

Of course there was no legal contest at Kapenguria between plaintiff and defendant of equal weight: as, for example, between nations with equal resources or financial empires of equal power, or individuals of equal social might. On the one side were limitless Imperial forces, an opulence of legal and military paraphernalia, abundant means to cloak repression in righteousness. The Defence had nothing more tangible than truth and justice with which to fight back. And the judgment of the Court, unencumbered by the need to take evidence into account, and unhampered by morality, was pre-ordained.

After pronouncement of judgment by the magistrate at Kapenguria, Jomo Kenyatta delivered a mitigation address in the following words:

'On behalf as well of my colleagues, I wish to say that we are not guilty, and we do not accept your findings. During the hearing of this trial — which has been so arranged as to place us in difficulty and inconvenience in preparing our cases — we do not feel that we have received the justice or hearing which we would have liked.

'I would also like to tell your Honour that we feel that this case, from our point of view, has been so arranged as to make scapegoats of us in order to strangle the Kenya African Union, the only African political organization which fights for the rights of the African people.

'We wish to say that what we have done, in all our activities, has been to try our level best to find ways and means by which the community of this country can live in harmony. But what we have objected to — and we shall continue to object — has been the discrimination in the Government of this country. We shall not accept that, whether we are in jail or out of it, because we believe that this world has been made for human beings to live in happily, to enjoy the good things and the produce of the country equally, and to enjoy the opportunities that this country has to offer

'While I will not say that you have been misled or influenced, the point that you have made is that we have been against the Europeans. You being a European, it is only natural that perhaps you should feel more that way. I am not accusing you of being prejudiced, but I feel that you should not stress so much your view that we have been entirely motivated by hatred of Europeans.

'We ask you to remove that from your mind, and to take this line — that our activities have been against the injustices that have been suffered by the African people. If you think that in trying to establish the rights of the African people we have turned out to be what you say, Mau Mau, we are very sorry that you have been misled in that direction. What we have done, and what we shall continue to do, is to demand the rights of the African people as human beings, so that they may enjoy facilities and privileges in the same way as other people.

'We look forward to the day when peace shall come to this land, and when the truth shall be known: that we, as African leaders, have stood for peace.

'None of us would be happy about, or would condone, the mutilation of human beings. We are humans and we have families, and none of us will ever condone such activities as arson and other things that we have been found guilty of.

'Without taking up much more of your time, I will tell your Honour that we as political bodies or political leaders stand constitutionally by our demands, which no doubt are known to you and to the Government of this country. In saying this, I am asking for no mercy at all. We are asking that justice may be done, and that the injustices that exist may be righted.

'Certainly we have grievances. Everybody in this country, high and low, knows perfectly well that there are such grievances. It is these grievances affecting the African people that we have been fighting for. We will not ask to be forgiven for requesting that these grievances be righted.

'We feel strongly about the fact that, at this time, the Government of this country should try and strangle the only organization — that is, the Kenya African Union, of which we are the leaders — that has been working for the betterment of the African people, and seeking harmonious relations between races.

'With these few remarks, your Honour, I may say that we do not accept your findings of guilty. It will be our duty to instruct our lawyer to take this matter up, and we intend to appeal to a higher Court. We believe that the Supreme Court of Kenya will give us justice, because we stand for peace. We stand for the rights of the African people, that Africans may find a place among the nations.

'We hope that you, and the rest of those who are in authority, will seek ways and means by which we can bring harmony and peace to this country. We believe that peace through force from any quarter is impossible, and that violence of any kind — whether from Europeans or from Africans — cannot bring us peace.'

There have been other instances in Colonial history — whether Britain or some other Power was involved — of intrigue and calumny, martyrdom and false banishment. But few have captured public imagination, or have lingered more avidly in venomous mis-statement, than the Kenyatta case.

The time has now arrived, in a phrase from the mitigation address, "when the truth shall be known". At Kapenguria, the man who might have stopped a conflagration was accused — by those guilty of fanning it — of providing its spark. This was the ultimate irony.

Subsequent appeal proceedings, which were mainly on grounds of jurisdiction or procedure, came to nothing, and their detailed course need not be traced.

But one point must be emphasised here. The substance of this case was never at any time heard by the Privy Council on appeal. The assumption or belief that it had been may perhaps have arisen initially, in some report or article, through sheer misunderstanding. Thereafter, almost more than any other monstrous distortion, this became a skil-fully-propagated untruth that was allowed to endure for years. It was taken up and repeated in parrot style by commentators and newspapers and reviews, from the shod-diest tabloids to publications that pride themselves — in Kenya or overseas — on accuracy and fairness. There was never an official disclaimer.

For this made it all look right. This was the final touch of genius that cemented the whole conspiracy. So justifiably vernerable is the Privy Council, as the epitome of justice and the rule of law, that seizure of a prospect, through fortuitous error, of persuading the world to believe that the Privy Council seal had been set on this verdict, made the perpetration of this dubious enterprise look even more watertight than might have been hoped.

But there are many precedents for the belief that sooner or later, despite the scrabblings of guilty men, the truth will be exhumed.

In fact, it was petitions to appeal to the Privy Council that were twice dismissed, in October 1953 and again in July 1954. The grounds for such dismissal will be discussed later in this work . . . (*in a trial lawyer's parliamentary speech in May* 1961) . . . But consideration of such petitions at no time involved or touched upon the facts or issues of the case.

Chapter 2

PRISON IN THE WILDERNESS

BANISHMENT MADE COMPLETE

Branded as a convicted felon, following the Kapenguria trial of 1953, Jomo Kenyatta began to serve his sentence at Lokitaung, in the hot and arid Turkana region of northwest Kenya.

Although blessed with a name — as though it were Los Angeles or Leningrad — the amenities at Lokitaung consisted virtually of a Police post and a Prison compound, the latter thoughtfully constructed while Appeals were being heard. All around was spindly bush and semi-desert; a lifeless place except for the occasional *manyattas* of nomadic herdsmen, who lived alongside insects, snakes and birds. Maybe ten miles to the east was a shore of Lake Rudolf. Less than twenty miles north was the Sudan. Discomfort, both for body and intellect, was absolute. And isolation was complete. Apart from a specially mounted and equipped safari, the place was barely accessible except by air.

This should not be presented as a kind of Devil's Island, with floggings and tortures and wanton neglect, although conditions were bleak. Kenyatta suffered from eczema badly, brought on first by deficiencies in diet, then aggravated by the flies. At one stage, he ripped off some bandages and applied a mud pack made from black-cotton soil, which afforded a little relief. Classified as "fit for light duties", he acted as cook for the group, which meant that for some of the time he was permitted to sit in the shade.

But there are more subtle ways of breaking a widely-travelled man whose life had been rich, and dedicated, and full of promise: the psychology of nothingness, the impeccable correctness of prison discipline and nomenclature, like a slap of contempt, the absence of human contact, slow passage of remorseless days of torridity and dust and meaningless surroundings. There was nothing green, nothing cool, nothing creative, nothing demanding, nothing at all.

For a long time, beyond occasional leakages and whispered rumour, he had no close knowledge of what could be happening outside. Towards the end of 1954, he was allowed by his own request to read selected religious books, including the Bible and the Koran. This study of religious philosophies left him with the conviction that all were rooted in one common theme: love your neighbour as yourself. In 1957, access to some newspapers was permitted, usually a month or two old when they arrived.

Mzee Kenyatta was at Lokitaung for six endless years. Only passionate conviction that his cause was just, and that justice would one day become manifest, kept him serene.

Meanwhile, in the heart of Kenya, anguish and effort went on.

In April 1954 in Nairobi, the biggest sweep of the whole Emergency — known as "Operation Anvil" — was launched, and before this was finished some 35,000 men and women had been scooped up and detained. Later in the year, the Colonial Secretary — Mr. Oliver Lyttelton (who became Lord Chandos) — visited Kenya and drafted, in consultation with the Governor and senior advisers, a new constitutional Plan.

On September 7, 1954, the Governor — Sir Evelyn Baring (now Lord Howick)—addressed a carefully arranged baraza at a place called Wangige in the Kiambu District. There he announced that, after serving his prison sentence at Lokitaung, Kenyatta would be sent to live "indefinitely" in some selected and remote area within the Northern Province. This was taken by clear implication to mean that Kenyatta would never be permitted to return to his home.

Then on October 4, 1954, under the Forfeiture of Lands Ordinance, the Governor signed an Order setting apart land that had been owned by Jomo Kenyatta in the District of Kiambu. An official statement said that this land consisted of four plots totalling about 31 acres, and it went on: "It has been suggested that the land forfeited will be used as experimental, demonstration and model smallholdings".

It is worthwhile considering the Governor's motives at that time, at least as speculation. Governor Baring was not a vindictive person. He is easily recalled as a man capable of almost Edwardian grace and courtesy, though with the hard eye and keen mind that could subjugate intricate finances, and grasp the whole sweep of great national or supra-national developments.

His was a basically constructive philosophy, of a yeoman and a man of peace, sometimes almost a visionary. He found violence, and the reprisals that must spring from violence, personally distasteful. But in his duty, which to him was paramount, he too often permitted his advisers to chart an inflexible course, which might have been better tempered to the winds and currents if compiled by the instruments of his own piercing intellect and innate understanding.

Governor Baring can never be disassociated from Kapenguria and its outcome. He was Governor and Commander-in-Chief. To what extent there may have been affront to his personal sense of logic and rationality, and therefore of justice, cannot here be surmised. It seems doubtful whether, professionally or academically, he can have been deeply stirred. At all events, at best, he was carried with the stream.

It must be supposed that, from such a standpoint, he forced official harshness upon himself, to counteract any reluctance to rule. He was urged to be harsh, and was ordered to rule. He lived in a world not of his making, and thereupon gave himself more to the seeming tasks of repair than to searching analysis of causes of decay. Thus, out of more vivid qualities, stepped the figure of a ruthless and rarely-emotional man . . .

Kapenguria was brought back into the wider public gaze in 1955, through publication of a book entitled *The Trial of Jomo Kenyatta,* by Montagu Slater. Sundry critics and observers found themselves making uneasy comments about the trial itself, after studying this work. In London, a leading article in the *New Statesman and Nation* of June 4, 1955, had this to say:

> I have always found it difficult to believe that Jomo Kenyatta, an able, highly educated and much-travelled African nationalist, could really have been guilty of "managing Mau Mau". After reading this book, I am even more surprised that he should have been convicted on that count.
>
> The evidence for "managing" Mau Mau produced at the trial did not seem to me to be worth tuppence; some of it, indeed, could have been obtained for a smaller sum. But it was the magistrate's comments that I found most disturbing. He seemed naively indignant because the Kikuyu believe they had been robbed of their land — something that seems obvious to almost all Africans because otherwise how do the British come to own land in Kenya at all? — and surprised that Kenyatta had an "obsession" about the "colour bar or alleged racial discrimination".

On the whole, no great or lasting stir was caused by Slater's book, and certainly none was officially encouraged.

But with Mzee Kenyatta still 450 miles as the crow flies from Nairobi, and very much more by any conceivable land route, there were three other events of note — which might here be mentioned for the record — during 1955.

First, and after a considerable lapse, Africans were again permitted under new regulations to organize political Parties. But the regulations were careful to insist that these must be on a District and not on a national basis. And thus were sown the seeds of organized tribalism and regionalism that were destined to bedevil Kenya through many ensuing years.

Secondly, the report was published of the Royal Commission on Land and Population in East Africa, which had taken nearly three years to prepare. And almost coincident with this report was the launching of the Swynnerton Plan for an agrarian revolution in African areas.

Then finally in this year, the report of the Lidbury Commission led to abolition of salary scales based on racial origin in the Civil Service, although Africans were still the most poorly paid.

THE PRESSURE BEGINS

By 1957, it was hoped in various Official circles that the Kenyatta issue was being forgotten, and that — in the context of some generally harmless practical reforms — political evolution could be geared to slow motion, if not actually contained.

This was, quite literally, a remarkable delusion. The human complex of Colonial Administration, distributed between Nairobi and London, almost totally failed to understand the mentality or the psychology of the Kenya Africans, and the Kikuyu people in particular. Certainly, during the whole long period of Kenyatta's imprisonment and banishment, the Colonial Government utterly failed to convince the people that Jomo Kenyatta was "finished", or that whatever he had been or had stood for was (*de facto* if not tangibly) dead and buried. The most curious phenomenon was not this lack of success, but that it should have been seriously imagined that such acceptance — especially among the Kikuyu — could ever be won.

In March of that year, under a restricted franchise suggested by the Coutts report, eight Africans were elected to the Legislative Council to represent the whole of Kenya. They at once relieved the Colonial authorities of any comforting misapprehension.

The new politicians immediately formed an African Elected Members Organization, which debated and appreciated the need for florid gesture, kept on the tight reign of longer-term strategy. In this light, they declared the Lyttelton Plan to be null and void. This was, they said, not an agreement with any responsible and accepted African leaders, but an imposition on the African people brought in without their consent.

There can be no doubt that African parliamentary presence and pressure at this time, blandly assembled and exerted in the knowledge that the group would be swamped by the surrounding hostility of the House, marked the first critical milestone on the road to Kenyatta's release and Kenya's independence.

For the purpose of tracing events over the ensuing four-year period, whenever reference is made to debates or events in the Legislative Council, the distraction of stipulating names or titles or constituencies — except where such detail is purposeful — will be avoided.

The point is that here was the overt arena, utilised more keenly as time went by, of conflict between the Official side, with all the arts and means of dominance, and African pressure. This was the one place where a great movement and great feeling among the African people could find an outlet and could let off steam.

Representatives put in to convey this deep feeling, and to pursue some strategic objectives using parliamentary talent quickly enhanced by some tactical experience, worked closely together within the African Elected Members Organization. It was A.E.M.O. as a whole which mapped out all courses of action — frequently assisted by due consultations outside — and the spokesmen in any given case may simply and truly be characterised as the A.E.M.O. voice.

Much the same applies on the Official side.

The issue of Jomo Kenyatta — and the other detainees — was first raised in Legislative Council on May 23, 1957. It is difficult to realise now, in sensible terms, what a shock at that time the very mention of such names could represent.

There was debate then on a Motion urging the Government to take all possible precautions against a resurgence of terrorist activity. The A.E.M.O. view was represented by this comment: "There is the general question of detainees as such, and there is also the question of certain more prominent cases . . . I think that rather than state that the process of release should be restricted, I would have said that the Government should be encouraged to accelerate the process of release."

Hansard for October 29, 1957, then records that African Members (through one of their number) put down a Question to the Minister of Local Government, Health and Housing, asking if the Minister would make a statement on the health of Jomo Kenyatta and his colleagues at Lokitaung.

The Minister replied that all the convicts referred to in the Question were in normal health. As a supplementary, the Official side was asked whether it would be possible for the Government to arrange for any African Elected Members to visit Kenyatta at Lokitaung. This — it was proclaimed — was Another Question, which might be addressed by an Honourable Member to the Minister for Internal Security and Defence. The parliamentary exchange ended on this note, but in the corridors, and even far beyond, was some buzzing.

In March 1958, Africans were given a further six elected seats in the Legislative Council, under the terms of the Lennox-Boyd Constitution for Kenya. This was the year that saw the formation, at Mwanza, of the Pan African Freedom Movement of East and Central Africa. The United Nations also entered Africa, through the establishment of the Economic Commission for Africa in Addis Ababa.

But 1958 must be principally remembered, in the context of this work, for acceleration of the parliamentary demand — which served both to inspire and to support a wider demand — for Jomo Kenyatta's release.

It should be re-emphasised that over an important period (broadly stretching from 1957 to 1960), the Africans who took their seats and were able to exert some pressure in Legislative Council were not speaking for themselves, or solely for their variously-designed and unwieldy constituencies. They were reacting, as front-line spokesmen, to the pressures and demands and emotions outside, among the people everywhere, but perhaps especially those in Central Province and in neighbouring portions of the Rift Valley.

None of the senior Kikuyu leaders were in Parliament throughout this time, being mostly in restriction or (by decree) overseas. But despite such physical absence, the real fulcrum — almost, in a sense, the technology — of political initiative and drive was still in Central Province, expressed most ably through the voices of those who responded to and represented this living initiative in its spell of absentia.

On June 11, 1958, the Chief Secretary found it appropriate to make a Ministerial statement in the House on the treatment of convicts at Lokitaung. The gist of his statement was this:

> Allegations regarding conditions in a prison in the Northern Province which accommodates a few Mau Mau convicts have been given fairly widespread publicity. The allegations related to lack of adequate water supplies, visits from relatives, censorship of mail, rations and medical facilities. As a result of the investigation which has been completed, the Government is satisfied that the allegations are unfounded.
>
> In making these allegations, the convicts concerned described themselves as political prisoners. That is quite incorrect. All of them are serving sentences following convictions in Courts for criminal offences. They include some of the most dangerous leaders of the Mau Mau organization.

It is difficult to look upon this statement, and the condition of mind which it embraced, with anything but repugnance. It was clear to some already at that time, as it must now be clear to all, that Kenyatta and his colleagues were the victims of a tortuous and reprehensible political conspiracy. It follows that they were political prisoners. And to describe them as "some of the most dangerous leaders of the Mau Mau organization", in face of background with which the Chief Secretary was all too familiar, evokes suspicion either of blind effrontery or of purpose that was now desperately malign.

A fortnight later, on June 26, 1958, African Members contrived to take this matter further in the Legislature. To do this, in a way that would open up the whole subject for wide-ranging debate, a Motion was introduced that: "this Council, not being satisfied with the statement made by the Chief Secretary on June 11th, regarding allegations made by certain convicts in Her Majesty's prison at Lokitaung, and also being concerned about allegations from other prisons and detention camps, calls on the Government to institute an independent Inquiry into the conditions obtaining in prisons and detention camps with a view to making a report to this Council."

The debate was continued on June 27, 1958, when a nominee of the fourteen African Members delivered a series of observations which appeared to have only limited appeal to authority. These are the vital extracts from this speech, as recorded in Hansard:

These African prisoners at Lokitaung — and maybe even in other areas — were, when they were arrested, the political leaders of the African people, and the African people respect them as such. As the leaders of their community they deserve that, when they are in prison, they should be treated with some respect. When Archbishop Makarios was arrested by the British Government, he was taken to the Seychelles and he was put in the Governor's Lodge there. Exactly the same thing should be done with Mr. Jomo Kenyatta.

When I say these people are the leaders of the African people, I do not take into consideration the recent violence in Kenya; I take into consideration the past deeds of these people in fields of politics, economics and social advancement. Until you realise this, you can never get the co-operation of the African people.

The Member was ruled out of order by the Speaker of those days, while (as Chief Secretary) Mr. Coutts remarked: "I regard this statement as almost incredible. I am completely dumbfounded." On or off the parliamentary stage, Coutts never loosed his grip on the shield of outraged virtue.

The Motion was then put and negatived. But from that point onwards, cracks in all but the most stubborn of ivory towers were widened by the freshening gales of challenge . . .

There was a mass meeting in the Kaloleni Social Hall at Kisumu on July 6, 1958, where the recent debate in the Legislative Council was discussed, and the meeting passed a resolution which read, in its principal part:

> Africans knew Kenyatta from the year 1929 as a devoted champion of their cause in demanding political freedom, economic opportunity and social advancement for his people. From a very early stage, he noted the manifold problems forming the basis of mass grievances, and called upon the Government to remove them constitutionally. This was to a large extent ignored, and as the result of an overstretched frustration it all ended in the Mau Mau outburst. Kenyatta was neither responsible for creating these problems, nor for refusal to remove them. In fact, he denounced terrorism and violence. It would be mere self-deception to think that any true and honest African can ever forget the leadership of Jomo Kenyatta.

In August 1958, a book called *Here I Stand* was published by Paul Robeson in London, and included this passage: "In Kenya Colony, the people's leader — Jomo Kenyatta — is jailed. I knew this brave man well in the years I lived in London; like Nehru of India and many others from Colonial lands who were my friends in England, he dreamed of freedom for his people. Well, Nehru was jailed in India, and many thousands more; but the road to independence and power ran through those prison walls, and Kenyatta too will travel on."

This was a prophetic observation. And in Kenya, with Mzee Kenyatta still in Lokitaung, the pressures mounted.

On August 26, 1958, the African Elected Members Organization issued a statement saying: "The arrest and confinement of Kenyatta left a big wound in African hearts, which will only be cured by his return to normal life among the African people of Kenya. Jomo Kenyatta and others at Lokitaung are still the real political leaders of the African people."

On September 7, 1958, the Nairobi District African Congress held a meeting in the Kaloleni Hall. Members present passed a resolution that: "we, the African people of all tribes assembled here, do solemnly reaffirm our confidence in the leadership of Jomo Kenyatta, now languishing in imperialistic jail for relentlessly fighting against injustice, settler domination and the colour bar."

And a fortnight later — on September 21, 1958 — the Nairobi People's Convention Party held a meeting in the same Hall. They decided that October 20 . . . (the anniversary of Kenyatta's arrest) . . . would henceforth be observed as a day of fasting and meditation, for "so long as our struggle for freedom continues". Thereafter, this date would be observed as a Kenyatta National Day.

Declarations and decisions of such kinds were not really directed at the British people en masse, who had no means of forming a judgement, but towards those few Colonial Officials — patronised and championed in all the right Clubs by European leaders and settlers often of foolish rather than extreme pretensions — who still held Kenya in a vice. Some of these officials had inherited a situation, and felt it their duty to live with its tradition. A handful, indeed, were bitter. Others simply brainwashed themselves, in a peculiar way, into believing that whatever was done must be right, or that from whatever had been done there could be no respectable, and certainly no career-forwarding evasion.

One of the considerable breakthroughs in Kenya's political history really occurred around this time. As 1956 had moved into 1957, the whole enormous issue that surrounded the person and purposes of Jomo Kenyatta had been tightly clamped behind a local iron curtain, as a subject officially disposed of, militarily safeguarded, and socially taboo. But as 1958 began to approach 1959, an assault had gained a foothold: a psychological bridgehead in which were almost equally compounded the elements of political pressure built up, and the hostile wall of social outrage clawed aside. There was still no easy way to get finally behind the rigid curtain. But what lay behind was brought, discursively and with lessened affectation, into the light of day.

In November 1958, the 14 African Elected Members walked out of Legislative Council while the Governor was reading his speech from the Throne. This was not firmly planned in advance, but was spontaneous, unanimous reaction. Governor Baring had just reached a point saying — in effect — that the Lennox-Boyd Constitution was going to endure, and that his Government would still proceed to govern regardless of what the African Members thought or did. This was considered by the 14 Members to be an insulting response, both inherently and by its indirect (public rebuke as distinct from private reply) nature, to their efforts on Kenyatta's behalf and their request for a Conference to discuss the Constitution.

On December 5, 1958, a delegate in London — on behalf of the African Elected Members — had an interview with Mr. Lennox-Boyd himself. After reviewing all recent events, the spokesman complained to the Colonial Secretary that the Administration in Kenya was still making it impossible for African politicians to hold meetings at key points around the country. He further urged that the Emergency, which had then lasted for more than six years, be at once ended. And finally, he handed over papers casting fresh doubts on the validity of the Kapenguria trial, by virtue of a confession of perjury by a witness . . . (to be reviewed in detail in the final section of this chapter).

Seven Kenya representatives then attended the first All African People's Conference in Accra. This Conference called for the immediate release of Kenyatta, and declared that people shown to have given false evidence should be punished.

All Kenya delegates found themselves freshly inspired by their time in Ghana, and returned to Nairobi more determined than ever to secure the release of Kenyatta, and work through constitutional advance and reform of the franchise towards the goal of complete independence.

On January 5, 1959, the Nairobi People's Convention Party passed a resolution demanding the immediate formation of an African Government, and that Jomo Kenyatta should be free. This was publicised in the Party's cyclo-styled newspaper — *Uhuru* — which for some time had been seeking to codify and discipline the new political awakening in Kenya, and attach it to meaningful slogans, so that people could feel the comfort of familiarity and widely-shared ambition in all that they were struggling for. The paper was also used to keep the name of Kenyatta in the public gaze, to support the campaign for his release, and restore him as a symbol of leadership and purpose for the people to keep always in their minds.

In March 1959, *Uhuru* was banned.

REVELATION OF PERJURY

Reference was made earlier to the weight attached by the Kapenguria magistrate — in the absence of anything else which might ostensibly justify the ordained verdict — to the evidence of a man named Rawson Macharia, who testified to the participation of Kenyatta in an oathing ceremony. This was one of the principal tactical presentations of the Prosecution. It was referred to by Counsel for the Defence in the words: "We have the Rawson Macharia incident resting on one weak witness countered by ten good witnesses, and I submit this incident is now completely dead."

The evidence by Macharia was always suspect. It is now known that he was simply bought, for money. For Kapenguria purposes, his demeanour and contribution were rehearsed time and time again at a mock Court established at Kiganjo. Macharia subsequently appeared as a student at Exeter University College.

All this began to come out into the open on December 3, 1958, at a special press conference in London, where there was made public an affidavit signed by Rawson Macharia. What generally transpired and was revealed at this press conference is taken now from London newspaper accounts:

Macharia's affidavit admitted that his evidence was false, and particularly in regard to an alleged initiation ceremony on March 16, 1950, at Kiamwange implicating Jomo Kenyatta. The affidavit said that, to the best of Macharia's knowledge, Jomo Kenyatta was neither a participant in nor present at any proceedings of the nature described at any time or place. The affidavit added that a number of other prosecution witnesses were procured and suborned to give false evidence.

Macharia has also revealed the contents of a letter allegedly written from the Attorney-General's Chambers in Nairobi on November 19, 1952. It confirmed the alleged offer to him of (a) an air passage to the United Kingdom at £278; (b) a two-year course in local government at a University at £1,000; (c) subsistence for his family for two years at £250; (d) a post in the Kenya Government at the end of his course. He added that he was duly flown to London on January 1, 1953, and took the course mentioned.

Mr. Mboya said: "In view of the serious nature of these allegations, I call on the Secretary of State and the Kenya Government to institute at once an impartial, judicial and public Inquiry, so that the truth or falsehood of these allegations can be ascertained".

All this, of course, created a noticeable stir, and sparked off a resurgence of doubt in many London quarters — more widespread now than at any time — about the legal validity and underlying justice of the Kapenguria operation. But officialdom in Kenya remained outwardly unmoved.

On December 4, 1958, the day following the initial press conference, the *Manchester Guardian* published the following comment in a leading article:

> The Kenya Government should lose no time in carrying out the fullest inquiry into allegations of perjured evidence at the trial of Jomo Kenyatta.
>
> One Rawson Macharia, a witness for the prosecution, has sworn an affidavit declaring that he gave false evidence against Kenyatta, and that to his knowledge other witnesses for the prosecution were "procured and suborned to give false evidence". Nor is a possible motive omitted from the statement. Mr. Macharia was promised before the trial, and received after it, a two-year course in local government in Britain at the Kenya Government's expense, and other advantages.
>
> One should not make too much of this. Nevertheless, such grave and precise allegations cannot be left unsifted. To fulfil its purpose the Inquiry must have such judicial standing as will enable it to call for testimony from whoever may be able to throw light on this affair. Its findings will carry more conviction if it is drawn from outside the ranks of the Kenya Administration.

There was much hasty consultation of files and cuttings about Kapenguria, with enterprising journalists becoming immersed, and often interested, in personal and cabled researches. As an outcome, a question — with genuine puzzlement — was posed. How could the magistrate, any magistrate, have attached so much weight to Macharia's evidence when deciding on conviction, in face of contrary evidence by a whole assembly of witnesses of higher credibility and standing? The sticky tape covering fissures in the edifice of this whole intrigue was beginning to be peeled away.

(By this time, more than two thousand days and nights of a man's life, of Kenyatta's life, had been endured at Lokitaung).

More forthright comment appeared in a leading article in the *New Statesman* of December 6, 1958:

> The trial of Jomo Kenyatta has always held an element of mystery. It was conducted far from Nairobi where close scrutiny of its surrounding circumstances was not easy, and it took place at a time of extreme tension in Kenya. Most Africans believe it to have been rigged, and many Europeans consider that Kenyatta was not guilty at least of the offences with which he was actually charged.

> Now comes Rawson Macharia, an important prosecution witness at the trial, with the allegation that his evidence was false and that he was bribed by the Kenya authorities to give it. This is a challenge to the Government of Kenya which requires immediate investigation.

> In this connection, it is important that Parliament should press for a formal judicial Inquiry: no investigation conducted under the auspices of either the Colonial Office or the Kenya Government will any longer be accepted as adequate. Indeed, the incidents in which first malpractice and then deliberate deception have been credibly alleged against Kenya officials have now become so many that this specific case may prove a blessing.

Macharia swore his affidavit in Nairobi on November 22, 1958. On December 8 in London, *The Times* printed a news story revealing that Mr. Dingle Foot Q.C. — a distinguished advocate and Labour M.P. for Ipswich — had sent to the Colonial Secretary some details of a recent conversation he had had with this man. *The Times* then quoted Mr. Foot as saying: "A fortnight ago at Nairobi, I had a lengthy interview with Mr. Macharia. I examined him in considerable detail about his allegations regarding his own evidence and that of other witnesses for the prosecution. I did not have the opportunity of interviewing other persons implicated, so of course I cannot say whether he was telling the truth. But I was quite satisfied that his narrative, which was extremely circumstantial, called for the closest investigation."

The Times was now moving, with the repute of an elder statesmen and at the gathered but inexorable pace of a cricket umpire, towards more Delphic comment. A leading article in this newspaper of December 10, 1958, should be quoted at substantial length:

'The announcement in Kenya that Jomo Kenyatta will have served by next April three-quarters of his sentence of seven years imprisonment, and will then be eligible for release, follows closely upon the assertion that evidence given at his trial was false.

'The original trial was fought out with the peculiar bitterness that the campaign of outrage and the measures taken to repress it had engendered, and the subsequent proceedings followed a complicated course. The defence contended throughout that Kenyatta had no connection whatever with Mau Mau; one Rawson Macharia, for the prosecution, testified that he had seen the accused administer a Mau Mau oath. Whether relying mainly on this evidence or not, the Resident Magistrate convicted Kenyatta.

'Now Mr. Macharia has sworn an affidavit that he gave false evidence and that the Mau Mau ceremony he described never took place. A witness who has admitted to perjury and corruption sets up no presumption that his second statement is more truthful than that which he originally made on oath. But in a case so serious as this, unless it is immediately self-evident that the confession is frivolous, the question needs to be determined judicially.

'It is immaterial that Kenyatta's imprisonment is near its end. Kenyatta's guilt has not been affirmed at a higher level than the Supreme Court of Kenya. It should now not be impossible to bring the substantial issue of guilt or innocence, in the light of the new evidence, before the Court of Appeal for Eastern Africa, and it would be reasonable that any such proceedings should be conducted at the expense of the Crown.'

6*

This statement by *The Times* meant a great deal. It was valuable not least for its perceptive introduction of the word "corruption"; and for presentation of the simple but shattering truth that Kenyatta's guilt had never been convincingly established; and for being meticulous in nailing the skilfully-perpetuated lie that the Privy Council had confirmed the findings in this case.

As a reflection, much might have been different if many other newspapers and reviews, both local and overseas, while forming such opinions as they wished upon the facts, had emulated *The Times* in the accurate recounting of such facts.

On December 16, 1958, Mr. Lennox-Boyd received from Sir Evelyn Baring in Kenya the Government's initial observations on the Macharia affair. An interlude in excess of three weeks between the signing of the affidavit and the official riposte was understandable. It may perhaps have been anticipated that, given an interval of time, public curiosity or connscience might well be switched elsewhere. But beyond this, with immediate denials or explanations clearly difficult to frame, it was somewhat awkward for the Governor and his official advisers to know quite what to say.

That same day in the House of Commons, it became evident that this whole matter would not be allowed to go by default. Supported by the signatures of ten other Labour Members, Mr. Dingle Foot put down a Motion outlining in detail the assertions made by Macharia, and demanding a public Inquiry. His Motion clearly mentioned the fact that the magistrate who conducted the Kapenguria trial expressly accepted Macharia's evidence in preference to that of ten witnesses for the defence.

In the Commons on December 18, 1958 — replying to a Question by Mr. Foot — Mr. Lennox-Boyd stated: "I have not yet completed my examination of the Governor's observations". This aroused such acrimony as led the Leader of the House (Mr. Butler) to remark that a request for debate after the Christmas recess was reasonable, although it would not be possible to discuss the matter before. He added: "Meanwhile, the seriousness of the matter is realised by the Colonial Secretary."

After the Christmas recess in Kenya — on December 31, 1958 — an A.E.M.O. statement again demanded a public judicial Inquiry into the allegations advanced by Macharia. It went on to say that, since the evidence on which Jomo Kenyatta was convicted was now said to be false, his imprisonment should be promptly suspended and a re-trial held.

By now, it may be fair to comment, the Establishment — spread between Nairobi and London — had had time to close its ranks. An official statement was issued in Nairobi on January 4, 1959. It read: "The Government of Kenya, having exhaustively investigated recent allegations made by Rawson Macharia, has decided that a judicial Inquiry should not be held. The Attorney-General has decided to institute criminal proceedings against Macharia, for allegedly having sworn a false affidavit containing these allegations, and Macharia has been arrested on this charge in Nairobi."

Proceedings against Macharia began at the end of January, and at the beginning of April this man was sent to prison for 21 months, following his conviction for having sworn a false affidavit. The magistrate, Mr. Isaac Rosen, who had the unenviable task of trying to separate truth from falsehood in anything the accused man said, or had ever said, described Macharia at the end — almost despairingly — as "a latter-day Judas".

But this was not the end of the affair.

On April 10, 1959, in the House of Commons, the Colonial Secretary rejected a suggestion by Mr. Stonehouse that he should still order a judicial Inquiry into the trial of Kenyatta, in view of issues raised during the Macharia hearing.

Then on April 12, 1959, there was published in London a searching article in *The Observer:*

> The Colonial Secretary last week declined to order a judicial Inquiry into the trial of Jomo Kenyatta. However, he recognized that the Nairobi magistrate had found Rawson Macharia a pathological liar; and that, not only had this man sworn a false affidavit, but he had lied at Kenyatta's trial.
>
> Mr. Lennox-Boyd contended that Macharia was not the most important Crown witness at the trial of Kenyatta. But on one vital point Macharia was the only prosecution witness. He gave evidence of an alleged initiation ceremony on March 16, 1950, at a place called Kiamwange in the Kiambu District, which implicated Kenyatta. This essential linch-pin in the prosecution's case against Kenyatta would appear now to have been seriously weakened.
>
> Apart from considerations of equity, there is a political reason why it is important that justice should be seen to be done to Kenyatta. Rightly or wrongly, his trial is widely regarded by politically conscious Africans throughout the continent as having been unfairly conducted. Nothing would do more to win respect for British justice than the appointment of a Commission of two trusted lawyers, one European and one African, to inquire into the conduct of this case. Indeed, this is almost an essential prerequisite to attempting a convincing New Deal for Kenya, which the Government shows some signs of contemplating.

There was little overt enthusiasm, in official circles back in Kenya, for the thesis that "justice should be seen to be done to Kenyatta".

But three days later, he was moved from Lokitaung.

Chapter 3

INTERLUDE AT LODWAR

THE WIND OF CHANGE

On completion of his prison sentence, which was officially deemed to have occurred on April 15, 1959, Mzee Jomo Kenyatta was transferred to compulsory confinement at Lodwar. He was destined to remain there for eleven days short of two years.

Sir Evelyn Baring's announcement in 1954 will be recalled, to the effect that Kenyatta would be sent to live "indefinitely" in some remote area of the Northern Province. Lodwar clearly filled this prescription. About ninety miles due south of Lokitaung, this place was three or four times as far from a shore of Lake Rudolf, but otherwise much the same thing.

However, Lodwar was (as it still is) the administrative centre of Turkana District, and thus was a little more urban in character. While still accessible from the world outside only with hazard, there were at least a few houses, built to the P.W.D. economy design, and a duka or two. The water supply was then quite frequently in operation. And for intellectual recreation, it was possible to stand and watch the District Commissioner coming and going in his cloud of dust. Kenyatta had to report to this man at 10 a.m. daily. Happily, Mr. District Commissioner Hill believed that duty should be reconciled with humanity, and his name may here be recorded with respect.

Apart from this, Kenyatta had some measure of comparative freedom in daylight hours. He was given a small two-

room house, built for the purpose towards the end of the
Lokitaung period, and thrice weekly was allowed to do
some shopping. But talking to the people was forbidden,
and under a curfew arrangement between 6 p.m. and 6 a.m.
he was confined to the compound of his house . . .

In Kenya at large, always in the shadow, if it could not
be in the substance, Jomo Kenyatta continued to dominate
the scene.

Although the Question was put in at an earlier date, it
was on May 27, 1959, that African Members finally managed
to ask in Legislative Council what amenities and facilities
were afforded to Jomo Kenyatta in exile at Lodwar. The
reply from the Minister for Internal Security and Defence
was: "the same as for other Lodwar residents, except insofar as these are legally curtailed. He is housed, and receives
a subsistence allowance."

There was nothing unusual, or especially resented, in a
parliamentary Reply being smooth or circumlocutory. But
more than one Member of the Council felt puzzled by the
ambiguous quality of the phrase "except insofar as these
are legally curtailed". There was some desire as well to
probe Cusack's answer for other grains of detail.

In response to a supplementary question, the Minister
revealed that the amount of the subsistence allowance to
Jomo Kenyatta, paid in monthly instalments, was £72 per
year. Then, when it was asked whether detainees were
allowed to have their families at Lodwar, the Minister —
master of the pose of inscrutable weariness — replied:
"within reason". Finally, a questioner wished to know what
specific facilities there were for detainees to bring grievances to the notice of the Government. The Minister advised
him that such opportunities existed during the obligatory
daily report to the District Commissioner.

Other Members did their best to catch the Speaker's eye,
to raise such questions as: "would the Government consider
transferring Jomo Kenyatta to a less strict place?" The
House was assured through the Official spokesman that:

"the Government is satisfied that Lodwar is a suitable place."

On April 14, 1959, in Zanzibar, a Conference of PAFMECA passed a resolution which demanded the unconditional release of Jomo Kenyatta, so that — as the resolution put it — he could take part in policy discussions already under way in Kenya about measures of constitutional change.

On the day after his Lodwar arrival — April 16, 1959 — Kenyatta received a cable from Dr. Azikiwe, who later became President of Nigeria, but as President, as he then was, of the National Council of Nigeria and the Cameroons. The cable read: "We are happy that you have been discharged from prison, but are sorry you are still being restricted in your movements. Have faith that these reverses are temporary, because those who struggle for human freedom are always immortals in history. Africa is on the move, and no Canutes can hold back the waves from rushing shorewards."

A great deal in fact happened in 1959, including (as tangible events) the opening of Nairobi's international Airport, and the opening in distinguished company of the new Headquarters of the Kenya Federation of Labour. But also, although Azikiwe had no means of knowing this, the year ushered onto the Kenya stage a new Canute, or a new kind of Canute, named Patrick Renison.*

Around the middle of this year, calls for the freedom and leadership of Jomo Kenyatta were continual. So when on

---

*(Note: The death of Sir Patrick Renison was announced while material for this volume was being assembled and arranged. There is no wish now to transgress any norm of good taste through the critical references that must come. And certainly there is no desire to belittle those manifold personal qualities of charm and gallantry, and his sense of service, for which he was widely mourned. But it is inescapable, in a work of this kind, that the professional and political impact of Sir Patrick as Governor of Kenya — over a crucial period — should be honestly presented. Renison himself would have held this to be fair).

July 25, 1959, the President of the Nairobi African District Congress declared that Kenyatta should be allowed to travel to London as constitutional spokesman of Africans in Kenya, this was one of many analogous proposals or demands.

And it is important to recall how — throughout all these Lokitaung and Lodwar days — the anchorage of political struggle and aspiration, even of rationality, remained firmly embedded in Kikuyuland: in the forests, in the camps and villages, and in the impassive faith that could never be deadened by the everyday sufferings of the people. The Kikuyu always remembered Kenyatta's words, and his personality, and the disciplined hopes that he held out to them. And while the means of fulfilment were then enshrouded in misery and hazard, in the bare material and moral subsistence of their contemporary lives, they still believed.

The next important event marked something between an experimental and a staggering concession, in the atmosphere of those days, with friction moving ever closer to impasse. Daniel arap Moi (today Vice President of the Kenya Republic) was allowed to visit Jomo Kenyatta at Lodwar on November 3, 1959. He travelled there — a detail mentioned as a human touch — weighed down with fresh vegetables and fruit.

Moi was selected as a prominent parliamentarian who was non-Kikuyu; as a shrewd man, respected by his people. It was undoubtedly hoped that he would return either as a substantial African spokesman in favour of confining Kenyatta, or with the view — almost equally malleable in official hands — that Kenyatta was so physically enfeebled, and so out of touch with the contemporary political scene, that whether he was in Lodwar or Legco was empty of significance.

In the event, Daniel arap Moi was greatly moved by this experience, and made public on his return a straightforward account of his impressions. He told correspondents that, in his judgment, Kenyatta should be released at once.

He was convinced that racial harmony and mutual understanding in the country would be furthered if Kenyatta
were granted an immediate interview with the Governor,
and could openly express his views on the question of land.
Furthermore — he went on — it could only be helpful for
Jomo Kenyatta to have an early opportunity of meeting
the British Government's official constitutional adviser.

It was against the new timbre of this background that
important contributions were made to the debate on the
Speech from the Chair, which took place in Legislative
Council over the period November 11 to November 19, 1959.

This occasion featured parliamentary announcement of
the legal ending of the Emergency, and an early contributor *Mboya ?*
to the debate was the Member for Nairobi area, serving as
spokesman for the African people as a whole:

> There is a point, Sir, which I would like to emphasise,
> relating to Jomo Kenyatta. We want to say in no un-
> certain terms that this release is an important factor in
> any attempts to bring about cordial relations, harmony
> and confidence between the Africans and the Govern-
> ment, and between the Africans and the other racial
> groups. We want to leave no one in any doubt on this
> particular question, and we do not consider steps will
> have been taken to end the Emergency if Kenyatta is
> not released, not only because we think it is right that
> he should be freed, but also because — if the Govern-
> ment insists that he has to be punished for anything —
> he has been punished. There is no justifiable reason or
> right on the part of the Government for his continued
> detention. We also submit, Sir, that facilities be made
> available for Kenyatta to be able to be consulted on the
> question of the constitutional development of this
> country.

A number of other African speakers also figured in the
Hansard record, making such comments as these:

> In the minds of many Africans, it is completely
> impossible for us to disassociate Jomo Kenyatta from
> the Emergency, and for this reason we would have liked

to see that the declaration of the end of the Emergency went with the release of Kenyatta and his other colleagues at Lodwar. This could have brought a real sense of relaxation on the part of very many Africans in the country. We believe very strongly that it is characteristic of the British Government to review aspects from time to time, and I hope that this characteristic will be applied on behalf of Jomo Kenyatta.

The fears which exist in the minds of many Government people were all unwarranted. It is incomprehensible for anyone to say that Kenyatta — a person who is acknowledged by all as the leader of the Africans in this country, the leader of the Kenya people — could never assist in the solution of Kenya's problems.

Then of course it was time for what had been called "the minds of many Government people" to manifest themselves.

As Chief Secretary, Mr. Coutts bleakly observed: "The Government will not release Jomo Kenyatta. It will not let him go to the Conference — in any case he is not an Elected Member of Legislative Council — and they will not let him see Professor McKenzie" . . . (Constitutional Adviser appointed by the British Government) . . . "because the latter's main duty when he is here on this trip is to discuss points with the participants in the Conference."

This was as flat and as uncompromising as ever. Having taken up his position much earlier, Coutts stood on it to the end, as immutable, as richly smug, and mostly as hilarious as the Victoria-and-Albert Museum.

But then perhaps the classic contribution came from the Minister for African Affairs: "Nor, Sir, do I believe that Kenyatta is the acknowledged leader of the Africans in Kenya, and I flatter myself, Sir, that I am in reasonably close touch with the opinions of responsible and mature Africans in this country."

Rather like the Shakespearean gentleman who did protest too much, the Minister's flattery here was a trifle opulent.

(One characteristic of a whole long era was that Colonial officials generally, in the context of any subject taken at random — politics, economics, agriculture, ecology, sociology — could not conceive of a situation in which their opinions or wishes could possibly be wrong, or in which they could properly be challenged by any of the unfortunate mortals not specially groomed and briefed by the Almighty to become Colonial officials. They had a particular kind of superiority complex, often accentuated by the queer comfort of hue. Some of them of course were very able and dedicated men, with even brilliant minds. But in the instance quoted above, a less complicated truth can be seen to speak for itself: This Minister was an ass).

That debate in the Legislative Council ushered in the fateful year of 1960, with Mr. Harold Macmillan speaking in South Africa of "the wind of change", as background to a Lancaster House Conference presided over in London by Mr. Iain Macleod. It was acknowledged at this Conference, for the first time, that Africans were soon to gain political power in Kenya, and that the "White Highlands" would be thrown open to all races.

"DARKNESS AND DEATH"

The first few months of 1960 saw and heard a continuation of pressure, from many sources and in all quarters, for Jomo Kenyatta's release.

As one example, another All African People's Conference — this time in Tunis — passed urgent resolutions on January 28, 1960, calling for the freedom and leadership of Kenyatta.

On March 10, 1960, the President of the Mombasa African Democratic Union announced that his Party had begun to organize a "Release Kenyatta" campaign. He made the point that Jomo Kenyatta was the only leader acceptable to all the tribes of Kenya, and said they would petition the Governor regularly until Kenyatta was released to lead the country as Kenya's first Prime Minister.

Then in the House of Commons on April 14, 1960, Mr.
Stonehouse asked if immediate arrangements would be
made for the release of Kenyatta and others still under
political restriction in Kenya. The Colonial Secretary (Mr.
Macleod) replied: "No, Sir. The case of each person under
restriction is regularly reviewed. It remains the policy that
no person will be released while he is a danger to security."

President Tubman of Liberia made public on April 16,
1960, the text of messages he had sent to Kenya, saying —
in effect — that it was gratifying to know the people of
Kenya had launched an appeal to the British Government
for the immediate release of Jomo Kenyatta.

The Budget debate in Legislative Council, when there is
traditional tolerance for discussion of all matters affecting
the state of the nation, offered a further opportunity for
raising this issue yet again. On May 3, 1960, an A.E.M.O.
spokesman delivered some comprehensive and graphic
remarks:

'Let me state here and now and publicly that we intend
to continue in the campaign for Kenyatta's release until he
is released, because we refuse to believe that the Government's present policy of his continued restriction is the
right policy. We refuse to believe that this policy is in fact
helping in terms of security, law and order. I want to
suggest, in fact I want to state, that Kenyatta's continued
restriction is a greater menace to security than his release,
and that these arguments about security, law and order
are completely out of date. Kenyatta should be released to
put an end to all this uncertainty, all this insecurity.

'Anybody who suggests that he will never be released is
dreaming, because he will be released one day. We are saying to you that it should be now and not tomorrow, because
in view of the stability that is necessary for this country,
so long as Kenyatta remains in restriction it will continue
to be an issue, a source of misunderstanding, a source of
friction between the Government and the people of this
country. If anybody doubts that the entire African community wants Kenyatta released, then I think he ought to
have his head examined.

'I say to the Government: release Kenyatta and remove a big burden from your consciences and from your minds, and help this country at least to achieve stability. Whatever the Government may say, whatever the British public may think or say, ultimately and indeed even now the position and status of Kenyatta can only be determined by the African people, and so long as the African people call him, refer to him, think of him, accept him and recognize him as their leader, no one can change that fact.'

Yet just a week later (May 10, 1960) the still-quite-new Governor, Sir Patrick Renison, made one of the most astonishing and notorious statements in all history. For sheer clumsiness and discord, the baseless nature of its catalogue of untruths, and its utter futility as a contribution to the stability and progress of a territory for which he was responsible, it would seem impossible to surpass this blundering assembly of assertions. In the most critical passage, condensed for sharpness but with nothing relevant edited away, Renison said:

> Jomo Kenyatta was the recognized leader of the non-co-operation movement which organized Mau Mau. Here was an African leader to darkness and death. With the assistance of the researches carried out by Mr. F. D. Corfield, I have very carefully studied his life and modes of thought and speech and action. He planned Kikuyu domination; he was an implacable opponent of any co-operation with other people, tribes or races, who live in Kenya. From the security viewpoint, I think that Jomo Kenyatta's return to political life in Kenya at the present time would be a disaster. We are not yet far enough away from all the tragedies, the hatreds and the passions of Mau Mau. I ask those who have been leading the campaign for Jomo Kenyatta's release to ponder deeply what I have said about light and darkness.

It is important (in the sense of the footnote printed earlier) to try and understand why Sir Patrick Renison should have made so grotesque an assessment of his duties,

and of their whole environment in both political and
psychological terms.

When Renison arrived in Kenya, to succeed Baring, he
knew nothing whatever about African affairs. He was, in
fact, the epitome of a long held Colonial Service assumption
that a man trained by the Code of Regulations, and who
had risen through approved steps, showing no nasty
tendency to think for himself, could serve with equal
effectiveness in Singapore, Kenya, South America, West
Africa, New Guinea or Ceylon.

Familiarity with the historical and political background
of a territory, with its peoples and languages and culture,
with its economy and resources and national personality,
was considered irrelevant. A Governor was an instrument
at so high and unquestionable a level that petty details
need hardly colour his functional activity or advice to his
superiors, and if he did ever need to base some pronouncement on facts, then their provision was what his officials
and advisers were for.

It was therefore understood, as part of the custom, that
Renison would really know nothing about the subject for
which he would stand as spokesman and ultimate authority.
But the grapevine gossip which preceded all such appointments intimated as well that in place of Baring, a man of
great economic talent, Kenya would have in Renison a
coldly-skilful political Governor, "a tough number who
had put Jagan in his place", a man who could unravel
intricate knots with their flair of political acument, or —
when that failed — with sudden charm.

In the event, throughout his time in office, Renison was
defeated both by his catastrophic lack of understanding of
— or sympathy with — Kenya, and by himself. At professional root, he was an unsure, baby-faced man. And
behind his bland expression lurked not (as was expected)
the mind of a supreme political strategist, like Macleod,
but the mental apparatus of a Boy Scout.

Renison made a fetish, in all his modes of thought and
action, of the word "honourable". This can hardly be

faulted, although it blunted him too frequently to reality and truth. The Corfield report will come to be considered in a later section of this chapter. Renison swallowed Corfield whole. His God was The Service, and anything contained in the files of The Service was automatically respectable and right.

In saying, therefore — as he did on May 10 — that "I have very carefully studied his life", Renison was speaking within his own limitations. He honestly regarded his super-ficial and unscholarly browsings among irrelevant or carefully-selected or deliberately-biassed material as being an objective appraisal, leading him into paths of duty from which he would not flinch. He would have accepted, as a thesis, that all the people of a country could be wrong, since it was clearly laid down in the Regulations that a Governor could not be out of step.

There was another factor as well. So steeped was Renison in procedure and protocol that the appreciations and urgings of his official and executive advisers were to him considerations of ultimate weight. Thus, men who had carried on the tradition of distorted administration and abuse of power, which began with Kenyatta's arrest in 1952, inserted Renison into this sordid picture, and filled the gullible mind of a man whose judgment was never robust enough for politics with their pyrotechnical displays of darkness and light.

It is obviously impossible to declare with certainty here, in respect of the "darkness and death" utterance by Sir Patrick Renison, that Coutts (himself a man of calvinistic inclinations) in fact drafted this phrase and placed it in the Governor's hands. But it would seem remarkable if it were ever established that Coutts was very far away.

Immediate reaction to the Governor's statement — that is to say, in the first hour or two — was as much bewildered as outraged. In the Budget debate in the Legislature, which was continuing on May 10, 1960, two African Members made some remarks indicative of contemporary thinking: "Jomo

Kenyatta kept on reminding people of all these problems
in Kenya. He kept on doing this year after year, year after
year, and when things came to a head then he was arrested,
and now he is taken to be the worst man that ever lived.
I do not agree with His Excellency the Governor in his
thinking that this question is not political. It is real politics
in Kenya. Without his release, the Lancaster House agreement is not complete. There is someone who holds strong
grudges against Jomo Kenyatta in this country. That is the
man I am warning and requesting to reconsider his position.
I hold very strongly that Jomo Kenyatta is innocent. But
what will help us all in this dilemma is to forget the past".

"The Governor's statement has been most unfortunate.
The Government must be more realistic. Everybody in this
country wants peace. Everybody in this country wants
security. You want economic stability, but you will never
have this without political stability, and I cannot see how
you can have political stability when Kenyatta is further
detained. Let us have Kenyatta back."

(By this time, Mzee Kenyatta had lived through nearly
four hundred days of his exile at Lodwar).

On May 11, 1960, James Gichuru, following his release
from restriction, trenchantly announced that he would seek
permission from Sir Patrick Renison to go up to Lodwar.
He declared that Kenyatta was not a threat to security, and
that once he was released the African leaders could begin
to plan constructively for the future.

On May 13, a delegation of African Elected Members
went to Government House with an official request that
African Members should be allowed to visit Lodwar. They
wanted to prove — as a Document put it — that Jomo
Kenyatta would not be a threat to security.

Nobody within or on the fringes of Government House,
then, had the kind of comprehension that would enable
them to put all the Emergency years and happenings in
perspective. They were simply unable to appreciate that
— whatever recent history had to tell about the "shooting

war", the incidents and round-ups, the screening and rehabilitation — there was never any possibility of getting the Kikuyu (in particular) to change their minds about Jomo Kenyatta.

The terrible occurrences at Hola had sprung from attempts to get detainees to stop singing songs about Kenyatta. All over Kikuyuland, the songs and dances which had endured throughout many bitter years were still on the theme of Kenyatta: not only on the impulse of the men, but also through the inspiration of the women, who were deeply imbued with the fervour of nationalism and whose solid influence was often under-rated. And whatever overt impressions may have been created, the Chiefs were still loyal to the Old Man: to Mzee.

All the mature political leaders in Kenya currently realized one thing. With Kenyatta at liberty and in command years before, the Emergency need never have happened. Now, without Kenyatta free and in command, it would never (except as legal technicality) be finished, since only this one man could so subjugate rubble and chaos as to lay bare horizons of national unity and dignity, economic prosperity and social purpose.

On May 14, Kenyatta was elected in absentia as President of the Kenya African National Union (KANU), at a special meeting of African political leaders convened at Kiambu. The Acting President, James Gichuru, told reporters that he was "keeping the seat warm for Jomo's return". Mzee Kenyatta's daughter, Margaret, attended this meeting as a guest.

At least some qualified support for the African attitude at that time was provided by a leading article in the *East African Standard* of May 17, 1960, from which the following extracts are taken:

'Demands on behalf of the African Elected Members to see Kenyatta, and the threat of resignation if they are not allowed to do so within the month, are neither so outrageous nor so bellicose as many people might suppose.

'Visitors have already been permitted at Lodwar — Mr. Havelock and Dr. Walker on one occasion and Mr. D. T. Moi on another — so there cannot be any very strong reason for refusing a repetition.

'They would see for themselves the state of Kenyatta's health and hear his views on recent developments. No doubt they would bring back some sort of message, and if that message indicated his willingness to help the African people along the ways of co-operation, so much the better for the people and for the personal chances of release.

'The overriding concern in making a decision is public security, with the paramount necessity for all the citizens of Kenya to live in peace, without fear for their safety. This was made perfectly plain by the Governor, supported by the Colonial Secretary. The impact of Kenyatta on security, therefore, is the criterion, involving the looked-for advancement of the African people. Any talk of civil disobedience can only jeopardise all these hopes.

'What happened last weekend, in substance, was to answer the Governor's declaration against Kenyatta's release at this time by electing Kenyatta President of the Kenya African National Union — a Party in process of formation for it is not yet registered — coupled with the demand for the visit. Is this not really just another skirmish in a planned offensive?'

On May 19, when Dr. Banda (now President of Malawi) called in at Dar es Salaam, he joined Julius Nyerere in publicly urging the release of Jomo Kenyatta — "our friend and colleague, whose leadership alone can bring peace and tranquillity to Kenya.'

A few days later, on May 31, the National Executive of TANU passed a resolution in Dar es Salaam calling for Kenyatta's unconditional release — "in order that he may, with fellow leaders, bring freedom to Kenya."

But for more than four weeks after the May 10 statement by Sir Patrick Renison, both the Governor and the

Government remained silent. Statements, petitions and delegations all addressed themselves alike to impassive and impermeable ears.

However, on June 12, 1960, an official statement was caused to be issued, opening up perhaps a millimetre of frigid concession at a time when both justice and tactic might have gained lustre from a mile of human balm. The statement read:

> African Elected Members and others have asked to be allowed to visit Jomo Kenyatta at Lodwar. In keeping with the Government policy of regular review, a series of visits of members of the Council of Ministers has been arranged and has been taking place to the remaining detention camps and places of restriction throughout Kenya. In the course of these visits, members of the Council of Ministers including African Elected Members of that Council, will at a suitable time visit Lodwar and see Kenyatta.

CORFIELD ON THE BANDWAGON

One of the publications which became notorious in this whole period and context was a report by Mr. F. D. Corfield, introduced in mid-1960 to the world at large, entitled: "Historical survey of the origins and growth of Mau Mau". It is doubtful whether any more pretentious document — or anything more blatantly fraudulent in design and conclusion — could be found in all the archives of Government-sponsored appreciations.

Let it be freely recognised that Frank Corfield's career, in war and peace, showed him to be an Officer of courage and an administrator of skill, often exhibiting the very antithesis of the wooden mind so generally regarded by the Colonial Office as a satisfying utensil. Moreover, it is apparent from the record that he knew the Sudan very well, Palestine almost equally well, and Ethiopia in some degree. But when accepting the burden of this task, to compile an "historical survey", he knew virtually nothing about Kenya at all.

This fact must have heightened the comfort of those officials who urged him on, and it is thoroughly regrettable that — at such behest — Corfield should have done so much less than justice to his own propriety.

He was apparently required, since this was evidently his method, to string together by means of qualifying phrases, and arrange into competent-seeming paragraphs and chapters, such past reports and observations of the Administration and the Police as (superficially) would offer *prima facie* justification for the reprehensible official intrigue which began in 1952.

He was apparently convinced, by the officials of the day, that Kenyatta was some kind of composite of Machiavelli, Hitler and Genghis Khan, since he sought only to uphold such a travesty, and whenever he stumbled on contrary facts these were either ignored altogether or decried in some derogatory phrase.

Corfield made a fool of scholarship, and of himself. But he produced a document which officialdom was overjoyed to lionise.

As background now to contemporary criticism of the Corfield report, it may be as well to recall the social conditions and considerations which could — in their aggregate — be described as the fundamental origins of Mau Mau. These were reflectively summarised by Tom Mboya in his book *Freedom and After*, from which the following passages are taken:

'Mau Mau was the child of economic and social problems which had accumulated over the years, and which had not found any solution through constitutional channels. They were nearly all problems of discrimination against Africans in different forms — discrimination in employment and in salaries; refusal by Government to let Africans grow cash crops like coffee, tea, sisal and pyrethrum; discrimination in Post Offices, hotels and restaurants, supported by a Government which had made liquor laws on racial lines; discrimination by Government in giving aid to schools and

hospitals on a racial basis; the absence of African representation in the Legislature or of any voice at all in the Government; the indirect rule of the African people through
Chiefs and Administrative Officers who did not reflect any
local African opinion. All these irritations went together
to create frustration which accumulated over the years.

'There was also the sensitive problem of land. The
question of land helps to explain why the Mau Mau revolution was largely contained in one area of the country —
Central Province and the Rift Valley — rather than covering Kenya.

'By the time of the Emergency — as the Royal Commission on Land in East Africa showed — out of the 20,000
square miles of land in Kenya with a rainfall of more than
20 inches, 5,900 square miles had been reserved for
Europeans who formed less than one percent of the
country's population.

'An atmosphere was created over the land question in
which it was no longer possible to reason. The matter
became so emotional. Many families were removed from
their land to give way to white settlement, and Africans
never accepted the settler argument that the land had
been found empty and uninhabited. Most Africans argued
that, although it was not our system to fence land, each
piece of land was claimed by some tribes, even if at the
time they were not actively using that land. This particularly applied to the pastoral tribes who moved from one
area to another, but also the Kikuyu, who were not culti-
vating some areas into which the first white settlers moved
because they had at that time suffered a series of catas-
trophies, including rinderpest.

'For a long time, the sensitive land question was more
an issue for the Kikuyu than for the rest of Kenya. Most
of the other tribes were unaffected by white settlement,
for there was hardly any settlement in Nyanza Province
or at the Coast or in other areas. The irritations of the
colour-bar and race discrimination, although felt almost

equally throughout Kenya, were more intense in the settled areas and in the towns.

'Incidentally, in the Corfield report it is argued that the KAU never spread its following beyond the Kikuyu. Corfield might have some difficulty in explaining why seven of the nine office-bearers of the KAU were non-Kikuyu.'

That passage can serve the cause of historical perspective, and bring down to earth a presentation by Corfield compiled while seemingly in orbit, round turgid planets of invective and whimsy.

It was not only in Kenya that the glaring bias of this Corfield submission was condemned. On June 5, 1960, a leading article in *The Observer* (in London) had this to say:

> Mr. Corfield's report could not be called an objective study. Indeed, no attempt at judicial impartiality is made. Kenyatta's guilt is assumed from the start. Neither the shaky structure of evidence on which Kenyatta was convicted, nor the Corfield report, can be said to satisfy beyond reasonable doubt that Kenyatta was the brain behind Mau Mau. Before his arrest, Kenyatta's attitude to Mau Mau was equivocal. He publicly condemned it at large public meetings on several occasions. It should also be remembered that Mau Mau became a violent revolution only after Kenyatta and the majority of African political leaders were arrested.

The matter was debated in Legislative Council in Kenya on June 16, 1960, on a Motion seeking to record the appreciation of the House to Mr. Corfield for the production and content of this report.

All the anguish of the past, brought into new and vivid focus by the impact of this gutter journalism masquerading as historical survey, was expressed by two selected spokesmen from the African benches:

> There has never been a more unfair, a more partial and unbalanced report than this one. If there is anybody

who should be taken as having tried to warn the Government to take heed, to try to rectify the grievances of the African people in order to avoid bloodshed, I think Jomo Kenyatta should be number one. He was the man who did all that he could. He stayed in Great Britain for 16 years trying to plead with the British Government, but no one listened. He came back to this country, but he did not go to violence. He came to form a constitutional organization, which later on sent a delegation again to Great Britain, and to the United Nations, to plead for the African development. Yet no one really listened to him . . .

In my own considered opinion, the Corfield report qualifies for either the wastepaper basket or just being banned. It has not helped at all in any sense. It is a doctored report. We would have liked to have seen also some of the speeches made by European politicians from time to time, produced as the basis on which some of the African reactions during all that period may have come. I discount completely any serious suggestion on the part of the Government that we should give any serious consideration, or attach any significance, to any of the so-called evidence at Kapenguria. The assumption that formed the basis of the Corfield report is that — when anything goes wrong — it must be the African who has done it, because he is the only black person in this country. There are many black people among the Europeans in this country. It is not a one-way traffic, this whole question of peace, harmony, friendship and so on. A lot of responsibility rests with this Government.

On the Unofficial side of the House, at that time, it was not unknown to rub up against conscience, or moderation, or rationality. But any such observations or appeals from the African Members were regarded, by the officialdom of the day, as routine agitation quite unworthy of appraisal or analysis. The Officials would play out the game. For however much longer, both within and outside the Legislature, an impregnable bluff was maintained.

At this point, however, the Council was galvanised by a speech from one of the European Elected Members — Mr. S. V. Cooke, the Member for the Coast. Shirley Victor Cooke, an Irishman by ancestry but Kenyan in spirit, is now retired but still living in Kenya today. In a speech of great courage, with sparks of that satirical honesty of which he was so capable, he flayed the Corfield document. These lengthy extracts are taken from the Hansard report:

'Mr. Corfield, to my own certain knowledge, has omitted many facts and committed a good many errors. He omits many cases which were in favour of Jomo Kenyatta, and he puts emphasis on any others which are against Jomo Kenyatta.

'Now this is a very important matter. In 1951, Mr. Jomo Kenyatta and Mr. Peter Koinange came to several of us — including myself and Mr. Vasey . . . (*Now Sir Ernest Vasey*) . . . and Sir Charles Mortimer — repeating that there was a grave danger of serious unrest, and we formed then what was called the Kenya Citizens Association. What I want to emphasise is that this Association was formed on the initiative of those two men, not on our initiative, as one would be inclined to infer from this report. Jomo Kenyatta and Peter Koinange were sincerely anxious to warn Government that, unless some action was taken, there would be great trouble in this country, and I think it would be grossly unfair not to reveal that to the House.

'Jomo Kenyatta went to Kaloleni Hall and denounced Mau Mau in a way that satisfied all the Europeans who were present at the meeting. He denounced it very vigorously. Later on, I saw several educated Africans who had been at Kaloleni, and they said they were perfectly satisfied with his denunciation of sedition in this country.

'Corfield always tries to see the worst side of this man. He said that Jomo Kenyatta was useless on the African Land Utilisation Board, because he never talked anything but politics. Well, I was on the Board at the same time, with Mr. Eliud Mathu, and we both resigned as well,

because we thought that Kenyatta was never given a fair
hearing when he made his protests about agriculture and
so on. Mr. Frank Joyce also threatened to resign, so
Kenyatta was not the only person dissatisfied with the
working of the Board.

'As another instance of unfairness, Corfield said that
"without a shadow of doubt" Jomo Kenyatta expropriated
the funds of the Teacher Training College. Well, Sir, if
there was not a shadow of doubt, I must say the then
Attorney-General showed a dereliction of duty.

'Right throughout the report he depends on hearsay, so
people must be warned not to give too much credence to
some of the conclusions.'

With that, the Corfield report may now be left to lie
forgotten, as the shabby interjection it was proved to be.

PRESSURE BECOMES CLAMOUR

There was no sign in ensuing weeks that the Government
really intended to implement the hint (embodied in the
official statement of June 12) that African Members might
be allowed to visit Lodwar. But Mr. Coutts (as Chief
Secretary) went up there in August 1960, and — after
some formal discussion — Mzee Kenyatta handed to him
a petition asking that a visit by African leaders should be
permitted, in order that talks on the future of Kenya could
begin.

This petition was unavailing, and more weeks went by.

On October 20, 1960, a procession made its way up to
Government House and presented yet another reasoned
letter on the subject of Kenyatta's release. This again had
no effect, and the whole climate of this pressure called for
the kind of patience that a man or a movement would need
in seeking a decision from the Sphinx.

On November 1, 1960, the then Deputy Leader of KADU
arrived in London and had a meeting with Mr. MacLeod.
He told the Colonial Secretary that intensity of feeling
among the Africans had currently reached such a pitch that

some public statement on the question of Kenyatta's release had become an urgent need. He affirmed KADU's belief that Jomo Kenyatta and all other African detainees should be freed before elections under the new Constitution were held in February. He also said they should be allowed to stand as candidates if they wished, and he made it clear that KADU would not oppose Kenyatta in whatever seat he chose to contest.

There is no means of knowing precisely what effect the whole current campaign may have had on Mr. Macleod's own thinking. In retrospect, there can be little doubt that the Macleod of 1960 was greatly impressed by James Gichuru, who was released from restriction early in that year and travelled privately to London for an unpublicised discussion with the Colonial Secretary. But the British Government as an institution still felt bound primarily to rely on their man in Nairobi: on Renison.

Back in Kenya, one of the local newspapers — the *Daily Nation* — came out strongly in favour of Kenyatta's release, in an editorial published on November 22, 1960:

> The only possible justification for keeping him in Lodwar now would be firm evidence that his release would lead to renewed strife. There is no such evidence and, in fact, those most concerned with keeping the peace in Kenya — senior Officers in the Police force — are understood to be of the opinion that Kenyatta would be far less of a security risk out than in. The release of Kenyatta might remove tribalism and factionalism at one stroke, allowing the Africans to go forward to independence in unity, a development which — although seeming to threaten some form of totalitarianism — is the only guarantee of a really safe transfer of power and sound government.

On the following day, November 23, a statement issued by KANU examined the nebulous factor of "security risk" customarily advance in the course of infrequent official statements on the Kenyatta issue. KANU could see no firm evidence or practical ground for upholding the existence of such an alleged risk, and commented at one stage: "It cannot be said that the situation of law and order in the Colony is the same as it was last May, unless the Government wants to admit that it has failed to improve that situation."

On November 28, 1960, the *East African Standard* published a news report from its correspondent in London:

> Soundings taken in the City yesterday confirm that there is a general feeling that the sooner Kenyatta is released the better. Even among those with personal, as opposed to merely trading, experience of Kenya, there is recognition that his release would allow the political dust to settle. Most support the view of the City merchant whose Company has large investments in Kenya, and who said: "Any factor hindering the economic development of Kenya must be swept aside. I believe the continued rustication of Kenyatta is hindering such development, and he should be taken back to Nairobi as soon as possible".

Christmas came and went, the time — supposedly — of goodwill to all men, and another year dawned . . .

On January 10, 1961, Sir Patrick Renison had a meeting with a KANU delegation in London. The following official statement on the outcome of these talks was issued immediately thereafter:

> This morning at the Kenya Office in London, the Governor received a delegation from KANU consisting of Mr. James Gichuru, Dr. Njoroge Mungai and Mr. W. C. M. Chokwe.

> The delegation put to the Governor new evidence of what they thought to be the feeling of the people in Kenya in support of the release of Jomo Kenyatta, and particularly mentioned a meeting at Nyeri which took place after the Governor left Kenya in December, at which representatives of the Church, loyalists and chiefs were present.

The delegation also showed the Governor a telegram of support signed by the Kenya Indian Congress, the East African Goan League, and the Kenya Freedom Party.

The Governor undertook to consider the evidence put forward, together with all the other evidence available to him.

That official statement, which offered no useful commitment in its concluding observations, made especial reference to a meeting at Nyeri. The following comment is by a man — currently a distinguished journalist in Kenya — who was present at Nyeri, and who is qualified to take an objective view of the occasion's significance:

Dr. Mungai convened a meeting of all Kikuyus — that is, ex-forest fighters, ex-home guards, leaders of the Church, pacifists and agnostics — and he secured a unanimous resolution that the return of Mr. Kenyatta among them would not cause a deeper division of the Kikuyu tribe. To my mind, this factor constituted a crucial determinant of Kenyatta's release. The Government continued to advance the argument that Kenyatta's return to the Kikuyu country would cause an inter-tribal war, between the loyalists on the one hand and other sections of the Kikuyu population on the other. By persuading the various factions to consent to the release of Kenyatta, Dr. Mungai managed to explode the last Imperialist myth that Kenyatta was unwanted.

Members of the London delegation — and their KANU colleagues — were completely dissatisfied with Renison's response, and so a further group went up to Government House in Nairobi on January 19, 1961. As before, an official communique was issued thereafter:

The Governor of Kenya, Sir Patrick Renison, received at Government House this morning at their request a delegation consisting of Mr. James Gichuru, Mr. Tom Mboya, Mr. M. Chokwe and Mr. J. Mathenge. Dr.

Njoroge Mungai and Mr. Arthur Ochwada joined the delegation just as the talks were finishing.

The Governor listened to the arguments put forward for the release of Jomo Kenyatta. He said that the delegation in London and today's delegation could not have made their feelings more clear. The Governor said he fully understood that the responsibility for the decision in the Kenyatta case rested on his shoulders, and he was under no illusions about the importance of the issue to the future of Kenya. But having made that clear His Excellency told those present that he had nothing to say on this issue at the present time.

And there, in a nutshell of his own manufacture, was Renison: widely spaced utterances that could hardly have been more maladroit, interspersed with long periods when, shielding himself in the verbose qualifications of a man beyond his depth, His Excellency had nothing to say.

While all this was happening, the pressures continued elsewhere. In Dar es Salaam, Julius Nyerere (then Chief Minister of Tanganyika), accompanied by Kenneth Kaunda (now President of Zambia), and Joshua Nkomo (one of the nationalist leaders of Rhodesia, today in detention), arrived back from a PAFMECA Conference on January 13, 1961. They told reporters: "The first thing we did was to send a very strong resolution to the Colonial Secretary for the immediate release of Jomo Kenyatta. There is not the slightest doubt that the only person who can unite Kenya is Kenyatta".

KENYATTA'S MOUNTING SWAY

Elections were held in Kenya in February 1961, under a system which engendered some political-bazaar bargaining, seen through generally in an atmosphere of excitement but good humour, with no ugly incidents at all. It was necessary for European and Asian (Muslim and non-Muslim) candidates, with their eye on Special Seats allotted to them, first to triumph in "primary elections" held within their own communities, and then to present themselves for confirmatory election on a much wider franchise bringing in African voters. In practice, this required them to obtain endorsement and support either from KANU (as the "national front") or from KADU (as a then opposition Party).

The scene and implications were described in a shrewd comment by Colin Legum in London, published in the The Observer of February 26, 1961:

> The attempt to keep Kenyatta out of Kenya's first nationwide elections has been a complete failure. Even from his remote, sun-baked residence of detention in Lodwar, Kenyatta dominated the election hustings as none of the politicians actively engaged in the hustings has done. This has, in fact, been Kenyatta's election. His picture looks down from the hoardings in every constituency. "Uhuru na Kenyatta" is chanted at all political meetings. Even the European and Asian candidates — who for the first time must woo the African voters to ensure their election for the special seats — have been compelled to some extent to climb on the Kenyatta bandwagon.

Campaigning very largely on the issue of Jomo Kenyatta's release and national leadership, KANU won these elections with about two-thirds of the popular vote.

It then became, prima facie at least, the task of Sir Patrick Renison to form a Government and to institute such policies as would reflect this national mandate and give some expression to popular will. But in the event, due in whatever proportion to his own obduracy or the enduring clamp of his officials, Renison simply embarked upon another wounding gambit.

The Governor staged this most theatrically. Early in March 1961, he invited Gichuru and Mboya (representing KANU), and Ngala and Muliro (representing KADU) up to Government House. When they were seated, Sir Patrick consulted his watch and then switched on a radio. His voice came out, in a statement to the nation, saying at the critical stage:

> In spite of the great difficulties of conscience after the Mau Mau horrors, it is not my view that Jomo Kenyatta should be kept in restriction indefinitely. I do not, however, propose to release him until the new Government is working well, and until I think that the security risk can be accepted and contained, and that the danger that his return presents to the economy and administration and to our whole constitutional progress towards early independence has been minimised. I care for Kenya too much to contemplate his stepping from restriction to a position of authority. I accept that the responsibility is mine, and mine alone. I ask you to read again my statement of last May. Nothing has happened since to make me wish I had worded the statement or any part of it differently.

It would be difficult to think of any complex of action and attitude more utterly extraordinary than this.

Instead of summoning the leaders both of the majority Party (KANU) and the minority Party (KADU) for frank and private discussions — which they had expected — on steps to be taken as an outcome of national elections, Renison presented them with the fait accompli of this broadcast speech. He was then seemingly naive enough to suppose that KANU could and would rally to his need to form a popular and stable government, having campaigned for office on the platform of Kenyatta's leadership, and then having heard the Governor reaffirm his description of Kenyatta as "leader to darkness and death".

Ordinary rational scrutiny of this sort of behaviour must leave any interpreter adrift. The Governor's statement again associated Kenyatta with Mau Mau, which was a lie. He spoke of "the new Government", which was neither in existence nor then in conceivable prospect. He mentioned "security risk" and "danger", with which, after careful schooling, his imagination was obsessed. And he referred to "constitutional progress" as though this could even

coherently begin before the one obstacle to its very com-
mencement was cleared away.

Renison asked the four delegates, at the end of the
broadcast, what they had thought of his speech. They
pointed out that there was no purpose then in asking for
opinion or advice. The speech had already gone out to the
country, and was in the public record. There was nothing
they could do, except completely disassociate themselves
from the sentiments expressed.

The delegates then requested that representatives from
both Parties should be allowed to visit Lodwar and discuss
the situation with Kenyatta, before Sir Patrick called on
anyone to form a Government. His immediate reaction was
refusal, clearly feeling it would be an embarrassment for
Kenyatta to be consulted in such a context, implying as
this would do that Jomo Kenyatta was in fact the real
leader of Kenya.

On the following morning, Renison changed his mind.
He advised that the four delegates who had been at Government House could go to Lodwar, but imposed a condition which Gichuru and Mboya were clearly unable to
accept, as Renison must have foreseen. And there the
matter rested for some time.

By pursuit of this remarkable strategy, the Governor
made it impossible for KANU to assist in the formation of
a Government that would honour the Party's election
pledges. After six weeks of hiatus, which ripened into seeds
of crisis, a minority Government was eventually composed
of a partnership between KADU and the New Kenya Party.
The effect of this manoeuvre on the pace and serenity of
Kenya's constitutional advance was not inconsiderable.

There was puzzlement as well as outrage in appraisal of
the Governor's attitude. Many of the African leaders,
almost from the day that Sir Patrick Renison landed in
Kenya, had urged him to go and see Kenyatta, or to accom-
pany them on a visit to Kenyatta, or even to send for
Kenyatta. It was made abundantly clear to the Governor
that Jomo Kenyatta would — soon or later — become

the leader of Kenya. All the time, as one of many tactics, the Governor complained that he had no means of knowing, and could never be certain, what was in Kenyatta's mind. Yet he appeared to have neither the resolution, nor the proper curiosity, nor the ordinary aplomb, to find out.

When Renison left Kenya eventually, it took the mature wisdom and humanity of a Malcolm Macdonald to rescue Britain from the harm and discredit, which threatened to be lasting, that Renison had engineered.

While all these events were taking place, or hanging in the balance, protestations on all sides about Mzee Kenyatta's continued detention went on.

On March 2, 1961, Milton Obote (now President of Uganda but speaking then for the Uganda People's Congress) publicly urged that Jomo Kenyatta's release would consolidate African public opinion, remove the bitterness of the past, and contribute greatly to stability in Kenya.

On March 10, a leading article in the *Daily Nation* made this point: "It is time for the Governor himself to have a meeting with Kenyatta. If he really wants to know what is in Kenyatta's mind, would it not be better for them to meet man to man, rather than for the Governor to get his information secondhand from sources which cannot be described as totally disinterested?"

On March 12, the *Sunday Post* published a statement by the Secretary of the Masai United Front, representing one of the minority tribes allegedly in fear of domination following Jomo Kenyatta's return. This read:

> Kenyatta is not bitter, he is not against his enemies, he is no racialist, he is no alcoholic wretch, he is not senile, he is not ignorant of political development in Kenya for the past nine years; in short, he is no danger to security as has been alleged. Jomo Kenyatta is the Gandhi of Kenya. His continued restriction is therefore an unparalleled injustice and will end in chaos.

On March 13, in Britain, *The Guardian* included an article by its resident Kenya correspondent, Clyde Sanger, saying the Governor should make an undisguised climb down and release Jomo Kenyatta unconditionally. Sanger then went on: "A major block to rational action over Kenyatta is the denunciation of the man himself over the last nine years. He is commonly referred to in newspapers as the manager of Mau Mau. Sir Patrick has added his own phrases to reinforce this attitude, yet evidence to support this vilification is extremely scanty".

On March 15, on behalf of KANU, James Gichuru issued this statement: "There can be no stability in this country unless Kenyatta is unconditionally released. It is unfortunate that the exemplary behaviour of the African people and political organisations during the recent elections should have been rewarded with a rebuff by the British Government, on an issue which is of paramount importance to the African people".

On March 20, on behalf of KADU, Ronald Ngala made it clear in an analogous statement that his Party also wished to see Kenyatta free.

And on March 27, in a leading article, the *East African Standard* complained that — since 1957 — that newspaper had pressed unrewardingly through official channels for permission to lift the veil that had been created around Jomo Kenyatta.

Before the month ended, a delegation consisting of six nominees each of KANU and KADU was authorised to visit Kenyatta at Lodwar. When they returned (March 23, 1961) a joint statement was read out to correspondents. This said it had been agreed at Lodwar that unity among Africans was essential, and should be pursued relentlessly, in the struggle towards independence. In the meantime, KANU and KADU should work in full consultation, on the question of full independence for Kenya and the immediate unconditional release of Jomo Kenyatta. But this was not the only outcome of the Lodwar safari. A tape-recorded greeting was made there, and was played back at the All Africa People's Conference, in Cairo on March 26. The text of this message, symbolising despite its brevity much of the philosophy of Mzee Kenyatta, was:

> This is Jomo Kenyatta speaking from Lodwar. I am very happy to send you my greetings and best wishes for the success of the Conference. I hope the All Africa People's Conference will work for the unity and strength of our people, and that unity will hasten the liberation of our people everywhere. The time has come when Africa must stand with other nations and show that she has something, not only to receive, but also to give to the world. I hope peace and prosperity will come to our people, when all of us can unite and work for the purpose of uplifting our people who have been struggling so hard for centuries.

This recording — which endangered the blood pressure of sundry officials who heard about it afterwards — was introduced and operated by Tom Mboya, who told the Conference: "I can assure you that Kenyatta is still alive and fit, and still leader of Kenya. Whether the British like it or not, no real Government will be formed in Kenya unless it is led by Jomo Kenyatta".

Nine days later, though still restricted, Mzee Kenyatta was moved away from Lodwar, and another chapter in this saga dawned.

Chapter 4

SPELL AT HALFWAY HOUSE

THE PRESS CONFERENCE

On the evening of a Tuesday — April 4, 1961 — a pithy but momentous press release was issued from the Government machine. It read: "Mr. Jomo Kenyatta arrived at Maralal by air from Lodwar this afternoon with his family. Mr. Kenyatta has moved into the house at Maralal where he will continue to be under a restriction order".

Maralal is the headquarters of the Samburu District, about 180 miles south-east of Lodwar, and 180 miles (in a straight line) north of Nairobi. In a perfectly accurate sense, therefore, this was a "halfway house".

The basic feature of Maralal is a pot-holed and dusty main street, flanked by Administrative offices, a small hospital and sundry stores, the whole surrounded by manyattas and the schools and other premises of Missions. The township itself is in the grip of hills, on the sides or summits of which are perched the houses of local officials: the District Commissioner, the Game Warden, the senior Policeman, the Forestry and Veterinary Officers, the Road Engineer. Kenyatta lived in one of these houses throughout his stay here of 130 days. He found it a steep journey up and down the hillsides when visiting the duka, being allowed no access to any wheeled instrument or vehicle. But the traders in the township, and the local Samburu, were generous and helpful.

In terms of surroundings, Kenyatta found himself now in a starting-off place for safaris into some of the wildest and most magnificent game areas of Kenya. And in one direction there was daily balm for eyes accustomed to the desert. Looking straight down the main road from Maralal, south-east as it runs in its initial phase, the clear light and limitless horizon of many an African morning give rise to a breathtaking skyline view, in which the principal resident of this period found enrichment for the spirit at the end of long and barren years. Mzee Kenyatta was once again facing Mount Kenya.

The decision to transfer Kenyatta to Maralal was a timorous one. He was still in an Outlying District, with restriction easy to maintain. At the same time, he was now only 70 miles from the outskirts of the settled areas, allowing much easier access — by air or by road — both to his physical presence and to the content of his mind. This desire, by the Governor and officialdom, to enjoy a closer scrutiny, was generally presented and regarded as the purpose of the move. Almost, this was like a swimmer who, knowing he must shortly take the plunge, first tests the water's feel and temperature by dabbling his toes in the pool.

But there was really more to it than this. Renison was under immense and growing pressure to release Kenyatta, locally and in Africa at large. Beyond, the sense in this issue of executive futility and moral outrage were spreading — through London, Washington and New Delhi — to the world outside. The nettle was there to be grasped, and he had to face up to decision.

True to his professional stature, he made this gesture instead.

The Governor was still bemused by his intractable officials. He was influenced as well by the intransigence of those — comparatively few in number but sinuous in voice — who dwelt in nostalgia for the Delamere days when white settlers and hidebound officials were lords of all of Kenya. This total collection of arid and narrow-minded men heaped disrepute upon a whole community, very many of whose members, on their farms or in their urban households, had by now developed views that were both tolerant and fair.

Through the implacable system of the Colonial Service, and the social influence — in Kenya and Britain — of vehement spokesmen for themselves, the Governor was kept in a political vice which he lacked the moral courage to elude or even to examine.

Even the critic-pacifying contrivance of this move to Maralal inspired such heated or sanctimonious riposte, from some, that the Corfield report was flung back into the ring. However, in public correspondence on this matter, Clyde Sanger of *The Guardian* — writing on April 7, 1961 — helped to reduce this to the perspective it deserved:

> I have of course studied the Corfield report, but I am bound to say that my first belief that this report was a rounded account of "the origins and growth" of Mau Mau was completely undermined by the later discovery that Mr. Corfield, in assembling his material, only had interviews with or accepted memoranda from exactly four Africans — including two Chiefs and one District Officer. This fact was excised from the published version of the report, but shows clearly that the report cannot claim to be anything but a presentation of the Government's side of the case. It is certainly not the last authentic word to be said on the subject.

Of course the tremendous event of this Maralal interlude, still talked about by aged Samburu who had never seen such a concourse in their lives, was the Press Conference of April 11, 1961.

Eight years had gone by since Kenyatta had spoken at his Kapenguria trial. In the four most recent of these years, pressure for his release, demands for his leadership, and avowals of his innocence, had reached a crescendo. This was no longer a routine political problem in a small Colony, something which the world might yawningly notice before passing by. Now this was international drama, with both principle and practice built in.

Just a week after Kenyatta's transfer to Maralal, arrangements were made for the world Press to visit him. Meticulously planned and directed by the Information and

Security services, an enormous convoy just descended on the place. Jomo Kenyatta then found himself besieged by news editors and reporters, resident correspondents and specifically-flown-out correspondents, feature writers, radio reporters, radio commentators, batteries of microphones, newspaper photographers, magazine photographers, cameramen, television newsmen, television teams.

The world wanted to hear something — almost anything quotable, after all this long time — from a man who had already become by record and repute a leading figure on the modern world stage. The Press of many countries therefore gathered, some representatives hoping for the droll stimulus of sensation, nearly all curious and a few genuinely anxious for the truth. They spent many feverish hours on a quest they would remember all their lives.

Uncounted thousands of words were written and spoken afterwards about this Maralal Press Conference: what transpired and what it all meant. The passage that follows, selected for its accuracy and as a model of objective reporting, is a condensed version of the story that was published in the _East African Standard_. Just two sentences have been interpolated, to elaborate points, taken from the tape of a radio interview brought back by the Kenya Broadcasting Service team.

These, then, were the views and responses of Jomo Kenyatta at the Maralal Press Conference of April 11, 1961:

'Before he answered questions, Kenyatta made a short statement in which he referred to his "position of disadvantage" as a restricted person. He hoped one day — "and this will not be very long" — that he would be able to meet the Press as a free man. He added: "I trust that in asking your questions, you will bear in mind that for more than eight years I have been bottled up in remote Districts away from public life and world affairs. During that time I have been greatly misrepresented by some of you, but today I hope you will stick to the truth and refrain from writing sensational stories about me".

'Kenyatta said he wanted to thank the millions of men and women, of various races and nations, who were fighting gallantly for his release. He also wished to thank his brethren who had kept up the struggle for Uhuru, and said: "I shall always remain an African nationalist to the end".

'First of all — he declared — Africans wanted political freedom. They wanted equal opportunities and rights, and an end to the colour bar. He favoured democratic Government with a Parliamentary system, and said the advance to independence must be through constitutional methods.

'The Governor had been badly advised and very obstinate, by accusing Kenyatta of refusal to speak. Far from refusing to give his views on various matters, he had expressed a desire on many occasions to meet the Governor. As recently as March 18, he had told his lawyer — Mr. Dingle Foot — that he would like to see the Governor, if the Governor wanted to know his views, but nothing had happened.

'Kenyatta said he believed in freedom of the African people from Colonialism and Imperialism, and felt he could achieve his objectives constitutionally.

'He had seen a copy of the Lancaster House Constitution and thought this was a step forward, but on the other hand it had — in some of its aspects — the kind of delaying tactic employed by colonial Powers. He felt it had served its purpose, and it was time another Constitution was brought into being.

'He said: "I do not think I am — and I never have been — an enemy of the Europeans or the white people, because I spent many years in England or in Europe, and even today I have many friends in various nations".

'Kenyatta said he had never had any Communist affiliations. He had visited Russia — "just like anybody else" — for educational purposes. He had been keen to see many countries in Europe, and one of them happened to be Russia. But Communism had no place in African society as it was today.

'His aim was to advance his people to better conditions — better schools, hospitals, roads and houses, and improved farming. Africans had some very fine customs which they could teach other people, but there were some customs which were not so good. His policy still was that some could be kept — and some European and Asian customs could be adapted — to build a new society based on the African mode of life.

'Questioned in general terms about respecting European land titles in Kenya, he said: "That would have to be gone into by a free Kenya Government after independence". Kenyatta said he had never advocated the eviction of Europeans from the Highlands. He had advocated that land which was not used — and there was a lot lying idle — should be taken over and given to landless Africans. People whose land was well farmed and yielding revenue should be encouraged. European land titles would be perfectly safe in all cases where land was being properly used.

'Under a future Kenya Government, all people — Europeans, Asians or Africans — accepting Kenya citizenship would have equal rights and equal protection in all spheres.

'Kenyatta said he had seen the Corfield report and it was "a pack of lies", a one-sided document with the single purpose of crushing Kenyatta. Much of the information was collected from needy informers, who said what Corfield wanted to hear. But he had no grudge. He could borrow from the New Testament philosophy: forgive them, for they know not what they do. He added: "I have never been a violent man. My whole life has been anti-violence, and will continue to be when I am free".

'He was then asked a particular question: "you have stated that you were opposed to oathing at the time, and that you made statements to that effect, and yet the oathing went on; so why did these deaths happen despite the great respect in which you are held by your people?" Kenyatta replied that many people respected the Queen, but nevertheless there were still gangsters in Britain. This, however, did not mean that the Queen was responsible for what they were doing.

'Asked what he would do to bridge the differences between KANU and KADU, Kenyatta said he had urged them — and still urged them — to come to some understanding. If one looked at their policies, one could find no difference between their demands. They should work together. He did not think the pastoral tribes in KADU were frightened of being submerged by the Kikuyu and Luo — "we want independence for all the people, not just for the Kikuyu and Luo" — but were the victims of some propaganda of divide-and-rule.

'It was not for him to decide whether he would be Chief Minister or anything else when he was free. It was for his people to decide what they wanted him to be.

'Asked for his views on the conflict between East and West in Africa, Kenyatta said the two blocs were like hungry dogs over a bone. When two elephants were fighting, it was the grass that suffered; and in the East-West struggle for power in Africa, it was the Africans who suffered. He thought the time would come when Africans themselves would realise this and act accordingly.

'Confidence in the economy of Kenya could be restored. People who were wanting to run away, or were waiting to send money away, were just being afraid for nothing.'

That report gives a faithful account of Jomo Kenyatta's own presentation of his views and objectives in April 1961.

What the report illumines, perhaps more than anything else, is the steadfastness of Mzee Kenyatta throughout his long political career. This happened to be 1961. But in terms of philosophy and approach and belief, he might have been speaking four years later or forty years before. As he himself was to observe, a few months after this tremendous Maralal occasion: "I have never changed".

Government House was quiet for the ensuing 48 hours. But then on April 14, 1961, this statement was issued:

The Governor has studied carefully the reports of the Press Conference held by Mr. Jomo Kenyatta at Maralal on April 11. The views expressed by Mr. Kenyatta will be of assistance to the Governor in considering when it will be possible to release Mr. Kenyatta from restriction.

The employment of "Mr." thrice, in such an otherwise sterile pronouncement, could be taken to embody the turning point implications — according to analogies chosen by various correspondents — of Trafalgar, Waterloo or Alamein.

"IN DUE COURSE"

This critical event at Maralal did not take place in utter isolation. Some most important elements of public opinion and judgment were contemporaneously being fomented and formed around the world outside.

In London, the annual conference of the Movement for Colonial Freedom (April 16, 1961) had passed a resolution demanding the immediate release of Kenyatta. On April 18, Mr. Stonehouse raised this matter in the Commons, and received from Mr. Fraser an entirely negative reply. This seemed strange.

For on this same day in Kenya, an official statement that — while far from being positive — was a fraction less than negative, was issued in the following terms: "The Governor has agreed that the Government will now begin to build a house for Mr. Jomo Kenyatta and his family, on a site to be agreed in Kiambu District, in readiness for Mr. Kenyatta's return from Maralal to his home in Kiambu in due course".

The phrase "in due course" was not altogether pleasing to Kenyans themselves, or to dispassionate commentators outside. In its London issue of April 22, 1961, *The Economist* made some unusually devastating observations on current affairs:

> Twice this month, the Governor of Kenya, Sir Patrick Renison, has injected such farce into the drama of Jomo Kenyatta's release that no political commentator could pass these banal moments by.

The first came when the Governor sent sixty journalists up to Mr. Kenyatta's new fastness at Maralal, to take for him the measure of the nationalist leader's intentions. Sir Patrick gratefully commented that he would study the reports carefully, and they would help him in considering when it would be possible to release Mr. Kenyatta. Another journalistic expedition is planned for May; but there is no whisper yet that the Governor intends to have his own first meeting with Mr. Kenyatta — and judge for himself.

The second moment followed when the Governor announced that a new house was to be built for Mr. Kenyatta a dozen miles outside Nairobi. While the house is to be tangible evidence of the Government's intention to remove the physical, if not the political, restrictions on Mr. Kenyatta, no time limit has been set for its construction. To suit Government policies, the builders could go slow; or else the house could be generously extended or embellished to delay Mr. Kenyatta's return to his people.

KAPENGURIA: FURTHER EXPOSURES

In the event, there was no new "journalistic expedition" to Maralal in the month of May, and no further inching towards decisiveness on the part of the Governor. But the month was distinguished for an important debate on a Government Motion in the Legislative Council.

This began on May 17, 1961. A Motion was moved that: "this House notes with approval the progress made by the Government in returning the large numbers of detained and restricted persons to normal life, and that the Government is making all possible efforts to the end that Mr. Jomo Kenyatta and all other such persons may be released as soon as possible, and calls on everyone, both in this House and throughout the country, to co-operate in establishing and maintaining stable conditions and assured security so as to enable these objectives to be achieved without delay."

One of the National Members expressed himself as entirely dissatisfied with such phrases as "all possible efforts" and "as soon as possible", as well as with the whole cautious attitude of the Government. He quoted from a document which had been handed to the Colonial Secretary in London in April, and was released to the Press. A part of this document read: "We strongly feel that no stable Government can be formed before Mr. Kenyatta is released. We believe that the Governor's decision has been based on wrong advice given by top Kenya civil servants who are not alive to the realities of the political situation in Kenya. Mr. Kenyatta no longer presents a threat to security, so he should be free".

James Gichuru proposed an amendment to the Motion, in the simple terms that: "this House, being convinced that Jomo Kenyatta is not a danger to security, calls upon the Government to release Jomo Kenyatta now and unconditionally".

Speaking to his amendment, Gichuru declared: "We talk about political stability, economic stability. I am as much interested in economic stability as anybody else. But how are we going to get this stability? I feel, Sir, that we shall not get political or economic stability so long as Kenyatta is still in detention. I have maintained right from the very beginning that Kenyatta was not a threat to the security of this land. I still say so now".

The House was then electrified by a powerful contribution from another National Member . . . (today Deputy Speaker of the House) . . . Fitz de Souza. In what was then (May 1961) a maiden parliamentary speech, and drawing on his first-hand knowledge as one of the defending lawyers at Kenyatta's trial, de Souza unfolded more of the discreditable travesty that passed for justice at Kapenguria in 1953. So illuminating was this portion of his speech, to which cross-reference was made in the opening chapter of this volume, that it must be held to merit (from Hansard) a lengthy quotation:

'Those of us who had the privilege of defending Jomo Kenyatta have always considered that this was one case

where there was a miscarriage of justice. We feel, Sir, that
this was one case which does not do any credit to the high
standards of British justice that otherwise have existed in
this country.

'I want to amplify what I have said by giving some
illustrations. In this particular case we had a picked
magistrate; we had a picked prosecutor, a picked interpreter and a picked venue. In this particular case, Jomo
Kenyatta was arrested at Githunguri, and by all rights he
should have been tried at Githunguri. But what did the
Government do? They took him down to a place called
Kapenguria, in a closed district, and said: "Jomo Kenyatta,
we hereby release you". But before he had gone one step
forward, they said: "Jomo Kenyatta, we arrest you". Then
they said that they wanted to try him at Kapenguria
because he was arrested in Kapenguria, knowing very well
that no person was allowed to go into the area, being a
closed district.

'Counsel had to go all the way from Nairobi to
Kapenguria under most difficult circumstances. Lawyers
who came from all parts of the world had to spend two
months in a garage 25 miles away from the place where
this case was being heard. Does this lend itself to the
support of justice? Every time we needed a book, every
time it was necessary to get a witness, people had to drive
more than 250 miles. With the resources available to the
defence at that particular time, this became almost impossible. We could hardly compete with the number of
men or the finances that the Government had at its
disposal. We did not have walkie-talkie sets, direct telephone communications to Nairobi, planes running to and
fro when we wanted them.

'The amendment asked for the immediate release of
Jomo Kenyatta. I am saying that we are not satisfied that
he was in fact guilty of the offence of which he was
convicted.

'I want to give one further illustration, since this House
is the court of public opinion. One of the most important

items of evidence against Jomo Kenyatta was the evidence of a particular oath ceremony in which Jomo Kenyatta, personally, was supposed to have given an oath to one Thiongo Waithaka. The man who gave evidence said that he knew Jomo Kenyatta for years, and that they had in fact given evidence together before the Carter Commission in 1932 or 1933.

'When we asked Jomo Kenyatta, he said he hardly knew this man. On cross-examination, Sir, we found that on the date stated in 1932 or 1933 this particular person was 13 years of age, and — what is more — Jomo Kenyatta was at that time in London, and proved conclusively so to be by passports and immigration records, while this man was in Kenya.

'The witness went on to say there were eight other persons present at the alleged oathing ceremony, and even with our limited resources we scoured the countryside and found them. They included a Minister of a Church, some teachers, and a person who had recently been appointed a Government Chief for his loyal activities and anti-Mau Mau sentiments. We brought every one of these eight persons, who swore that Jomo Kenyatta had been with them that evening, and that no Mau Mau or any other oath ceremony took place. Now it was a question of eight persons or a single person; one would have thought the magistrate would have considered these eight persons worthy of belief.

'There have been statements that this case of Jomo Kenyatta was decided in the Supreme Court and in the Privy Council, and that that is why we must accept the finding. Sir, the Supreme Court made a finding of fact, but as is known to all lawyers they cannot interfere when a magistrate says that this finding of fact has been based on the demeanour of a witness. That is the ground on which the Crown fought the Appeal, and they won, because the magistrate said his finding was based solely on demeanour.

'The second question, Sir, is that this case is supposed to have gone to the Privy Council, where the Privy Council decided that Jomo Kenyatta was guilty. Nothing of the sort. The Privy Council never heard this Appeal. All that happened was that they refused leave to appeal, which is a totally different thing. They did not go into the facts of the case, and were not really interested, because they said — and quite rightly — that on questions of fact your Court of Appeal is your Court of Appeal in your country, and not us. They did not find in this particular case whether Jomo Kenyatta was guilty or innocent, but found that there was no departure from the processes of law.'

The debate that was adjourned soon after de Souza had finished this speech was resumed on the following day — May 18, 1961. But the Government steamroller, however chipped and warped and painfully anachronistic in design, still had weight and momentum left, and lumbered on. Despite the quoted pleas and speeches, and all the other arguments that were raised in the course of the debate, the Gichuru amendment was austerely negatived, by a voting count of 43 to 26.

EXCURSIONS TO MARALAL

On June 1, 1961, the Leader of Government Business caused to be issued a statement, announcing that arrangements had been made for a Gatundu farmer, Paul Muigai, to exchange his land for another plot, thus allowing Jomo Kenyatta's house to be built on its previous site.

Then on June 15, 1961, ten Party delegates — five KANU and five KADU — made a formal excursion to Maralal. An announcement afterwards said they would henceforth take joint action on such matters of national interest as the unconditional release of Kenyatta, and true and immediate independence for Kenya.

Ten days after that, a Kenya Indian Congress delegation went up to Maralal, and the following account of their impressions was given as a local press report:

The Kenya Indian Congress has added its weight to the argument that Kenyatta should be released as soon as possible because he represents no threat to security. They say he is the only man capable of pulling the different political forces in Kenya together, and creating a truly national drive towards an independent State

After their return from Maralal, the Congress spokesmen stated that Kenyatta's approach to land was not racial. It was prompted entirely by considerations of economic benefit to the country, so that land — whether alienated or not — which remained idle and undeveloped ought to be made available by the Government for the settlement of landless Africans.

The Congress also reported that, on the question of the Civil Service, Kenyatta made the point that independence meant a change of authority. Those prepared to continue to serve faithfully under the new authority would be welcome to stay, and their rights would be protected.

It might become wearisome for such accounts to be reproduced, in respect of every visitor (or visiting group) to Maralal. The 'bon mot' of the time, when acquaintances met in any street or bar or office, was simply: "have you been up yet?", or maybe: "which day are you going?" One feature writer somewhat sourly observed that journalists — to simplify their task — might switch to covering the background and the purpose of those few members of the populace who had not been to Maralal at all.

During his 130 days in Samburu District, and apart from the one massive Press Conference occasion, Mzee Kenyatta was visited by a constant stream of persons and delegations. There were Party nominees, and groups of Members of the Legislative Council. There were officials of the Chambers of Commerce, and of the Kenya Federation of Labour. There were delegates of teachers, of women's organisations and of religious organisations. There were doctors and lawyers. There were members of the Consular corps, representing the United States, France, West

Germany, Italy, Ethiopia, Somalia. And there were private individuals whose rank or profession or concern, while taken to be relevant, could not always clearly be established by those whose fascinating duty it was to report on this human migration . . .

Meanwhile, on June 24, 1961, Prime Minister Nyerere (as he then was) arrived in London in good time for a scheduled Conference there on the formation of the East African Common Services Organisation. He at once submitted a strong plea — noticed by *The Times* — for the release of Jomo Kenyatta from restriction. Nyerere said the people of East Africa were anxious to determine their own future, and Britain should do whatever she could to help. In the case of Kenya, if Jomo Kenyatta were released the whole position would change for the better overnight.

On successive aircraft over the period of July 2 and 3, 1961, Kenya delegates began to arrive back in Nairobi from this EACSO Conference. At the Airport, they all said a word to correspondents —

"KANU demanded the immediate and unconditional release of Kenyatta. I am hopeful he will be released this month."

"Kenyatta will be free to attend the Conference on Kenya's constitutional progress which is to follow immediate discussions in Nairobi".

"It will only be a short time before the Old Man is back at Kiambu".

"After talks with the Conservative Party, political fears over the release of Kenyatta have disappeared, and businessmen say his return will speed up development".

The Governor also returned, but merely observed that — while in London — the two political Parties and the Government had all made their views on Kenyatta clear to Mr. Macleod. This was a good poker-table observation. But it was acidly received, by all those capable of feeling any compassion for the human stakes.

For this particular poker game, in which (to pursue the analogy) officials in the name of their Monarch had employed such guile and falsehood and venom as must draw in retrospect a Royal flush, had been going on for nine long years . . .

The whole contemporary scene was summed up in a neat conclusion, by Colin Legum of *The Observer*, writing on July 5, 1961: "The two-month-old attempt to carry Kenya forward towards self-government, while keeping Mr. Jomo Kenyatta in detention, has failed. It is now widely recognized that no real political progress can be made until Kenyatta has been released. In a sense, therefore, it appears that Kenya is Kenyatta's prisoner rather than the other way round".

On the following day — July 6 — Legislative Council was asked to declare that: "this House, being desirous to enable Jomo Kenyatta and other leaders — who due to their political activities in the struggle for Kenya's independence have served two-year sentences or more — to be Members of this Legislative Council, calls upon Government to take the necessary steps immediately to have revoked the section of the Order-in-Council which now bars such persons from being Members of this House".

This became the first of a number of debates on this issue. The present Motion was seconded by another African spokesman who stated: "Should this section be removed, we are willing to take whatever measures are necessary to have Mr. Jomo Kenyatta as the Prime Minister of this country. The leadership of Mr. Kenyatta will magnify the unity in this country. He attracts the unity of the people because he is universally respected in Kenya".

An amendment was put in by the Leader of Government Business to the effect that the House should recommend that the provision of the section be amended, and should request the Government to convey this recommendation to the British Government.

The amendment was carried by 42 votes to 27, when the debate was concluded on July 13.

Events thereafter moved, by contrast with the torpor of the nine previous years, with comparative celerity.

First portents of some pending break were signalled in the House of Commons. In place of routine phraseology, when replying to the latest in a persistent series of Questions about the release of Kenyatta, Mr. Iain Macleod — on July 21, 1961 — incorporated this remark: "In all races and all communities, there has been a considerable change of thought in this matter quite recently".

London correspondents were quick to pounce on the expression "change of thought", in juxtaposition with or as prologue to the "wind of change". And in one newspaper, the traditional 'authoritative sources' were quoted for the prophecy that August 15 would be the date for Mzee Kenyatta's move to Kiambu.

In Kenya, there was still the groundwork to be got through, and the final soul-searching, and official procedure . . .

On August 1, 1961, a formal statement was issued by the Leader of Government Business. It said:

I now have great pleasure in announcing that the Governor has decided — in consultation with the Council of Ministers — that Jomo Kenyatta will be moved to Kiambu about the middle of August, when the house which has been built is ready for his occupation, and that his restriction order will be revoked a few days thereafter.

A copy of His Excellency's Despatch to the Secretary of State for the Colonies informing him of this decision is published today in the Gazette for general information.

The Secretary of State is making a statement in the House of Commons today, and is laying before Parliament a copy of the Governor's Despatch as a Command Paper.

Sir Patrick Renison's formal communication to the Colonial Office was a remarkable document. It made self-satisfied reference to the background of his attitude over the previous eighteen months. It grudgingly allowed that Kenyatta might conceivably become a stabilising influence in contexts of unity and progress. It reproduced arguments — presenting them as though they sprang from original mental process — that had been put to the Governor for a long time past. And it embraced, as an unconscious irony, Renison's discovery of how much weighty consequence for the future of Kenya there was in this whole question.

In a somewhat condensed form, but with nothing material omitted, this Despatch is reproduced below:

'On the 31st March, 1960, and again on the 10th May, 1960, I stated publicly that it was my view that in the then prevailing circumstances the release of Jomo Kenyatta would be a danger to security. On the 1st March, 1961, immediately after the general elections, I said that it was not my view that he should be kept in restriction indefinitely; I did not, however, propose to release him until the new Government was working well and until I thought that the security risk could be accepted and contained, and that the danger which his return presented to the economy and administration and to our whole constitutional progress towards early independence had been minimised. I also then announced that he would be restricted at Maralal instead of Lodwar, and that more people would be allowed to visit him.

'Since his move to Maralal, Kenyatta has spoken freely to the many people who have visited him, journalists, politicians, diplomats, churchmen, writers, relations and friends, of all races and political persuasions. He has spent much time trying to effect greater unity among the African political Parties and leaders. His very early release is now widely expected in Kenya.

'Only events can establish the facts but, since his move to Maralal, Kenyatta has given every indication that he is now in no way irreconcilable to the maintenance of law and order, and to the association of all the peoples of Kenya

with its progress to independence in an East African setting
and based on a sound economy.

'I am confident that, with my Government behind me, I
can accept and contain any extra security risk which now
remains on Kenyatta's release. It is arguable that the
economy is likely to be more damaged by the uncertainty
caused by his continued restriction. The officials in the
Government Services are among those who are now widely
expecting his release, and there is general agreement among
my senior officers (including the Commissioner of Police)
at headquarters and in the field, and among representatives
of the Kikuyu who steadfastly supported the Government
during the Emergency, that the timing is correct. Even
those — and there are still many — who have deeply felt
anxieties about the possible consequences of his release
have come to realise that, in the changed political circumstances in Kenya, the wiser counsel is to release him at a
time when Great Britain is responsible for law and order.
They realise also that his continued restriction is an impediment to good relations and orderly progress.

'The African Elected Members of my Government have
continuously advised me that Kenyatta should be unconditionally released. Indeed, they agreed to join the Government in the belief, which was certainly correct, that the
formation of a Government would lead to his earlier
release. All other members of the Government join them
in recommending that Kenyatta should be returned to
Kiambu as soon as the house which is being built for him
is ready for occupation. The Council of Ministers recom-
mends that he should be released after only a few days'
period of limited restriction in Kiambu, which will be
necessary in order that the Police may control the
immediate public excitement on his return.

'You will appreciate how much anxious thought I have
given to this question, which has such weighty consequences for the future of Kenya. I have now decided . . . '

By the nature and content of this Despatch, the Governor
disowned in advance all the calamities and contingencies

that the most morbid imagination could forsee. It was noticeable, moreover, that while referring to Kenyatta's continued restriction as an impediment, there was nowhere the slightest hint of feeling that it was also fundamentally unjust. And a somewhat snappish reference, to the effect that this present grace was reward for formation of a Government, merely reflected Renison's pique at having — and knowing that everybody knew that he had — the façade of a minority Government on his hands.

On the following day — August 2, 1961 — the *East African Standard* published a leader from which this extract is taken:

> One man can play a part which could contribute to Kenya's greatness, a new greatness glimpsed on horizons which could progressively be brought into the forefront of the Kenya scene. In the affairs of a people who are striving to achieve those common ideals by which they can mould a pattern of society that is free from yawning disparities, but seeks to treat all men with equality and justice, no one man has had a greater chance. He has the chance to be big enough to overcome tribal prejudices, to be a leader not of one section of the community but of a forward movement that transcends sectional interests. He has had much time to ponder all this.

At Government House on August 4, a meeting was held between Sir Patrick Renison and the KANU Parliamentary Group. There was afterwards issued, by the Press Office, what was described as "the following agreed statement":

> The Governor expressed gratification that the joint KANU-KADU talks on land and property rights and on constitutional advance were about to begin. He emphasised that he was ready and eager to start the projected discussions under his chairmanship immediately thereafter. The following subjects were also discussed — arrangements relating to Mr. Kenyatta during the short period of restriction following his return to his home; the Constitutional Order-in-Council in relation to Mr. Kenyatta's future participation in

political life; and the future of persons still in restriction.

A few days later, the country heard the first direct message from Mzee Jomo Kenyatta for many years. Recorded at Maralal on August 9, 1961, the message was broadcast on August 10, in Kenyatta's own voice in Swahili and Kikuyu, and in translation over the other national or vernacular Kenya radio services. This was the English text:

'This is Jomo Kenyatta speaking from Maralal. My countrymen, in the name of Uhuru and the unity of our people I send you all my warm greetings. As you have already heard, I shall soon be returning to my home in Gatundu. With this in mind, I want to assure you that I am very grateful for what you have done and are still doing for me. But I am sorry to say that under the present circumstances I shall not be able to meet and greet every one of you immediately on my arrival.

'However, in a short time after my arrival home, I expect to have ample opportunity to arrange a number of public meetings in various places, where I shall come round and speak to you all. Until that time, I would most earnestly appeal to you to keep calm and wait patiently for a short time, until I can visit you all in your particular areas.

'In the interests of our dear country, I trust that wherever you are you will conduct yourselves in an orderly and dignified manner, for the sake of peace and unity of all our people. With this urgent appeal for calmness, and with my sincere good wishes to every one of you, I will say goodbye for the moment, hoping to be with you very soon. Let freedom, peace and prosperity be our aim.'

Four days after this message was broadcast, Jomo Kenyatta was home again.

Since his arrest when the Emergency was proclaimed, more than a hundred months had come and gone. He had been consigned to the wilderness, and confined when in that wilderness, for three thousand two hundred and eighteen soul-searing days.

Chapter 5

THE HOMECOMING

"CARNIVAL AND MIRACLE"

On the morning of August 14, 1961, three aircraft of the Kenya Police Airwing took off from Maralal at 0715 hours. They landed at Kahawa Military Airstrip at 0830 hours. After brief greetings there by political leaders, a convoy shepherded by Police vehicles left for Gatundu, a few miles away. Mzee Jomo Kenyatta and his family arrived home at Gatundu at 0925 hours precisely.

Such were the vital statistics of one of the most poignant days in the history of Kenya.

This was a Monday, following a weekend of high expectancy and false rumour, the assembly and dispersal of exuberant and patient crowds.

Early on this Monday morning, the Kenya Broadcasting Corporation — not without difficulty, in terms of manoeuvring bodies and equipment through successive shockwaves of impassive policemen and the solid phalanx of a multitude in high humour — had a full team at the site, some members within and some outside the wire compound which then surrounded the Kenyatta house. For the description that follows, therefore, memory has been refreshed by consulting the record (on tape) of this occasion, and the bulletins afterwards prepared.

This volume is not a novel. But it would still seem inadequate, in a work of this kind, to treat Kenyatta's homecoming merely as factual incident, without attempting to paint in something of the surrounding colour and reaction

and significance. Within this chapter, therefore, there will
be descriptive passages, but having positive interpretation
rather than pointless attempts at any artistry as their
objective.

For an hour before the arrival, more and more masses of
people came streaming from over the hills and from far
away. The area was jammed tight, broad smiles on all the
faces, the whole atmosphere and feeling something between
carnival and miracle, with those pressed stoically against
the wire, unable to move and almost unable to breathe,
indifferent to their agony: they were in the front row for a
special performance of the beginning of time.

Every now and then, at first spontaneously, but gathering
lather and moving to a competitive climax, village or Party
groups, under their cheer-leaders and conductors, would
burst into song. This became a cacophony of feeling, and
the words had just one theme — 'Kenyatta is our only
leader' . . .

At 0922 hours, a further huge crowd, full of more jubila-
tion and waving wildly, poured over the top of a ridge and
round a final corner towards the waiting house. In the
midst of this concourse, a Landrover station-wagon could
faintly be seen, with escorting vehicles, just managing
gradually to move, sometimes as much as three or four feet
at one bound. It seemed impossible that the critical car
could ever get through to the gate, but somehow it did. It
seemed impossible that this new crowd could mingle with
the existing masses without some popping of bones and of
flesh. But somehow they did. Specially trained and imper-
turbable Police units leaned back against the multitude,
forcing a path for the vehicles; the Landrover drove into
the forecourt, and thankfully came to rest.

Jomo Kenyatta alighted, and for two or three full minutes
he was surrounded by such a huddle of people — politicians,
journalists, wellwishers, relatives and friends — that everyone was rooted to their spot in space and time. But, then,
some energetic heaving cleared a human gangway, and in
brown leather jacket and corduroy trousers, fly-whisk

waving ceaselessly to the people, Kenyatta moved over to the doorway of his house.

There, he was besieged by reporters and cameramen and correspondents of many tongues and accents, all screaming questions at once. Their voices tried to rise above the total pandemonium around: the singing and dancing and ululations and shouts of delight. Over the next few moments, Jomo Kenyatta was able to make some faintly-heard replies:

> My immediate plan for the future is to unify my people, those who consider themselves Africans in this country or citizens of Kenya — I would like the two Parties to be working as one, because Kenya is one — I do not feel bitter towards anyone at all, because I know my cause and my activities were just — I regard everybody as my friends; you know the Commandment "love thy neighbour as thyself", well the world is my neighbour — I want security for all people — I will serve my people in any position or capacity.

Thereafter, by special arrangement and the process of quick scuttle to a strategic doorway, two members of a K.B.C. recording unit entered the house. Mzee Kenyatta, with his closest relatives and colleagues, was already inside.

Ignoring some initial courtesies, questions about the journey, and parochial matters, these exchanges figure in the first radio interview with Kenyatta at Gatundu, broadcast from Nairobi around noon on that day:

Question — Have you any general message, on your homecoming, for the people of Kenya?

Kenyatta — My message now is unity for all the people of Kenya, coupled with my thanks to everyone for what they have done for me.

Question — This is both the end of a road for you and the beginning of a road; which is uppermost in your mind today?

Kenyatta — I feel that this is the beginning of the road, so far as the progress and prosperity of our country is concerned.

Question — Are your thoughts now on Kenya or on pan-Africanism; must we solve one problem before we move to the other?

Kenyatta — Well, I think we must say charity begins at home; we must put our own house in order first, through unity in Kenya, and then move on to pan-Africanism.

Question — Now that you are back here, fit and well, how soon do you think your influence on affairs will be felt?

Kenyatta — This is really not for me to say, but I think it might have been felt already.

Question — What is the next step to take?

Kenyatta — The next step is unity.

Even at this time, less than an hour after his arrival, Mzee Kenyatta stressed the theme of unity that was to carry him — and carry Kenya — through to such hard-won triumph.

That evening, Mzee Kenyatta walked around the inside of the perimeter fence, to which he was still restricted, gazing out over well-loved scenes and surroundings that had lived only in his memory for so many years, and greeting old friends . . .

On the following day — August 15, 1961 — the *Daily Telegraph* in London published a leading article on the challenge confronting Jomo Kenyatta, and mentioned as well the constitutional clause which, by virtue of his prison sentence in excess of two years, currently prohibited his entry into parliamentary life. The newspaper said:

In a few days time, the last obstacles to his complete freedom of movement will have been removed. He must then get to grips with the formidable task for which he has been groomed — to lead a united Kenya, as quickly as possible, with due regard for economic realities, to independence.

Assuming, as the British Government evidently does, that Mr. Kenyatta is the only African who can carry through such a programme, there remains one difficulty. He is still disqualified from politics. It was bad enough when he was running the country from Maralal without responsibility. It would be absurd if he had to do the same from Nairobi. If we trust him to do the job, we should let him use the tools.

One of the earliest external visitors to Gatundu, during this first week, was the African nationalist spokesman of Southern Rhodesia, Joshua Nkomo. Speaking to correspondents afterwards in Nairobi, he remarked: "Kenyatta is a great leader of Africa, not just of Kenya. It was a great day for me to have met him and talked to him".

Local people flocked towards the house at Gatundu, in unbroken streams, on every day, anxious to see for themselves that Kenyatta was there. It was estimated on the Sunday — August 20 — that people crammed into comparatively small channels and vantage-points around the perimeter must have numbered thirty thousand.

It is important to understand not simply the cause but virtually the context of this mass pilgrimage. Why did so many thousands, day after day, make their way towards Gatundu, in buses and lorry convoys, in motor-cars, on bicycles or simply on foot?

Really, for all of these, and especially the Kikuyu, this was an emotional experience and almost a mystical urge. The phrase 'Father of the Nation' may sound trite to Western ears. But to the people of Kenya it rings true.

Jomo Kenyatta was home. The Mzee was with them again. The Old Man was back.

There were really three reactions, intermingled. First, there was rejoicing, the release of pent-up feeling at the end of bitter years of longing, of struggle and demand. Secondly, there was relief and the glow of new comfort: for here was the one man, the father of all the nation, who could take them in his hands, put an end to bickering, and bring them Uhuru, with new purpose and new hope.

But rejoicing and relief for all these tens of thousands were not — at a distance — enough. The event of Kenyatta's

return was of much profound tangible significance, and if
not strictly spiritual at least such boon to the national
spirit, that primary emotions hardly dare be given rein
until the eyes or ears of sense of touch had removed all
doubt from others' testimony. Disappointment could not
have been endured. So each man had to see, and had to
satisfy himself, that out of the hopelessness of waiting and
living the soul of a people could gather strength again.
Kenyatta was home, the living legend, and out of his
genius new life would spring . . .

On August 21, 1961, just seven days after his arrival,
Jomo Kenyatta was freed from all forms of restriction. An
official statement baldly observed that: "Mr. Kenyatta has
been restricted to his home plot — number 976 — in the
Kimunyu sub-location of the Gatundu division of Kiambu
district. The revocation of restriction order was served on
Mr. Kenyatta this morning by the District Commissioner of
Kiambu".

For the first time since early in the previous decade,
Mzee Kenyatta could walk out of his own garden gate and
proceed where he pleased.

BACK INTO HARNESS

The Governor, still Sir Patrick Renison, met Jomo
Kenyatta for the first time on the morning of August 22.

This was a remarkable occasion in itself, after all that
had passed, and it was remarkably staged.

Instead of summoning Kenyatta to Government House,
or sending a car for him, or travelling himself to Gatundu
— as a man with the presence to carry this off might have
done — or even arranging a meeting in somewhere like
Parliament Buildings or his Deputy's residence, Renison
contrived a somewhat furtive rendezvous amid the bare
amenities of the D.C.'s office in the boma at Kiambu.

The first the country heard of this was when members of
the Press were advised, in sibilant telephonic whispers,
that "something was happening", something so top-level
and top-secret that it could never be defined, out at

Kiambu. However odd it sounds in retrospect, this was literally the gist of an officially-conveyed all-round communication.

Mystified newspaper and radio correspondents who sped blasphemously to the scene were greeted with the intelligence that Jomo Kenyatta and the Governor were "together, inside". The Press, their numbers swelling, were invited to wait, in an unfurnished room, with one telephone (on the floor) between twenty. Remarks were occasionally offered about the scope of these facilities, as more than an hour went by.

Then there was a stir, and all were ushered to a larger room inside. Renison stood tight-lipped, and seemed under strain. Jomo Kenyatta stood quietly to one side, his feelings impossible to fathom. With a curt nod, Renison caused his Press Officer to read a bleak communiqué. They had discussed — it said — a variety of subjects affecting the future of Kenya, including constitutional advance, security, restoration of confidence, and the release of the few remaining restrictees.

No questions were permitted. There were no courtesies, no helpful or amplifying observations, no human-interest asides.

Renison retreated to Government House.

As Jomo Kenyatta got into his car — to the cheers of a crowd now outside — he confirmed on a tape that much ground had been covered in discussion, blandly described this as useful, and made it possible to speculate that such further meetings could and might be arranged . . .

More days followed of endless visitations to Gatundu. On August 23, Mbiyu Koinange — whose return to Kenya had been prohibited for many years — flew up to Nairobi from his office as General Secretary of PAFMECA in Dar es Salaam. He drove straight to see Jomo Kenyatta.

Another visitor on that same day was Mrs. Indira Gandhi (now Prime Minister of India) who brought greetings from the late Pandit Nehru.

On August 24, and incidentally while 150 lorryloads of people made their pilgrimages from all surrounding districts to Gatundu, a B.B.C. 'Face to Face' television broadcast quoted Mzee Kenyatta as saying:

> The most urgent task for the people of all races is to unite — without hatred — for rapid independence. An African Government will retain the services of British advisers and technicians, and will readily accept aid without strings. We want help, whether administrative or economic, from those who can give us help. We do not want to rob anybody of his property. What we want is the power of Government.

> We want to rule our country, and people who want to stay in this country can do so, provided they accept this.

And then came another historical milestone, another most memorable day, on August 25, 1961, when the released Kenyatta paid his first visit into Nairobi. Met on the Thika road by James Gichuru and other leaders, his car was escorted to Parliament Buildings, where he arrived some thirty minutes before (on paper) he was really due.

The excitement and the cheering at that stage were tremendous, as Mzee Kenyatta was formally introduced to Mr. Speaker Slade. And when soon afterwards Kenyatta made a balcony appearance, the astonishing sight was observed of Police barriers and all the parliamentary railings not being torn aside or trampled, but simply and with a sort of dignified helplessness bowing before the surging weight of thousands of widely enthusiastic people.

Parliament Buildings were stormed, in no sense by a mob but by a huge and good-humoured concourse, carrying reporters and photographers — and even policemen — with them like corks in the bosom of the ocean. Some time elapsed before Police reinforcements, with commendable aplomb, were able to restore to Parliament the dignity and prudence of a vacant forecourt space.

Kenyatta presided first at a meeting — watched by the Press — at which a memorandum detailed the agreements reached at recent KANU-KADU talks. For the record, he

proceeded to endorse this document, in the words: "I am
very glad that after some discussion between KANU and
KADU they have agreed to work together for the common
good of our country, and I hope that the spirit of unity that
is now being revealed will continue".

The content of this memorandum should here be briefly
sketched. It referred to or provided for such points as:
means to permit Jomo Kenyatta to secure a seat in the
Legislative Council; a constitutional conference followed by
general elections and declaration of a date for independence; an interim Coalition Government moving to internal self-government without a Chief Minister stage; land
titles — including tribal rights and private property rights
— should be respected and safeguarded in the interests of
the people of Kenya; fair compensation should be paid for
any land acquired by any future Government for public
purposes; the immediate release of remaining detainees and
restrictees; approaches to such problems as the Coastal
Strip and the Masai Treaty.

Mzee Kenyatta then took this opportunity, of his return
to Nairobi, to make some important general observations.
Ostensibly, he was speaking to the joint Party assembly,
but the presence of the Press ensured that these virtually
initial words were spread throughout the country and the
world. Perhaps his most important statements were:

> The Government of an independent Kenya will not be
> a gangster Government. Those who have been panicky
> about their property — whether land or buildings or
> houses — can now rest assured that the future African
> Government, the Kenya Government, will not deprive
> them of their property or rights of ownership. We will
> encourage investors in various projects to come to
> Kenya and carry on their business peacefully, in order
> to bring prosperity to this country. We are going to be
> an orderly and responsible Government, relieving the
> tensions which exist today. We want to run our country
> in the most peaceful and friendly way. I wish the pre-
> sent spirit of unity to continue, in order to meet the

constructive tasks lying ahead. The Press has an opportunity to help in making unity something that is alive.

And when the meetings and ceremonies were over, there
was an informal adjournment, to a place where there could
be proposed a toast to: 'the leader of our nation, Jomo
Kenyatta'.

On the following day (August 26), Press comment in
Britain was notably cordial. Prompted and almost persuaded by years of official propaganda that such outcomes
as chaos and confiscation were likely if Kenyatta were
ever released, the event found newspapers pleasurably
disabused. They remarked on this with innate fairness.

A leading article in *The Guardian* said: "It is less than
three months since Kenya was looking thoroughly unhappy.
It is not yet fully transformed, but the joint statement and
Mr. Kenyatta's commentary on it have made a new and
constructive spirit evident".

A leading article in the *Daily Telegraph* observed:
"Actions in the future will speak louder than words in the
present. But it would be churlish to deny that the released
Kenyatta spoke a lot more sensibly yesterday than many
with a less questionable record".

To round off this momentous month, an editorial note
was published in the *Christian World* of August 31, 1961,
and this is reproduced verbatim below:

When Jomo Kenyatta, the symbol of African nationalism in Kenya, returned to his home at Gatundu after
nine years' imprisonment and restricted custody he
immediately called upon his people to work for unity
and peace. "Then we will get our independence faster,"
he said to the thousands of Africans who greeted him.
"If there is trouble, violence or disturbances, our independence will be delayed. Whoever supports trouble or
violence is an enemy of our freedom."

Kenyatta had earlier met with two groups of Church
leaders in Maralal. He told a group of Friends that the
future of all minority groups in Kenya would be safeguarded, and that no one who accepted Africans as
equals had anything to fear.

BACK INTO HARNESS

The ensuing month was principally distinguished for journeyings and meetings, as Mzee Kenyatta went about the country to acquaint himself with the contemporary scene, to carry everywhere his message of unity and well-ordered progress, and to meet the people.

On September 3, 1961, Kenyatta arrived in Mombasa, and addressed a mass meeting in the Stadium that afternoon. What transpired there was sketched by the correspondent of the *Kenya Weekly News* in these words:

> The mass meeting repeated after Kenyatta pledges spurning autonomy for the Coast; the demand for complete independence for the whole of Kenya; the release of all detained persons.

> Mr. Kenyatta told the crowd that he had not changed, and still wanted what he had been fighting for: "to govern our country now". He urged the people of Kenya to respect individual property, adding that an African Government would respect foreigners' property and give them the same rights as Africans. He added: "We shall not steal anything from them except freedom, which is our right."

On September 4, Jomo Kenyatta was guest of honour at a luncheon given by the Ismaili Provincial Council. He said Kenya needed the help and experience of its immigrant communities; all the African asked was for some change of heart, and recognition that the time had come for African majority rule. Then he went on: "There are some who think African independence will mean taking away your property; but that is not what the Africans want. In an independent Kenya, we as citizens of Kenya will work as one team, pulling together for the benefit of Kenya. If you identify yourselves with Kenya, you have nothing to fear."

Later that day, he told members of the Mombasa Indian Association that they were welcome in Kenya as friends of the Africans, but they must show their friendship by

deeds and not words, doing more to teach Africans their
trading and professional skills.

And at a party that evening, he referred to the then
delicate and emotional issue of Coastal autonomy, by saying: "Mombasa is the gateway to and from East Africa. To
sever the Coastal Strip from the rest of Kenya would be
like someone saying that they want our head but we can
live with the rest of our body. If we give Mombasa away
we are finished, for those who possess her will control
Kenya."

While these events and subsequent private discussions
were taking place in Mombasa, the second day of constitutional and related talks came to an end in Government
House in Nairobi on the evening of September 5, 1961. An
official communiqué that night said the meeting had considered the first item of a memorandum submitted jointly
by KANU and KADU: Mr. Jomo Kenyatta.

It was decided — this communiqué revealed — to request
the Secretary of State to take action on the Legislative
Council resolution of July, regarding amendment of the
Order-in-Council. There should be introduced the power of
discretion vested in the Governor — in consultation with
the Council of Ministers — to remove in individual cases
the disqualification prescribed by Section 28 of this Order.

On this same day, incidentally, Mrs. Gandhi returned to
New Delhi, where she described Jomo Kenyatta to correspondents as: "a wonderful person, giving the impression of
great gentleness and understanding".

Back up-country again, Kenyatta appeared at Nairobi
Airport on the morning of September 9, 1961, for the arrival
of Julius Nyerere as a guest. On the next day — a Sunday
— it was estimated that 100,000 people thronged the streets
of Nairobi to greet Mzee Kenyatta as he toured the City
by car.

By early afternoon, most of these people had flocked to
the Stadium in Doonholm Road, where Kenyatta addressed
his first mass political meeting in the Capital for roughly

ten years. The account of his speech on that occasion has been made up from local Press and Radio reports:

'Kenyatta declared: "I am still healthy. I am still the Kenyatta of 1952. I will serve you for the rest of my life". He went on to counter accusations that he had been an extremist, saying: "All I have been proclaiming is that our country has been taken away from us. We are ready for our Uhuru. We want economic development and better social services. I have always fought to bring about equality in this country, and for that I was called an extremist".

'Throughout his speech, Jomo Kenyatta made frequent appeals for national unity, beginning with denunciation of the multi-Party system, then returning to the point in other contexts: "If we are going to have the unity we are determined to have, then I see no reason for having two Parties. African Members were elected to speak on behalf of the people, not to argue amongst themselves. Unity is the only way for Kenya to achieve independence and an African Government. I have always preached unity, and until we attain this unity the imperialists will keep bribing you and delaying our Uhuru. Some people had been told they were small distinct tribes, or were somehow separate by being from the Coast. They should forget all this and be united".

'He told the mass meeting that independence should be granted at once, but while the Africans must demand Uhuru, they should not try and obtain it by violence. Former rulers of the country were invited to remain, but it was the people who would be ruling in the future. He added: "Uhuru is never given, but is achieved through struggle, and those who have been governing us for many years must accept to be under an African Government."

'Kenyatta warned against bribery and corruption, which he described as a disease facing Kenya that must be condemned by all: "We have got to forget the old saying that money is all that matters, and start thinking of our country which we love".

'On the issue of Coastal autonomy, he said people who thought they could keep the Coastal Strip separate from the rest of Kenya were deceiving themselves. Kenya was one country, and not a single inch of Kenya's soil would be given to anyone else. He commented: "The whole concept of Coastal autonomy might be compared with a man who has a beautiful house built for him, but is asked then to place the door keys in the keeping of some other person."

Over the following weekend, Mzee Kenyatta travelled to Kisumu, and addressed a rally in the Stadium there on September 17, 1961. The theme of his speech was once more unity and peace: "We must unite our country so that we rule in an orderly way. We must have the courage to fight for our country's riches, not with spears or arrows, but by demanding justice and our rights."

Subsequently, at an evening party for all communities and races in Kisumu, Jomo Kenyatta spoke informally and reflectively on the significance to all of independence. He told the Africans present that: "Uhuru does not mean that you will get good things given to you from Heaven. If you work hard, Uhuru will mean something to you, but if you are lazy it will mean nothing". Turning then to the Europeans and Asians, he advised them respectively that: "We Africans feel we must take the Government into our own hands. That does not mean we want to take over property. All we want is to have the deciding voice in Kenya's affairs." — "You have done good things. You should start having confidence in Africans, and try to take them into partnership. Teach them the tricks, and you have nothing to fear".

By this time, the whole pattern of Mzee Kenyatta's dynamic strategy was becoming clear, as he brought the country under his command. And on September 18, 1961, a leading article in the *East African Standard* made these perceptive remarks: "National unity alone can support national integrity, protecting the right of every citizen to live in peace. Kenya can prosper only if conflicting tribal animosities are smoothed out under enlightened leadership bringing national unity, along the lines of Mr. Kenyatta's appeal to the crowds at Kisumu."

After Mombasa and Kisumu came Nyeri, the scene of one of the famous pre-Emergency mass meetings in July 1952. Now, on September 24, 1961, Mzee Kenyatta addressed what was described at the time as the largest political rally ever held in East Africa. Local press reports give these glimpses of his speech:

> Jomo Kenyatta told the crowd: "When they arrested me, they expected me to repent, but I had done nothing. I had stolen nothing. I had killed nobody". But now the time had come to forget the past. People might have been Home Guards or Chiefs, they might have been detainees or in the forests, but they were all brothers and sisters and there should be no revenge.

> He said Kenya might have been independent by now if there had been one Party, and if KANU and KADU were not fighting amongst themselves. Until there was unity, the Colonialists would be able to say that Africans were not fit to rule themselves. And he went on: "We should respect other tribes, and not think of the Kikuyu as the big men".

> Kenyatta said some of the land that had been taken away was not properly utilised, and Africans would ask for this land to be returned peacefully. But nobody should say that Kenyatta had told them to break the law, because that was not what he wanted. He urged the people to pay their local taxes, so the salaries of teachers could be paid. And he denied that, after independence, taxes would be a thing of the past.

And so it went on, throughout the next week, in Central Province and in Nairobi.

Kenyatta addressed a meeting on September 28 at Kahuro in the Fort Hall District, and said: "Only disunity has prevented Kenya from attaining self-rule quickly. If we have unity, our independence will come very soon. In the Emergency, there were Home Guards, and others who fought, and others who were restricted and detained like me. I ask you to find a way that will make us all friendly and forget the past. Let us look into a bright future. When Uhuru comes, people should not expect blessings to fall like manna from Heaven. We shall have to work very hard."

At a Civic Luncheon on September 30, Kenyatta said: "Europeans will not be chased from the country when Uhuru comes to Kenya, and land and property rights will be respected. A free Africa will bring more security to all races in the country. We Africans feel the time has come when we can be the directors of our own destinies. Please forget about the past, and remember we are all citizens of Kenya of equal status. If you do this, you have nothing to fear. But those who cannot accept this should go."

Then in an address to a crowd of 30,000 at Meru on October 1, 1961, Kenyatta said: "The need now is for unity, for ending the divisions which are delaying Uhuru. All of us come from one mother. If you want freedom, you must eliminate violence. Now we have the chance to hold our meetings during the day. Those who want to hold them during the night should stop. We must be peaceful. We must be ambitious. But we should not be vengeful. The time for taking oaths is past. I have heard that some people giving oaths have said they were commanded by Kenyatta. Now I must say that I have never told them to do so. We must not use clubs, pangas or arrows, but one thing: logic."

AN ARMY FOR THE GENERAL

The unfortunate Renison committed another blunder on the morning of October 4, 1961, through the issue of what — by virtue of its tailpiece — might be singled out as one of the most extraordinary statements ever to emerge from Government House.

This statement read: "About ten days ago, Mr. Jomo Kenyatta asked the Governor, Sir Patrick Renison, for an interview. This interview was arranged at Government House on Tuesday evening, October 3. The Acting Chief Secretary, Mr. E. N. Griffith-Jones, and Mr. Achieng Oneko were present. Mr. Kenyatta did not stay to dinner."

The word 'classic' was employed more than once, in contemporary comment on this revelation. Plumbing the depths of his antiseptic social training, Renison went to some pains — first — to make it clear that he had kept Kenyatta on a string for the statutory ten days, about the length of time that a Colonial Governor should allow before consenting to see some bothersome minor personage. He omitted to mention that Kenyatta had been bustled in by a side door, nowhere near the main entrance. He avoided all indication of the subjects of discussion, or their outcome. But then of course, he emphasised, lest Senior Officials and Leading Families should be disturbed by such grotesque suspicion, that Kenyatta in Government House could simply never be — borrowing the title of the popular play — the man who came to dinner.

It is almost impossible to understand how Sir Patrick Renison interpreted his role in Kenya. Although he had discounted all past forecasts and advice, it must by now have been obvious even to him that Kenyatta was leading the country in the real terms of the popular will; and, moreover, leading it along paths of unity, security, and economic restoration. But just as he had refused to contact Kenyatta in detention, so now he reared away from any chance to get on human terms with this national leader, so that — retaining or yielding whatever proportion of initiative — there could be some mutual understanding. Here, it is apparent, Renison allowed his personal sterility, and social trepidation, to come before his duty. And he never understood Africa at all.

It was during this month of October that talks under this Governor's chairmanship, aimed at bringing KANU into the Government in coalition with KADU, again broke down.

Sir Patrick turned once more to the Radio. He said this failure was due to "fear of domination" among some minority groups, and went on: "This is no new problem;

indeed, we have already faced and overcome one major attempt to enforce domination over those who did not accept such domination, in what was called Mau Mau."

Yet again, Renison misread history, struck out at dawning harmonies with the lash of discord, and turned back the clock.

Unperturbed, Jomo Kenyatta travelled to Nakuru for the following weekend, and addressed a mass rally of 25,000 people — on October 8 — in the Stadium there. He told them:

> I want to warn you — all you people of different tribes — to beware of falling victims to the policy of divide-and-rule. If you are all united, Imperialism will have nothing which it can say. But if you are divided, the imperialists will move about telling different groups that they are better than the others. If you fall victims to Imperialism, you should not say that Kenyatta did not warn you. Unity is the only way to give us power.

On October 14, 1961, Mzee Kenyatta appeared at a mass public meeting in Dar es Salaam, as a guest of Julius Nyerere, and flanked as well by Kaunda, Banda and Nkomo. A huge crowd sang songs of praise to him, as he declared: "Fighting for freedom and unity is nothing new to me. I have been doing it for forty years, and I have never changed".

In Kenya, a fortnight later, on October 28, 1961, Jomo Kenyatta became President of KANU. The formal announcement was made in Parliament Buildings, at the end of a four-hour meeting of KANU Branch Chairmen from all over the country. The actual statement was issued in these words:

> This meeting of the KANU Governing Council records with deep feeling the reunion of our beloved leader Jomo Kenyatta and his other colleagues with the people for whom he has fought and who have awaited his leadership.

> This meeting, endorsing previous decisions of KANU in recognition of Mr. Kenyatta's leadership, records its

appreciation of Mr. Kenyatta's decision to accept the leadership of KANU, and accordingly unanimously resolves to give Mr. Kenyatta full powers to lead and reorganize KANU and all its sectional policy, and the Parliamentary Group, with a view to setting up an efficient, effective, disciplined Party determined to win Kenya's Uhuru now.

Thus, Jomo Kenyatta became the established Head of a Party institution that had earlier been described as "the national front". James Gichuru vacated his Acting Presidency, but remained as Chairman of the Parliamentary Group.

Most of the immediate reactions and surmises were covered by leading articles — and particularly by their conclusions — in the local press on October 30, 1961. The four paragraphs that follow are taken from the *East African Standard* of that day:

'As the KANU leaders had hoped and expected, Mr. Kenyatta has become their President and the die is cast. Henceforth, he will be embroiled in the political wrangles, and be Head of one Party ranged against its opponents.

'Having been accorded full powers, Mr. Kenyatta cannot now abstain from correcting his lieutenants when they transgress the Party line. As from this weekend, he has ceased to be "a General without an Army", which is how he described himself last week. He will be fully responsible for the political deeds and utterances of the KANU leadership.

'In the long term, Mr. Kenyatta's new role will make him the target for attack by political opponents, and this in turn will impede his emergence as a national statesman who can weld together the different factions into the national unity so urgently required for peace and prosperity after independence.

'Political and tribal differences having been thrown into sharper relief, Mr. Kenyatta can best serve the country's interests by striving to ameliorate the fears, exerting his influence in tireless attempts to win accord between the rival factions. If the tribes do not learn to live together in peace, independence can bring great tribulation to the land.'

In a shorter but hardly less penetrating editorial, the *Daily Nation* said this:

> Jomo Kenyatta's final acceptance of the Presidency of KANU came as no surprise to most of the country. The sweeping powers given to Mr. Kenyatta indicate that, right down to Branch level, there should be no difficulty in bringing to heel some of the unruly elements which have brought KANU's name into some disrepute. The actual Party organisation is not so important, perhaps, as the discipline in thought-lines which KANU must learn. It may truly be said that the opportunity which has been put into Mr. Kenyatta's hands can make or break this country. The eyes of the world will be on him as he sets out on his new task.

(Three years after such prognostications were published, Kenya had not only progressed through a period of full independence, but had achieved complete national unity under President Kenyatta, with KANU as the political vanguard of the new Republic.)

It was apt that Kenyatta's first public appearance as President of KANU was at Githunguri, where he was initially arrested many years before. On October 29, 1961, he urged the people there never to think of revenge, or to settle old scores, with real or imagined enemies of the Emergency days. He flatly condemned oathing, and all who wanted secret meetings, and called for a KANU recruiting campaign so that Kenya could move to independence through well-ordered Party discipline and in the clear light of day.

Emphasising the themes of tolerance, unity and effort, Jomo Kenyatta made two more public speeches then before he left Kenya for London.

Opening a Maternity Home at Eastleigh (Nairobi) on November 3, 1961, he said Kenya's citizenship after independence would be open to all races, and her racial policy would be an international example. He went on: "There must be no revenge against people who have discriminated against Africans in the past. We must set a good example. Our aim is to bring people of all races together."

Thereafter, on November 5, Mzee Kenyatta attended a political rally in Machakos, where he said again: "There must be no revenge on foreigners in a free Kenya. They worked very hard for what they have achieved, and when we get independence we, too, must work hard, if we are to get the good schools and hospitals and other things that we need."

Not even the most churlish comment on all these sentiments, not even the most scanty recognition of Mzee Kenyatta's work and purpose, not even the most fleeting gesture of co-operation in the contemporary task of putting together all that had been torn asunder, emerged from the portals of Government House.

LONDON AND LEGCO

A visit to London now was not only a rediscovery of old scenes, and appraisal of altered perspectives, but was also in the nature of a preliminary reconnaissance before the rigours of a full-scale Lancaster House Conference, which was still more than three months ahead. A comprehensive KANU delegation, led by Jomo Kenyatta, held talks (which served to stipulate a time and formula for the ensuing Conference) with the Colonial Secretary, who was then Mr. Reginald Maudling.

Press comment in London on the appearance and achievement of this delegation varied from faint praise to effusiveness, as these quotations from newspapers of November 11, 1961, reveal —

The Times observed: "Though KANU has been a far from harmonious team, in public Mr. Kenyatta gave an impression of confident leadership. He made his claim to national leadership also, as his colleagues were fairly representative of the tribes and races of Kenya."

The *Daily Telegraph* commented: "The tone of the statement is in keeping with the firm — yet shrewd and amiable — line that has been followed by Mr. Kenyatta and his advisers of all races during this London visit."

The *Daily Herald* declared: "Jomo Kenyatta and his KANU delegation have scored a triumph in their London talks with the Colonial Secretary."

On November 14, Mzee Kenyatta left London for Addis Ababa, and was welcomed at the Airport there — by members of the Government and diplomatic corps — on the following day. The villa of the Duke of Harar, opposite the Emperor's Palace, was thrown open for him; during his stay receptions in his honour were given by Emperor Haile Selassie and the Ethiopian Prime Minister.

The *Ethiopian Herald* marked this occasion in the words: "Jomo Kenyatta is not a President, nor a Prime Minister, nor even a Member of Legislative Council, but he is a leader to millions of Africans who know the sacrifices he has made. He has made his mark as a freedom fighter not only for Kenya but for the whole of Africa . . . "

Back in Kenya a week later, November 22 was for Kenyatta a busy day. First, as President of KANU, he responded to an invitation to meet — for private talks on land and agriculture — the Executive Council of the Kenya National Farmers Union. And then, as national leader, he delivered an address to the United Kenya Club, from which these extracts are taken:

'There is one thing I hate very much, and that is foreign domination. We have had that for long enough, and it is time the Africans took over the leadership of their country.

'When we say we want our Uhuru, many Europeans and Asians think we are meaning to seize their property and drive them away. But we do not mean that at all. What we mean is that Africans are the majority, and — this being a democratic country — it is our birthright to rule this country.

'When we have achieved our goal of Uhuru, Africans will welcome all other people to live with them, provided those people will adapt themselves to the idea of the African way of running things.

'Following our independence, we shall adopt a system of citizenship under which all citizens will be equal in the eyes of the law. It does not matter what race, what colour, or what religion they are, so long as they consider themselves as Kenyans.

'The aim of the African Government will be to run the Government in a decent way, to create friendships with other people.

'Kenyatta stands for the rights of the Africans, because they have been oppressed so much and for so long. But at the same time, I stand for the rights of all other human beings.

'Some of you have a notion that Kenyatta is a terrible hater of other people, especially Europeans. I am here to tell you that we do not hate anybody.

'Those Africans who think that when we have achieved our freedom they can walk into a shop and say "this is my property", or go onto a farm and say "this is my farm", are very much mistaken, because this is not our aim.'

Twenty-four hours after this major speech — on November 23, 1961, — Mr. Maudling made a statement in the House of Commons on the subject of the disqualification of persons who had undergone a sentence of two years or more imprisonment from standing as a candidate for election to Kenya Legislative Council. The Colonial Secretary said:

I have discussed the matter very fully with the Governor, and I have reached the conclusion that the Constitution should be amended so as to remove the provision in question. Accordingly, an appropriate amendment to the Order-in-Council will be submitted to Her Majesty in Council in the near future.

I am satisfied that responsible opinion generally in Kenya, and in particular the main political Parties, accept that in the developing situation in Kenya the Constitution should give all people — subject only to normal disabilities — the chance of pursuing their political aims by legitimate political means. I believe that this step will help us to secure our main objective in Kenya, which is to achieve constitutional advance on the lines generally acceptable to the people of the country.

The month of December for Jomo Kenyatta, following his tours both internal and external, was devoted to consolidation and planning. He steeped himself in the solid work of Party organisation, in blueprints for economic and social development, and in constitutional design.

On December 21, 1961, it was announced at the KANU Annual Conference that Mzee Kenyatta would stand for a Fort Hall seat which the sitting Member, Kariuki Njiiri, would vacate for this purpose.

So it was that, on January 12, 1962, Jomo Kenyatta was the only candidate who presented himself for nomination for a by-election in this Fort Hall constituency. He was thus declared elected unopposed. He entered the House on the following morning — which was a Saturday — and the Oath of Allegiance was administered to him as a Member of Legislative Council, almost exactly five months after his return home.

SECURITY AND LAND

Armed with gathering authority — now as a Party President and an M.P. — Mzee Kenyatta utilised the early months of 1962 to implement a further phase, transforming the overall image of his national leadership into its various components of practical impact and objective.

One important component was security, and Kenyatta at no time hesitated to impose rigorous discipline within his own ranks. Disturbed by reports from sundry areas of trespass and intimidation, and even oathing, by some younger members of the Party, he issued — on January 19, 1962 — a stern statement:

I have been deeply perturbed by the activities of some members of the Youth Wing, who are alleged to have taken the law into their own hands. Although youth has an important role to play in the future of this country, the primary duty of every citizen is the maintenance of law and order.

It is therefore vital that, while full importance should be attached to the part that youth can play in the constructive development of the country, they should essentially realise the necessity of working within the framework of the Constitution, and of the organization to which they belong, and generally behave as responsible citizens.

KANU is dedicated to the establishment of peace and stability in Kenya. We are opposed to the setting up of private courts.

In order to ensure that proper discipline is maintained at all levels, I have decided that a special meeting be convened of youth leaders from all Districts of the country. I wish to make it quite clear that any youth acting contrary to the rules and regulations of our Party shall be expelled forthwith.

Jomo Kenyatta understood that under conditions of population increase, accentuating widespread unemployment, with resettlement then barely in its infancy, and comparative (at that time) economic lethargy, there should be sporadic symptoms of unrest and disaffection. He realised as well that, in terms both of economy and of emotion, there was an urgent need for redistribution of land, creating opportunity for thousands of then-despairing families to work on holdings of their own.

During this month, therefore, he made two important statements on the settlement schemes. The first of these was issued (as President of KANU) on January 22, 1962:

In the allocation of land to the new peasant farmers, we shall bear in mind that our first duty will be to help those poor and landless people who today have no means of livelihood. I did not say — at a recent KANU rally — that such peasant farmers will get land free. I went to great pains to explain that the way our Government

would help such peasant farmers would be by giving
them loans on easy terms, to be repaid by the farmers
in instalments over a period of time.

I emphasised that KANU would never allow the mere
substitution of a new black landowning aristocracy for
the present white aristocracy. We are particularly
opposed to those speculators who are planning to buy
huge tracts of land in the hope of selling at a higher
price later.

On the question of compensation, I repeated the
declared KANU policy that the British Government,
which in the first instance encouraged and even financially aided the European settlement in Kenya, has a clear
moral responsibility to help pay such compensation as
has to be paid. For it is clear, in any case, that the future
Kenya Government would not by itself be able to afford
the cost of such compensation.

The second observation on this matter was made in the
Legislative Council on January 25, 1962, during debate on
a Motion dealing with land reform and resettlement.
Hansard has recorded Kenyatta (Member for Fort Hall) as
saying that:

'The schemes which we have in mind, or which we want
to see functioning, are schemes which will help landless
and unemployed and poor people, by giving them a piece
of land where they could earn their livelihood.

'We do not believe in being given this or that free. I do
not want Africans to adopt that attitude. I want them to be
able to work with their own hands on a piece of land.

'I think the landless Africans should be given so many
acres on loan for so many years, so they can start farming
with the help of the Government, and then when they start
earning some money they can start paying the debt back.

'I recall at one time seeing a similar scheme in Denmark.
I was informed that the Government in Denmark was

interested in collecting the unemployed from the towns, and they were given some pieces of land — somewhere between six and twelve acres — with a small cottage. The Government then gave these farmers more loans with which to build their farms, on easy terms. After 20 or 30 years, such small farmers owned not only the land but also the cottage. They were also helped to market their crops on co-operative lines. If the Government in this country could adopt a similar system of helping poor and landless Africans, it could work well.

'In the towns we have a lot of criminal elements, mostly due to the fact that these people have nowhere to live and nothing to eat. Necessity knows no law.

'We respect the right to land. When anybody owns land, we respect his right to it. But what we do not respect is people who have large tracts of land lying idle when our people are suffering because they have nowhere to live. We feel that such land should be taken by Government, and the compensation due in respect of such land will be a matter for the British Government. But we will definitely not interfere with the land that is producing for the benefit of this country. Nobody who owns such land need have any fears.'

These points about land and settlement were of such fundamental importance that Mzee Kenyatta stressed them yet again, when he addressed a political rally at Wundanyi in the Teita District on January 27, 1962. Comparing much of this speech with those made ten years earlier, or with arguments submitted twenty or thirty years earlier, there is ample evidence to support Kenyatta's frequent contention: "I have never changed."

A full report of this Wundanyi meeting is taken from the *East African Standard* of the following day:

'The KANU President said Africans would not be given land free after independence, but would be given Government help to buy it on easy terms over periods ranging from 20 to 30 years.

'He said many shambas had been taken away from African by settlers. Some of these farms were now well-developed and were bringing a lot of wealth to Kenya, but there was land which was lying idle and was not even used for grazing cattle — "it is this land which is lying idle that we want for the landless Africans". The British Government had sold land to the settlers, and it should be responsible for paying compensation for any unused land taken over by a future African Government.

'Mr. Kenyatta said this was a very important period for Africans, and it was time for them to be united. They should join together and demand Uhuru with one voice. For many years, Africans had been ruled by people who had never been invited to their country — "if someone gets into your house without your permission, you tell him to get out. That is what we are telling the British Government. Their period of ruling this country is over. But whenever I say this, they say Kenyatta is against Europeans. I am not against anyone. I am only against *Ubwana,* the boss mentality."

'The Africans had been ruled because people thought they did not know the secrets of the Europeans. Their brains were thought to be inferior. Children in African schools were given poor teachers and poor tuition, and so produced poor results. But children in European schools had been taught properly by good teachers, so that they became doctors and lawyers while the Africans lagged behind.

'Changes would not come from Heaven, but from hard work. Mr. Kenyatta then declared: "When I said Africans should demand Uhuru, I was taken to the wilderness to be taught a lesson. But all that I learnt was to say Uhuru more vigorously". All that Africans were demanding were their rights, which they were demanding without violence.'

With London now looming large on the horizon, Kenyatta addressed one more important public meeting — in his own Central Province constituency — on February 3, 1962. He laid firm emphasis on law and order in the course of these remarks:

Oath-taking, lawlessness and a return to the forests would only delay Kenya's independence. If you have a child who wants to go to the forests, tell him that Uhuru is near, and this not to be found in the forests. It will be brought by unity. I say that we should have only one Party: KANU. Let us be open and do things during the day, and not at night. Those people who tell you to go and take oaths and go to the forests are just misleading you. If you go back to the forests, those who can give us independence will say Kenya's people are mad and should not be given their Uhuru. Africans must develop their land without delay. Where there are grievances about land consolidation, these should be put right, but where land has been properly demarcated and all parties are happy, development should go ahead.

Referring to this meeting, the *East African Standard* commented in a leading article on February 5 that: "This was the first time he had addressed his Fort Hall constituents since his unopposed return to the Legislative Council, and he must have realised he was speaking not only to the crowds in front of the rostrum but also to the world outside, especially London on the eve of the Lancaster House Constitutional Conference. His straightforward delivery, and forthright condemnation of evil influences, are bound to make a favourable pre-conference impact."

There is no doubt at all that "he must have realised" every nuance of the occasion, including the ripples of consequences spreading way beyond Kenya. For this was the man to be described later on, by Malcolm MacDonald, as "the wisest old bird in Africa".

But it is also true that Kenyatta would have said all that just then, in any case, and irrespective of consequence, for the sake of his people.

CONSTITUTIONAL ARENA

This crucial Lancaster House Conference occupied Mzee Kenyatta and his colleagues for most of February and March. To set the stage, on the eve of his departure for

London, Kenyatta supplied to the *East African Standard* the first article he had written for a newspaper in sixteen years. In somewhat condensed form, but omitting no important declaration or viewpoint, this article (of February 9, 1962) is reproduced below:

'For fifty years, the African people have struggled against the Colonial regime. The nationalist movement in Kenya has passed through many phases in its history, but our determination to regain our liberty has never been lost.

'I go to London as the President of KANU, with the assurance that the overwhelming majority of the people of Kenya are with me. KANU's policy is based on the fundamental principle of complete equality for every citizen of Kenya. KANU will not accept any privilege for any tribe or race, and will fight against any individual discrimination based on tribe, race or religion. I believe in the complete integration of all the peoples of Kenya into one nation. I believe that in a free Kenya a person's loyalty must be to his country, not to his tribe or race. We must direct all our efforts and policies to building a strong, happy and prosperous nation.

'KANU will treat as a sacred provision of the Constitution a Bill of Rights which will guarantee to all persons the fundamental freedoms, and equality before the law. KANU will insist on a strong unitary form of Government, elected by the people on universal adult franchise. We believe that the independence of the Judiciary is a vital safeguard of democratic freedom. The Civil Service will also be protected from political influence.

'KANU will recognize and respect rights in private property. As I have often stated, the African people are not robbers. However, it is no use pretending that thousands of Africans can go on suffering from landlessness, poverty, hunger and unemployment, while vast areas of land lie completely idle and undeveloped. While we shall maintain and assist farmers who develop their lands, and who assist the economy of our country, we shall vigorously pursue a policy of land reform.

'Kenya is a small and not unduly rich country. We simply cannot afford six Parliaments and six Governments. It is a gross error to believe that the division of the country into "Regions" will in some way help to preserve individual liberties. On the contrary, it could easily lead to chaos and disintegration.

'Kenya is one nation with an integrated economy. It would be most unnatural and artificial to carve it up. No underdeveloped country has been able to expand its economy rapidly, without the economic planning and determined action that only a strong and well-organised Central Government can execute.

'We go to London not only to bring independence to our country, but to bring peace and brotherhood among its many peoples. We desire to bring love where there was hatred; peace where there was violence; confidence where there was suspicion.

'By achieving these ends, we will restore confidence in our economy, sadly strained by floods and natural disasters, and thereby make a start towards prosperity and a better standard of living for all people.'

That article launched the country into the constitutional conference and influenced thoughts and emotions throughout ensuing weeks.

The whole approach by Kenyatta and the KANU delegation was that of autonomy and self-determination for Kenya. Although such set meetings had slipped into their tradition of discussing "the next step towards" self-government and independence, it was made clear that the context now of hard negotiation, and the fulcrum of real thinking, must be the structures and the needs of Kenya when this ultimate stage had been reached.

In meeting the world Press — as he frequently did in London, on questions involving the Commonwealth, defence alliances, foreign policy, economic plans — Jomo Kenyatta was always at pains to create this picture of sovereignty, and the decisiveness which this must bring about.

This present work is a political portrait of one man. It does not pretend to be a political history of Kenya, except insofar as — with Kenyatta as the subject taken — such themes are indivisible. Certainly in regard to recent constitutional history, a separate operation is required. There is no intention of tracing here in detail the slogging work, the agreements reached, the bargains struck, the advances registered, the rulings imposed, the dissatisfaction or ambitions carried forward, the strategies then pursued, all of which distinguished in Kenya — from the day of Lyttelton to the days of the Republic — nearly ten years of constitutional negotiation and design.

Suffice it to say now that, in respect of this Lancaster House Conference of early 1962, there was progress. But it was marked again — from nationalist and patriotic viewpoints — by imperfection and compromise. This was no easy road.

In his pre-conference article quoted above, Kenyatta had poured scorn on the idea of dividing a country like Kenya into the domains of six "Regional Governments". Again, his words and warnings went unheeded. Pressures and advantages, in London, were smoothly disguised in the niceties of policy and conscience. Political opponents of that time were caught up, if not in delusions of grandeur, at least in conceptions of omnipotence. There was a great deal of emotionalism, spilled out as erudition, but rooted in selfishness or fear.

There emerged in fact, at this stage, the early skeleton of a Regional — 'majimbo' — Constitution. Covered then by the flesh of expediency, and fully clothed by Independence Day, such a Constitution of its own volition amply justified the view of Kenyatta and his colleagues at the start, that for Kenya it could only prove to be too cumbersome, too expensive, too frustrating. Following Uhuru, its unreality was increasingly tempered, until it was finally swept aside by the provisions — December 1964 — of the Republican Constitution. This in turn was adjusted and perfected, until by the end of 1966 there was evolved a document in full harmony with Kenya's traditions and needs.

However, the 1962 conference under present review also provided that there should be a Coalition Government in Kenya, prior to fresh elections in new Constituencies and Regions to be determined by Boundary Commissions. As another outcome of the London assembly, a Central Land Board mechanism was designed, in control settlement in parts of the former 'White Highlands' purchased for transformation into African farming areas.

By the end of March, it was all over. And in London, on April 2, the Chief Whip of the KANU Parliamentary Group paid tribute to Mzee Kenyatta as: "the living symbol of the movement for freedom, in Kenya and throughout Africa".

On April 10, 1962, Jomo Kenyatta and a number of his colleagues entered a transitional Coalition Government.

Kenyatta was sworn in — as Minister of State for Constitutional Affairs and Economic Planning — by the Acting Governor, Mr. E. N. (now Sir Eric) Griffith-Jones.

Chapter 6

MINISTERIAL MANTLE

STAKE IN THE LAND

The interim Coalition Government which Mzee Kenyatta joined as Minister of State was completed (April 10, 1962) after three days of active discussions and formalities. One of the earliest contrivances of the new Government was to set up a Working Party — announced on April 26 — to make proposals for provisions that should govern the franchise in ensuing Lower House elections.

The period beginning in April 1962 must in a real sense be considered as a phase — lasting for ten or eleven months — before the general elections dominated the entire Kenya scene between March and May of 1963.

Towards the end of 1962, Sir Patrick Renison, who had, perforce, found himself working with Jomo Kenyatta as a senior Minister holding the key Government portfolio, returned to Kenya from some London consultations. At Nairobi Airport, Sir Patrick told correspondents that he would shortly be departing for good, and — as he put it — "leaving my work here unfinished". Neither then nor now could there seem point in further embellishing for public scrutiny whatever Mr. Duncan Sandys (as Colonial Secretary) may have said to Renison in private meetings.

At the very beginning of 1963, Malcolm MacDonald arrived, as new Governor, to embark on his brilliantly-accomplished restorative duty.

Such was the bare background to the phase that is dealt with here. But the narrative at this point must divide itself, to trace first of all the pattern of Mzee Kenyatta's work and concerns as a Minister, and then to introduce a complementary account — inevitably overlapping in time — of his work and activities as President of KANU: "the national front".

As the Minister of State (for Constitutional Affairs and Economic Planning) Kenyatta at once evidenced and thereafter maintained his special interest in all questions and processes of land resettlement and agricultural advance.

Jomo Kenyatta toured a Settlement Scheme at Muguga on June 1, 1962, where five hundred Kikuyu families were being accommodated on 5-acre plots of land. Commenting that this was the right answer to the immediate problem of landless and unemployed families in the Kiambu District, he urged the new settlers to farm well, and by their example encourage the Government to start more Schemes for other landless people.

Schemes of this kind — Kenyatta declared — were important not least in that they helped people in despair to feel that they had now acquired some stake in the country.

Then on August 6, 1962, Minister Kenyatta opened a new factory belonging to the Gacharage Coffee Growers Cooperative Society in Fort Hall. Local newspaper reports give this account of his approach on that occasion:

> He said independence will mean nothing to Kenya if the people are not willing to work hard and work together. Uhuru could be destroyed by such evils as oathing, law-breaking, drunkenness, thriftlessness, idleness, jealousy and revenge. He added: "Some people go around saying they have been told by Kenyatta to take oaths. But I am against those who take oaths. I do not want to hear any more about oathing".

> The Minister said farmers should work hard on the land, for their wealth lay in the soil. Even the Europeans and Asians who had come to Kenya had had to work hard to make their money. Coffee planting would lead to

better education, better hospitals, better roads, and all the good things people wanted for independence.

Mr. Kenyatta said if there was a law that somebody thought was wrong, he should not break it, but should approach his representatives to see if it could be amended — "the Police are our friends and our servants".

Whenever possible, the Minister constructively broke away from his Departmental and Cabinet duties to get back to the soil. On August 23, 1962, he visited the Kaimosi Agricultural Training College, and spoke to the assembled farmers there: "You should be preparing yourselves to teach others the importance of improving the soil and of better farming. The country will need people like you when independence comes. But do not think that land will then be given free to anyone. It will be given to the landless only on payment of a deposit, followed by instalments over a number of years."

Mzee Kenyatta went on from Kaimosi to the Lessos Smallholder Scheme, and to see farms in the Nandi District on which some of the farmers were now growing tea. He was greatly impressed with the Lessos achievement, and told the settlers there: "All this shows that you really needed the land you have now occupied".

One of the great events in Kenya's agricultural — and social — year for more than half a century was the annual Royal Show (now entitled the Nairobi Agricultural Show). On September 28, 1962, Jomo Kenyatta — in his Ministerial capacity — paid his first visit to this Show since back in 1925. Conducted by colleagues and officials the Minister toured the livestock and trade sections, and spent some time as well at the Wildlife Society stand.

Telling correspondents how impressed he was, not least with the beauty of the Showground (Jamhuri Park), Kenyatta went on: "The Show must be expanded, and I hope this will be done after independence. It provides a great opportunity for encouraging higher standards in both agriculture and industry. The event can help the African farmer to raise his standards, particularly in his livestock and poultry. I hope European farmers will take a continued interest in the Show. They are part of Kenya; they are not going to live in isolation."

Three days later — October 1, 1962 — found the Minister on tour of the Wanjohi-Kipipiri high density Settlement Scheme. At that stage, about 12,000 acres (land formerly in European ownership) was being made available for re-settlement; it was planned eventually to have 1500 plots, with areas set aside for community centres, and premises for co-operative marketing.

Mzee Kenyatta met and talked to many plotholders — mainly landless Kikuyu families from Naivasha and Laikipia — who were preparing their new land for planting and building their houses.

The Director of Settlement commented that it was up to the politicians to make a success of these Settlement Schemes, since without political support such Schemes were bound to fail. Kenyatta instantly gave an assurance that the work of officials (in Land Settlement and Agriculture) was recognized to be "a most important task", and that politicians would fully support their endeavours.

PROBLEMS OF ECONOMIC TRANSITION

The assumption by Jomo Kenyatta of a portfolio which embraced Economic Planning came at a time when the economic fortunes of Kenya were still in a condition of some sloth. This was frankly recognized in a number of public utterances, and in a message to the *Sunday Post* of May 30, 1962, which is reproduced below:

'My Ministry has noted the series of articles which your paper has lately been publishing on Kenya's local industries. At this crucial time, when those lacking in fortitude and faith talk of economic despondency, we are indeed fortunate to have a newspaper seeking to tell the world that Kenya's economic foundations are still firm and secure.

'My Ministry considers the current economic difficulties to be a passing phase. Being responsible for planning to effect rapid economic recovery, we are determined to make sure that these difficulties are overcome in the very near future. To do this, our attention is directed both to appropriate investment from abroad, and to widespread expansion of local industries.

'There are many positive aspects of Kenya's economy which need to be repeatedly emphasised. It is true that unemployment has risen alarmingly in recent times. Money has also left the country in considerable quantities, due to the cowardice and pessimism of otherwise self-styled "lovers of Kenya". But we must never lose sight of the tremendous efforts currently in progress, which keep the spirit of home and faith.

'May I say, in conclusion, that it is very easy to blame others — and particularly politicians — for whatever economic ills the country may experience. But Kenya's economic wellbeing depends on all of us. Simply blaming the politicians and sitting idle until things improve is a negative attitude.

'Let all of us roll up our sleeves, and get on with the work for Kenya's economic advancement. Let us expand our local industries, and raise the people's purchasing power to create markets for our locally-produced goods. Above all, let us vigilantly safeguard high standards for our products, to command large markets overseas.'

Kenyatta was all along concerned with the confidence that must underlie investment, and with directing along lines of economic reality a unified national effort. Speaking (as Minister of State) in the Budget debate on June 12, 1962, he made these comments:

The Trade Unions, too, can help us create confidence. If they continue with this series of strikes, I do not think they will contribute to confidence in this country, because I feel the more they strike the more people will hesitate in investing their monies here. I want to assure the House and the public that we will do all we can to restore confidence, to encourage people from abroad to invest their money in this country. The ideal for the future is that we should all pull together and develop our only means of production: the land of Kenya.

Mzee Kenyatta was not wholly immune from the misunderstandings which beset, or may deliberately be read into, Ministerial utterances of unusual consequence. In the period which followed the Budget, there was frequent reference, on the one hand, to Kenya's need for and endeavours to secure overseas development finance. On the other hand, there was also public discussion or unease concerning quantities of money known or understood to be entering the country for dubious purposes.

It was not difficult, therefore, to discern motives behind such accusations, or misrepresentations, as led Kenyatta to issue the following statement from his Gatundu home on August 16, 1962:

I must refute categorically recent allegations levelled against me, to the effect that I am against seeking investment funds from foreign countries. As the Minister of State responsible for economic development, I know and appreciate fully Kenya's need for economic aid and capital investment from overseas.

I wholeheartedly support the efforts which have been made, and are being made, by my colleagues in the Council of Ministers to secure development loans from the United Kingdom, Germany and elsewhere. Such loans are arranged on honourable terms, and the uses to which the monies will be put are publicly known.

What I am against, and what I attacked at a rally last Sunday, is foreign monies which are given to individuals, for the purpose of helping them to corrupt leaders and people in an attempt to build themselves politically.

It is well known that this sort of corruption led — for example — in the Congo to the disintegration of the country and elimination of some of its best nationalist leaders.

In all my life in politics I have worked for the unity of the African people, not only in Kenya but in all Africa. I must emphasise that, at this time more than ever in the history of Kenya, we must each one of us work against tribalism, and for unity of purpose and action, in order to achieve our common goal of Uhuru.

A Committee of Supply debate in the Legislative Council on October 17, 1962, gave Kenyatta an opportunity to portray both the purposes and the difficulties of economic planning. Quite typically, he made no endeavour to gloss over the problems, and he was prompt to acknowledge such forms of external assistance as were appreciated when received.

A condensed version of the Hansard record of this particular speech is reproduced below:

'I am glad to have the opportunity of this debate on the Estimates of my Ministry, to explain some of the ideas on which the Government is working for the long-term development of Kenya.

'I have been approaching the problem of long-term planning with five main objectives in mind. The first is to associate the private sector and the general public more closely with the Government's planning machine. The second is to avoid waste of scarce resources of capital and skilled manpower. The third is to make as smooth as possible an economic transition from Colonialism to Independence. The fourth is to advise planning organisations and produce a plan which will prove attractive to overseas investment, essential if we are significantly to raise the standard of living in the near future. The fifth is to spread the benefits of development throughout the country, both in urban and rural areas.

'In approaching these problems, I have been extremely fortunate in having the benefit of advice from a mission of the World Bank.

'The economic transition from Colonialism to Independence is raising very great problems for Kenya. These arise from economic dependence on expatriate staff and European farmers as well as on overseas investors for our industrial development. Our next Development Plan will, I hope, reflect the tremendous effort which is being devoted to the settlement schemes, and to the training of local staff for senior posts in the Civil Service.

'It will not be out of place at this point to acknowledge the very large financial contribution which the British Government is making to the settlement programme, and to our general development.

'I hope my friend the Minister for Commerce and Industry will soon be able to announce new plans for giving a fresh stimulus to the development of industry, in which the Government will go forward in partnership with the private investor, thus assuring him of our goodwill and desire to give him every encouragement.

'The Government is greatly concerned with, and is giving all possible attention to, the problem of mobilising internal investment. Planning has little meaning if necessary resources to implement the plan are not forthcoming.'

Then on January 14, 1963, it was officially announced by the Press Office that "Mr. Jomo Kenyatta has, with the agreement of his colleagues in the Government, set up an Advisory Planning Commission, which has already held a first meeting under the Minister's chairmanship". The five terms of reference of this Commission were stated to be:

to examine and advise on plans for future development in both the private and public sectors of the economy, including short-term plans for promoting unemployment relief;

to consider the obstacles to quicker growth and to advise on what steps can be taken to improve efficiency and make a better use of resources, including greater co-ordination on an inter-territorial basis;

to promote a greater understanding of the problems of economic development;

to seek agreement with industry, labour, agriculture, public authorities and other important sectors of the economy on ways of increasing the rate of economic growth;

to advise on methods of implementing the agreements reached.

But apart altogether from his fundamental and allotted concerns during this period, Mzee Kenyatta also promoted or guided or clarified a number of other issues of national consequence. Two particular examples should be cited here.

On June 21, 1962, a Motion was moved in the Legislative Council that: "this House, being aware of the absence or grave shortage of scientists and technologists in this country, and being satisfied that the facilities generously offered to Kenya in countries abroad are not adequate to meet the present needs of Kenya, urges Government to establish co-ordinating machinery to facilitate the acceptance of assistance for suitable educational courses overseas to be taken by suitably qualified students, from whatever source offers may come, and to remove unnecessary or discriminatory restrictions on persons wishing to travel abroad for educational purposes."

There had been much contention — both on practical and emotional grounds — that Kenya's need for higher education, and for the accompanying cosmopolitan experience, was so critical that any hindrance to overseas travel and residence in such causes, hinged to political distaste, was a positive disservice to the country.

Jomo Kenyatta intervened quite spontaneously in this debate, offering some statesmanlike comment and advice:

I believe in freedom of people. So far as they are not infringing any law of the country, people should be free to move as they like. One of the greatest needs in this country at the moment is education, and I feel that any restriction which prohibits students from going abroad to study in any country is wrong. Students ought to have — and under a completely free Government students will have — the right to go and study in any country. Some people feel that if you go to Russia or East Germany or China, you are only going there to copy their ideology. This I do not think is right. Many Englishmen, Americans and Indians also visit those countries. They do not return as Communists or anything of that kind. They just go there for educational experience, or to see things for themselves. I am a strong believer in this kind of education; travelling is more valuable than just reading books. It is also the aim of this Government to approach various other Governments, and ask whether it would be possible for us to obtain money to build up the educational institutions which we need here in this country.

The second example of Mzee Kenyatta's widespread interests and duties as Minister of State was illustrated on July 16, 1962, when the following official statement was released: "The 1962 population census will take place in August, and will be the first census to be taken in Kenya since 1948. Because of the fourteen years which have elapsed since the last census, present-day population figures are now inaccurate, and it is most important for many reasons that these be brought up-to-date. The results obtained will be vital to the planning of Kenya's future economic development."

(The outcome of this census provided Jomo Kenyatta with data which has since coloured his views on proper land-use planning. Political solutions, compounded as they have been of triumph and stability and justice, are one thing. Still elusive then is the physical solution to an underlying problem: how to reconcile demands upon or damage to such life-sustaining resources as soils and water reserves and protective vegetation, with the implacable annual progression — especially in quantity but also in quality — of human need.)

THE PRESIDENTIAL IMAGE

Outside his office and aura as a Minister, throughout this comparatively short but intensive period, Kenyatta was concerned all the time — as President of KANU — with his work for national unity, with cementing the foundations of law and order, with Party organisation and discipline, with making the policy preparations and creating the images of thought needed to sustain independence, and with accelerating the pace of African initiative and responsibility in all constructive tasks.

He was not always assisted by the calibre of reporting — sometimes inaccurate; sometimes ballooning a sentence into a sensation — of what transpired at mass rallies, and on May 23, 1962, he felt constrained to circulate a message to the Press.

After dealing with a contemporary dispute about some alleged remark, which no longer has relevance, this message concluded: "I would further like to emphasise to the Press that they should not be concerned only with what may appear to be controversial statements made at public meetings. They should also bring out the positive and constructive statements. There were many such statements made at the Nakuru meeting which the Press ignored."

It was apt that, on this very same day, the KANU President sent a missive to the Kenya Federation of Labour . . . (this body has today become the kernel of the Central Organisation of Trade Unions) . . . which stressed — in its concluding paragraph — his underlying frame of mind:

I must congratulate the Kenya Federation of Labour for taking the initiative in publishing the weekly newspaper *Mfanya Kazi*. African-published newspapers are greatly required in Kenya today, and I welcome *Mfanya Kazi* heartily.

You have all heard the challenging slogan "Uhuru na Kazi". We say this because of our profound realisation that only our sweat and toil will provide us with better conditions of life when independence is achieved. Constructive work has dignity and national dedication, as the members of the KFL have vividly demonstrated.

I am a great believer in the freedom of the Press, and am therefore quite sure that the future of this weekly paper is going to be a prosperous one. I know that you will uphold truth and justice, both for your organisation and for our country as a whole.

Kenyatta then embarked on a tour of Central Province districts and Laikipia, addressing public rallies at a number of key centres.

At Fort Hall, on May 24, 1962, a huge crowd pledged themselves to work harder in the future, and to help build up Kenya's economy by planting more coffee, pyrethrum and tea. The KANU President said he was more concerned with the progress of all the people of Kenya than with anything else, and Kenya must learn from the fact that other peoples and countries had grown rich because they fully utilised their land. He spoke strongly against oath-taking, and said everyone should now co-operate with him in maintaining law and order and creating national unity. The crowd — at his direction — passed a firm resolution condemning those people who still believed that oath-taking was in any context a worthwhile practice.

At Thomson's Falls on May 27, 1962, Mzee Kenyatta again condemned oathing and secret societies of all kinds, describing anyone involved in such things as an enemy of Uhuru. He emphasised that the law of the country must always be obeyed, and told the people: "Get rid of the oaths from this country. We have no use for them. Let us have unity. There is no need to take oaths, because Uhuru is round the corner. You should work hard in your shambas, so we can attract overseas investors. Some laws may be bad, and if they are tell KANU. But while they remain, they must be obeyed. The Police must be known as the servants of the citizens. They are doing a job, and they must be helped as friends are helped. Robbery and violence must be outlawed, so we have a peaceful independence."

At Thika, on June 3, 1962, Jomo Kenyatta explained how KANU had decided to enter the Government to take part in drafting a new Constitution and thus speed up the country's independence — "If you are hoping to get Uhuru by waiting around and doing nothing, you will not get it; nobody has yet got Uhuru that way since the world was created". He declared regretfully that it was not the Europeans or Asians who were delaying Kenya's independence. The people who were now frustrating attempts to win freedom from Colonial rule were in KADU. In a reflective passage, Kenyatta then hit out at those who had sometimes described Africans as "inferior". It was lack of education — he stated flatly — and not lack of ability that had always held the Africans back.

The purpose — at this stage in the narrative — of introducing so many references to these public speeches and occasions is quite deliberate. In the British Parliament, on February 2, 1965, when formal cognisance was taken of the Republic of Kenya, tributes were paid on all sides to the "astonishing" or even "miraculous" way in which Mzee Jomo Kenyatta had succeeded in transforming and fashioning his country. Within three years — it was said — a situation of political conflict and suspicion, personal insecurity and economic despondency, had become a situation distinguished by enthusiastic political unity, the firm rule of law, and economic expansion. It is important, therefore, to follow and understand both the strategic and tactical steps that were taken to this end.

On June 29, 1962, Kenyatta as Party President delivered a major policy address to mark the beginning of a three-day KANU seminar in Nairobi. His speech on that occasion should be quoted at length, and for an accurate account of it recourse is had again to the *East African Standard*. He said:

'At the Lancaster House conference, instead of fighting with us for the immediate independence of Kenya, KADU concentrated on the demand for *"majimbo"*. They did not seem to appreciate that — even if you had *"majimbo"* — the African would still want to be free. Surely the most ignorant man must know that the immediate African demand is for Uhuru.

'At that conference, a number of concessions were made, but KANU's stand and efforts saved Kenya from disastrous disintegration. We came back with the promise of a strong and effective Central Government for the whole of Kenya, and additionally we won the points that Kenya's economy shall be planned centrally, with international trade and borrowing controlled by the Central Government.

'The purpose of our joining the present Government was to speed things up, and to watch over the African nationalist interest, as well as to provide Kenya with a stable transitional Government.

'We all know that what matters are the forthcoming elections. It was agreed in London that whichever Party secures a majority in the Lower House shall form Kenya's first internal self-governing Government, and that this — once formed — would approach the British Government to set the date for independence.

'KANU must win these elections. The secret of KANU's victory will lie in the unity of our leadership and Party. I must warn, as strongly as possible, against any elements in KANU who pay lip service to unity but engage in personal or tribalist manoeuvres. These are the enemies of the Party. Such elements, if allowed to continue, could disrupt our entire work for Kenya.

'Let us all look upon ourselves as servants of the cause and people we serve. Let us renounce selfishness and personal ambitions, and dedicate ourselves to the nationalist cause. Let us renounce any lust for power or personal material gain.

'I am shocked at stories and rumours of the prostitution of politicians and Party workers with money. Money seems to have become the God of some people, and stories of people being bought and paid for their services to individuals have become everyday gossip. Through this gossip, the Party's work has sometimes been undermined.

'If a person can buy another, he too can be bought. If a person can offer himself to be bought by a leader, he is no better than a prostitute and cannot be trusted. Let us serve the Party and be proud of this service even if we remain poor, for in the long run we will emerge victorious with a free conscience.

'KANU has always been concerned with the economic future of our country. In fact, the motive power behind our nationalist struggle is the deep desire to improve the lot of our people.

'We are confronted with the grimness of the boy who grows to be an adult and dies without ever having owned a pair of shoes; the man or woman or child who cannot be sure of eating even one square meal a day; the pregnant woman who dies in childbirth because she cannot get to a maternity hospital; the worker who is discarded in old age without care; the chronic indebtedness of most workers in the urban areas.

'These and many others are the grim realities that we must face. The challenge before us can only be met through our resolve to wage war against poverty. Our next task is the fight against illiteracy and ignorance. This is a task which only an African Government can carry out, for it would be a Government responsible to the people.

'We must vigorously exploit the African potential as a producer, worker and consumer. This has been tragically neglected in the past. We must encourage self-help projects and co-operatives. We must supplement the scarcity of capital with maximum use of the abundant labour available in our country. We must generate production by better use of labour, and efficient management and planning.

'KANU believes in African Socialism. We are not the slaves of Western capitalism or Eastern European socialism. We must develop our own standards and ideals, based on our own culture and the inherent African socialist philosophy, in which every man accepts his duty to his neighbours and community, and the community in turn is the source of his security.

'Let me make it clear that we in KANU believe there is a future for any European or Asian who wishes to stay in Kenya. All we ask for is that he forgets the arrogance of the past, accepts the new order, and makes his contribution like everyone else.

'Like many other nationalist organisations, we in KANU believe in the policy of positive neutrality. We start from the basis that we are friends of all nations and people, be they from the Eastern or the Western countries. We are prepared to acknowledge the good that may come from either the East or the West, and to reject and even condemn the bad and evil that may come from the East or the West. As an independent State, we shall deal with both sides on merit, but without strings or dictation from any side, and not backing one side against the other.'

In that major speech, at a deliberately-chosen moment, Jomo Kenyatta set out to accomplish three things: to surround the concept of national unity in a whole new climate of conscious and even subconscious thought; to bring political advance down to the earth of social purpose in confronting poverty, ignorance and disease; and to create from the idea of African Socialism an image of autonomy built on self-confidence and self-respect.

Three years later, in mid-1965, the full definition of African Socialism was published as a Government Paper — Sessional Paper No. 10 — with an introduction by Mzee Kenyatta. Described in one instance as "perhaps the most important document to emerge from Africa in modern times", this unique statement not only prescribed the detail of a new but attainable political philosophy; it met the challenge as well of how to translate principle into the hard realities of economic policy and social practice. The document is indispensable to full study of Kenya's image and Kenyatta's statesmanship. It towers over pronouncement or dogma in certain other States, which has merely reproduced the so-called "scientific socialism" in analogous word but clumsier posture.

PREPARING FOR TASKS AHEAD

In mid-August 1962, a Convention was held in Nairobi under the title "The Kenya We Want", and on its opening day the KANU President sent a message of greeting and good wishes.

I want to congratulate you most profoundly for arranging this Convention. We are now entering a new era in the history of Kenya, which may be called the nation building phase.

Within a very short time, the authority for running this country will be in African hands. It is, therefore, most fitting that a conference of this kind should be held now, to provide the people with an opportunity to express their views on the new Kenya.

At Lancaster House, we worked out a constitutional agreement. Now, at this Convention, the people of Kenya can produce ideas on the social and economic problems which will face us when self-government is attained. I have said before, and I say again, that the new era in Kenya must be economically prosperous, and must provide adequate social services for all sections of our population.

Your Convention, being non-partisan, will have an opportunity to discuss economic and social problems objectively. I wish the conference all success.

And then, over the ensuing period, there were many more public speeches by Mzee Kenyatta on the themes of national unity, maintenance of law, and ordered progress into and beyond independence. Some illustrative extracts should be given.

At Kericho on August 19, 1962, he said: "KANU wants unity, not only in Kenya but all over Africa. That is our aim — no discrimination and no regard for tribe. We have no hatred of Europeans and Asians, but they must obey our laws."

To a mass meeting at Githunguri on September 8, 1962, Kenyatta was more severe:

If reports in newspapers that some of you are going back to the forests, making guns, taking unlawful oaths, and preparing to create civil war after independence, are true, I request all Kikuyu to stop doing such things. Let us have independence in peace. I am requesting you

strongly not to hold any secret meetings or support subversive organisations. We are determined to have independence in peace, and we shall not allow hooligans
to rule Kenya. We must have no hatred towards one
another. Mau Mau was a disease which had been eradicated, and must never be remembered again.

In the course of a speech at Lari on September 14, 1962,
the KANU President declared: "Kenya will achieve independence in a few months, and there is no need for people
to go back to the forests or make illegal guns. I am told
some people are taking oaths and that they will kill me if
I disobey them. But I should not be the first man to die
in this world. The time when we used to blame Europeans
for delaying our independence is gone. It is only Africans
who can delay it now".

At a mass rally in the Nairobi (Doonholm Road) Stadium
on October 21, 1962, Mzee Kenyatta announced that KANU
would henceforth be open to members of all races — "From
today, those Europeans and Asians who want to co-operate
with us, who agree that the Africans should govern this
country, have the door open to them. I welcome them to
join our Party, if they will agree to follow our law". He
told the large crowd that this decision was made to show
there was no bitterness on the part of the Africans towards
other races. And in a further appeal for broader national
unity, Kenyatta invited the supporters of KADU to join and
strengthen KANU as the national front.

Addressing a meeting at Bahati on November 18, 1962,
he said again that this was no time to think of fighting with
spears, bows and arrows, or guns. The continuing struggle
was on the political front, and the greatest weapon that
could be used was that of unity — "We want one tribe only:
KANU. As long as we are divided, the imperialists will sit
and mock us".

And so it went on, as a fateful New Year dawned.

At Eldoret on January 6, 1963, Jomo Kenyatta spoke in
public and later talked to correspondents. He repeated his
call for unity among the Africans of Kenya, urging the

people not to listen to those preaching of tribal differences and tribal fears. Then he said that any white settlers willing to identify themselves with the Africans would be welcome in the new Kenya; they would be accepted as full citizens with full and equal rights.

Switching to the other end of the country — at a rally in Mombasa on January 20, 1963 — Kenyatta told the crowd that whoever indulged in tribalism was an enemy of the Africans and of Kenya. He urged them to prepare themselves, their minds and skills and energies, for all the increased responsibilities that would have to be assumed after independence . . . (at that time, internal self-government was just over four months ahead.)

THE EXTERNAL SCENE

Between his duties as a Minister and his task as Party President, there was little time for Mzee Kenyatta to travel far afield throughout this phase.

However, he did visit Somalia, and on July 26, 1962, cheering crowds lined the streets to welcome him to Mogadishu. Prime Minister Shermarke there described Jomo Kenyatta as "a man who sacrificed his own liberty, and endured great hardship, to defend the dignity of Africa". Kenyatta then received the Freedom of the City: the first time — according to the Mayor — that this ceremony had been performed since Mogadishu was founded about a thousand years before.

At a Reception that evening, given by the President of the National Assembly, Jomo Kenyatta urged the Somali people to join in the brotherhood of Africa, and added: "Try a new phychology, an African psychology. We have been fed too much with ideological ideas which are not African, not our own".

During his short stay in Mogadishu, there were discussions — generally described as "useful" in the jargon of diplomacy — with members of the Somalia Government, and broad areas of agreement or potential co-operation could seemingly be noted down in formal talks. But there was what must be called an astonishing rupture of protocol, at the end of Kenyatta's visit.

An appropriate array of dignitaries, with a large crowd behind, were assembled at the Mogadishu Airport. The customary brief and harmless farewell speeches — on both sides — were finished and Kenyatta then expected the parade out to the aircraft to begin.

In fact, there was an unexpected and an awkward lull. Then — without any warning at all — the Somali Prime Minister, sheaves of foolscap papers in his hand, climbed upon a nearby rostrum and delivered an impassioned address. This committed Somalia, beyond issues of legality or right, to the whole emotional concept of the "five-pointed star", to the policy of "redeeming areas from bondage", including some Districts of Kenya, and to the declared purpose of "uniting all Somalis under one flag".

After listening to this, with no outward display of feeling, Mzee Kenyatta firmly requested and was in fact given the right of reply. Without preparation, and simply as national leader, he said he merely wanted the people of Somalia to know that not an inch of Kenya's territory would be surrendered to any alien cause. But — he added — any Somali national in Kenya wishing to return to Somalia would be perfectly free to do so. The crowd applauded him.

On January 9, 1963, speaking as President of KANU, Jomo Kenyatta warned the Somali Republic that any aggressor who dared to enter Kenya would be crushed. He told a Nairobi crowd that — according to information reaching him — the Somali National Assembly had agreed to help Somalis in the Northern Frontier District who were wishing to secede. He commented: "Somalis must know that they are brothers of Kenya Africans. Nobody will be allowed to take any part of Kenya. If Somalis here want to join their colleagues in Somalia, they should pack their camels and go."

On March 20, 1963, Kenyatta made a formal protest to the Colonial Secretary, over a British statement that Somalia would be consulted on the future of the N.F.D. In a cable, he said such promises did not emerge from any agreement or consultation with the Kenya Government, and KANU would recognize no such promises. The Party stood firmly by its decision against secession in any form. He added that Somalia's constant interference in Kenya's internal affairs must stop, and Britain should refrain from the possibility of committing any future Kenya Government . . .

The other brief external visit by Mzee Kenyatta was to an Afro-Asian Solidarity Conference in Moshi on February 10, 1963. He told assembled delegates that: "this Conference has shown awareness of the need for us to get away from the virus of the Cold War, and establish our own objectives and standards".

Kenyatta then declared that people who propounded textbook ideas about democracy — such as those who believed that a two-Party system was sacred — should not be heeded too much. Democracy could be expressed in many different forms. In a particular country, it should be expressed in the form which the people understood, and not merely to satisfy foreign ideas.

Just 110 days later, the unleashing at last of democracy in Kenya swept Kenyatta from the fact of political leadership to the reality of political power.

KCA leaders in Nairobi, December 1928. (left to right) Jesse Kariuki, Joseph Kang'ethe, Jomo Kenyatta

Members of the KCA who welcomed Jomo Kenyatta on his return from England on 29th of October 1930. (left to right) Benedetto Wamutitu, Josphat Kamau, Amos Wangacha, Job Muchuchu, James Njoroge

Jomo Kenyatta as a student at the London School of Economics in 1935

Jomo Kenyatta at the Kenya African Teacher's College, Githunguri in 1948

Welcoming group at Dagoretti in 1946 after Jomo Kenyatta's return from England

Jomo Kenyatta speaking to the mass meeting held in Kiambu on 24 August, 1952

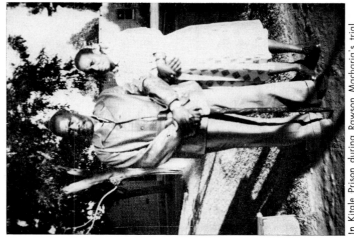

In Kitale Prison during Rawson Macharia's trial in February 1959

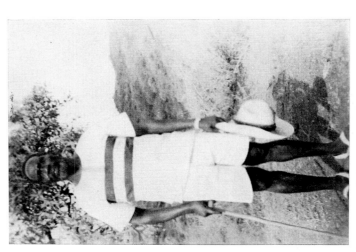

In prison at Lokitaung in 1956

Mzee in his house in detention at Lodwar in 1959

Mzee in his shamba at Lodwar in 1959

Mzee watching tenniquoit at Maralal in 1961

Mzee in the cobbler's shop at Maralal in 1961

Mzee reading in his house at Maralal in 1961

Mzee talks to a woodcarver at Maralal in 1961

Mzee at the Maralal Press Conference on 11 April, 1961

Jomo Kenyatta, then Prime Minister of Kenya, being sworn in at the Independence Day ceremony on 12 December, 1963

Jomo Kenyatta accepts the traditional symbols of a cloak, a shield and a spear from Chief Ole Sangale of the Masai at the Independence Day ceremony

President Mzee Jomo Kenyatta speaking to reporters after announcing the Republican Cabinet at Gatundu — December 9th., 1964

His Excellency President Mzee Jomo Kenyatta with Heads of States and Governments at the Nairobi meeting of Good Neighbourly Relations at State House — 31st March to 2nd April, 1965

Mzee pictured with delegates from Kenya's North Eastern Province on the occasion of KANU's Limuru Conference on 13 March, 1966

Mzee speaks at a Labour Day rally at Kamukunji, Nairobi

President Jomo Kenyatta acknowledges a salute from the crowd after visiting KANU HQ in Nairobi on Kenyatta Day in 1966

President Jomo Kenyatta lays the foundation stone of Alego Secondary School

President Jomo Kenyatta at the opening of the new extensions to Parliament Buildings on 2nd November, 1965

President Jomo Kenyatta on his shamba at Gatundu

Daniel arap Moi (now Vice President of Kenya, third from right) visits Jomo Kenyatta and the other detainees at Lodwar on 3rd November, 1959

His Excellency the President Mzee Jomo Kenyatta addressing the Reconciliation Committee on the Congo Kisangani (Stanleyville) landings

President Jomo Kenyatta with (left to right) President Kenneth Kaunda (Zambia), Prime Minister Egal (Somalia) and President Milton Obote (Uganda) in Kampala after the Summit Conference in 1967

Mzee Jomo Kenyatta is introduced to members of the Kitui Hospital staff in February 1968

Chapter 7

ELECTION TO DESTINY

BLUEPRINT FOR UHURU

The general elections conducted in May of 1963 — in an atmosphere of much excitement but in lawful tranquillity — were the first ever held on a full franchise in Kenya, and without communal representation.

The mechanics of the elections embraced some massive organisational challenges, all over the country, which were surmounted — by the Administration and the Police — with degrees of patience and good humour that deserved and won the highest praise.

Within periods of consecutive or well-separated days, varying with the numerical strengths and geographical problems of each constituency or district, voting had to be supervised for seats in the Regional Assemblies, and the 41 seats in the Senate . . . (now dissolved) . . . and the 117 seats in the House of Representatives. The admixture of differing electoral rolls, candidates, procedures, ballot-boxes, regulations, queries and objections, might have disturbed the serenity of a Trappist. But each day passed without real incident or upset. Officials and Party agents between them removed the spectre, which had haunted Returning Officers for weeks beforehand, of queues of voters outside the right Polling Stations on the wrong day, and next day the other way about.

The polling for the Lower House was, of course, the critical expression of the people's will and mandate. Here, KANU was returned with an overwhelming majority, both in seats and in popular votes. Mzee Jomo Kenyatta was swept to power as Prime Minister, and six months thereafter led Kenya into full and sovereign independence . . .

Although election fever was at its height in the period from March to May, the loom of the election was felt from the turn of the year. The report of the Constituencies Commission was issued at that time, and on January 17, 1963, speaking as President of KANU, Kenyatta had this to say:

Now that it is published, our immediate demand is that the general elections must be expedited. The interest, excitement and good humour of our people should not be allowed to turn into frustration because of delay and protracted electioneering.

To all our supporters, I have only one message. The hour of reckoning has now come. The unity and strength of our Party shall decide not only who wins the next election, but who governs thereafter and leads Kenya to independence. I must add that KANU is more united now than it has ever been before. I have every confidence that we shall win, but that alone is not enough: we have to be able to form a stable Government.

Once this stage had been reached, Jomo Kenyatta — assisted most notably in Party headquarters by Tom Mboya as General Secretary, and Mwai Kibaki as Executive Officer — approached the election as a General marshalling his forces for a planned engagement, understanding the advantages of strength, but knowing as well that there could be no effective exertion of strength without discipline.

On January 25, 1963, the KANU President, therefore, issued the following statement through the Press:

'After reading Press reports and listening to Radio broadcasts, I find it necessary to issue this statement as a means of giving information to those who plan to stand as candidates in the forthcoming elections.

'A good and loyal Party member is one who will abide by the rules and procedures of the Party to which he belongs. It is natural that a person should seek to be elected,

but the development of the Party system means that such
desire or ambition must be subject to Party rules. Already,
some people — especially in my own Party — are issuing
statements and making personal declarations. This conduct
is contrary to our Party Constitution, and must be brought
to an end.

'The procedure is that those who want to stand for
election should apply directly to the KANU Branch in the
area they wish to stand for. Such applications will be
considered by the Branch, in consultation with the constituency concerned. After reaching a decision, the Branch will
convey this decision to Headquarters, from whence all
announcements will be made.

'Where agreement is not reached, or grievances arise
over the selection, such disagreement or grievance must be
brought to the notice of Head Office, who will endeavour
to settle the matter. On no account will Branches or Sub-
branches be allowed to announce names of candidates, in
contravention of the Party Constitution.

'The enemies and opponents of KANU concede that we
shall easily win the next elections, but at constituency level
they nurse a secret hope that discipline within our Party
will break down. They hope that — as in 1961 — KANU
will have independent candidates, thus splitting the votes
to give victory to other Parties. This is the challenge to all
our members. The Delegates Conference decided to expel
any member who defied the Party on this question, and I
shall carry out this decision without fear or favour. But let
us, through self-discipline, disappoint our enemies by adher-
ing to Party decisions. This way, our victory will be
assured.'

This set the stage for decisive democratic contest, and for
some weeks the quiet work of preparation continued.

On March 21, 1963, there was a valedictory debate marking the termination of the Twelfth and last Legislative
Council. The Speaker, Humphrey Slade . . . (still Speaker
of the National Assembly in the Kenya Republic, attesting
to the popularity, integrity and outstanding intellectual

calibre of this man) . . . said it was improbable that "Legco"
would ever sit again under the old name, or as the sole
Legislature of the country. He recalled how the present
body — "in various forms which changed with changing
times" — had been the Legislative Council of Kenya for
more than 55 years. In his view, it had developed over that
long period, and now passed on as a heritage, "a tradition
and reputation of dignified and good-humoured conduct
second to no other Parliament".

In his capacity as Minister of State, Jomo Kenyatta then
rose to speak in tribute to this occasion, and adorn it with
perspective. He said:

The next Council will be the Legislature of a country
which will be internally self-governing. The Council of
Ministers will have the last say in matters which are
important to the daily lives of all of us. The composition
of the new Council will be in the hands of the people.
For the first time in the history of this country, it is the
people who will choose the Government they want.

We go to the elections as soldiers go to battle, determined to win but equally determined to fight according to well-known and established rules. Each candidate
must be prepared to give his best in the fight, but thereafter to accept the result cheerfully.

The country knows how much my Party and I have
fought to establish on a permanent footing the pattern
of parliamentary Government with which we are
familiar. It is not without reluctance that we have
accepted variations in that pattern to meet the views
and wishes of others. But let us now pledge ourselves
to uphold the dignity and prestige of the Parliament we
are going to set up. Let us agree to accept willingly and
wholeheartedly the decisions that it will take. Let us,
above all, agree to use the method of friendly persuasion
to iron out any differences that may arise in the country,
and faithfully submit ourselves to the vote of the people.

With the steady build-up of Party organisation and readiness, and the necessary formality of a parliamentary void,
electioneering — in April — could really begin. The next

tidy step was the printing and issue of the KANU Election Manifesto, which has remained ever since as a critical blueprint of Kenya's national purpose and progress.

Inevitably, this Manifesto in its final form was a detailed and intricate document, of a length that would make it unwieldy to reproduce here. But on the evening of April 18, 1963, its day of issue, a summary was prepared and broadcast over Kenya radio by the K.B.C. Political Correspondent, using the following script:

'The KANU Manifesto began by declaring that achievement of independence would not be an end in itself, but would give the opportunity to work unfettered for the creation of a democratic African Socialist country. The Party emphasised that the Government, and economic experts, could only show the way to social and economic advance. It went on: "Whether our country forges ahead, or whether its economy declines further, depends on the determination and hard work of every citizen".

'The KANU Manifesto described the family as the fundamental unit in the Welfare Socialist State of the future. The Party intended that every child in Kenya should have a minimum of seven years' free education. Moreover, KANU believed that non-racial education, and the growing together of the country's youth, must lead to national consciousness. The new Government must aim at free medical and hospital treatment for all citizens. And while anyone would be free to pay for medical services, racial health institutions or schemes would have no place in an independent Kenya.

'The Party said there was no desire to suppress any of the diverse cultures and communities which made up the Kenya nation. KANU would welcome non-Africans who chose to join in the new national task, recognising that their training, skills and knowledge would be of the greatest value. The Manifesto stressed that the Party would uphold the rule of law, and guarantee the position of every citizen in accordance with the Bill of Rights. The Judiciary would be independent of other branches of the State at all levels.

'On land ownership, the Manifesto said KANU would not tolerate the holding by anyone of large under-developed tracts of land. But those who had farms, estates or ranches making a full contribution to the economy need have no fear of expropriation. The Party recognised that production of crops for the market was the backbone of Kenya's economy, and that only by what it called "a dynamic breakthrough" in farming methods could the future Welfare State be financed.

'On land settlement, the Party said the problem of the unemployed landless must be vigorously tackled, and resettlement in the Scheduled Areas had a part to play in meeting desperate needs. But Kenya could not afford to fragment economic farms already making a vital contribution to national prosperity, into units producing little more than subsistence. The main solution — the Manifesto declared — was increasing agricultural efficiency in all areas, to provide a basis for rural and cottage industries and regular farm employment.

'It would be economic madness — as KANU put it — to continue importing finished goods processed abroad from Kenya's own primary products. Consumer goods made from raw materials locally available would therefore have priority in a programme of industrial expansion. The Manifesto said KANU believed in a wide measure of governmental control of the economy, but noted that there were many methods of participation without acquiring public ownership.

'The Party advocated what it described as "a high wage economy", for the good of the worker and his family, and to encourage the acquisition of skills. A skilled worker living in an urban society, and making the break with traditional social patterns of the rural areas, would have priority in the social security programme. Outside urban areas, the Community Development service would be of outstanding importance in building a new country. In all areas, Local Government — from village level to Regional level — would have an important place.

'While maintaining standards in the Civil Service, KANU policy would be to give first priority to indigenous Africans, until progress was made towards a structure reflecting the proportions of Kenya's society. Second preference would then be given to citizens of expatriate origin. The Manifesto added that non-citizens who were replaced would be protected by the agreed compensation terms.

'The guarantee for preservation of the rights of Trade Unions — the Party declared — would lie in their recognition of the responsible part they must play in building a prosperous Kenya. Some of the attitudes that were appropriate when Kenya was fighting for independence would have to be revised, and what the Manifesto called "an all-out war" by the Trade Unions now could only be waged against their own Government and fellow-citizens. The basis for settlement of disputes — KANU went on — was laid down in legislation and in the Industrial Charter.

'The Manifesto stated that an independent Kenya should adopt a Republican Constitution, as being a form of government appropriate to Kenya's conditions and meaningful to the people. Kenya should apply for membership of the Commonwealth. Beyond this, KANU would seek to build on pan-African unity, to make the whole Continent of Africa a force for good in world affairs.

'Finally, the Party accepted that Colonialism could take more subtle forms, and could come from Communist as well as from Capitalist sources. Externally, Kenya must follow an absolute policy of non-alignment. The country should support whatever was right and just in international affairs, judging each case on the facts and principles that arose.'

Rarely can there have been a Party Manifesto, at election time in almost any country, which opened with such a fusillade of undisguised reality, and which thereafter was prepared to commit itself — ignoring any backwaters of prudent ambiguity — on so many issues and unknowns.

Two days later — April 20, 1963 — was Nomination Day for the general elections. Jomo Kenyatta was the only candidate to present himself for the House of Representatives constituency of Thika-Gatundu, and was declared elected unopposed.

FOUNDATIONS OF THE FUTURE

During the following week, choosing this moment for his final shove and impetus as President of KANU, Kenyatta supplied an article to the *East African Standard* setting out his views on the Party and electoral issues then current, and sketching the foundations of philosophy and approach that must underlie the whole future of Kenya. In somewhat abridged form, this was the article as published on April 24, 1963:

'Running through the KANU Election Manifesto is the theme that only by the hard work of all our people, under the dynamic leadership which the KANU Government will give, can we make a success of independence.

'Freedom, equality and brotherhood are fundamental articles of KANU's political philosophy. We believe that only in a free and liberal society can each individual develop fully to serve his fellow-citizens.

'We live in Africa, and our policies, both internal and external, must reflect this fact. Our people must be given a pride in their own cultures, and we shall build upon all that is good and applicable in our traditional societies. That does not mean that we shall reject what the West and the East can offer.

'Those of our citizens who have come from other lands can play a special part in adapting the knowledge and the skills brought from abroad to Kenya's needs. We shall work for a united and integrated nation.

'Those principles of equality and brotherhood to be followed in the political sphere also apply to economic and social matters. While natural ambition must be harnessed to help achieve that economic advance we all desire, greed and exploitation cannot be the cornerstones of our nation building.

'Our message to the people is that, under their own leaders, they must work hard to make a success of independence, so that we can expand social services.

'In all my years in the nationalist movement, I have always believed in a non-tribal, non-racial approach. This is KANU's policy also. It does not mean that we wish to suppress or oppress any particular tribe or race. Indeed, the presence of different groups in our nation provides us with the opportunity to build a rich culture from these diverse elements.

'The position of every citizen, according to the Bill of Rights, will be safeguarded by the Government. Every citizen, whatever his tribe or race, must think and act as a Kenyan.

'The course leading to the achievement of our political freedom has been arduous, and much hatred has been engendered. Many Africans were so frustrated at the denial of social, economic and political rights that they resorted to violence. Inter-racial hatred reached a peak some ten years ago, and much suffering resulted.

'I myself suffered for long. But I promise you I am not bitter. I ask those of you who still have hatred in your hearts to cast it aside. We cannot build a happy and progressive nation as long as men harbour ill-feelings about the past.'

In the hustings sense, the battle then really commenced. But to trace all the tactics and submissions — and the appeals and protestations and counter-arguments and individual fortunes — of the whole general election would be beyond the scope and intent of this present work . . .

At this point, logical in timing, there must be a digression.

On May 10, 1963, Jomo Kenyatta broke away temporarily from the conduct and concerns of the election to send a message to Addis Ababa, to be read at the Conference there of Heads of independent African States. Explaining why it was impossible — at the height of the election — for him to leave Kenya, Mzee Kenyatta conveyed to the Conference some of his long-formulated thoughts on the prospects for and the practical objectives of pan-Africanism. These were his words:

'This is indeed an historic occasion. The long-cherished desire for a completely liberated Africa, united under the banner of pan-African brotherhood, is about to be achieved.

'Only a decade ago, flags of European colonial powers flew from east to west, and from north to south, throughout our motherland. It was only in the country of our gallant colleague and freedom fighter, His Imperial Majesty Haile Selassie the First, and in the Republic of our renowned brother President Tubman, and in the illustrious Egyptian State, that one found truly African independent Governments. But the spirit of African freedom continued to burn in our hearts and minds.

'Our long struggle for African freedom has finally achieved most of our cherished desires. Neither persecution nor deprivation, nor torture nor banishment, could ever kill that deep-seated longing to be free.

'The presence of 32 independent African States in this Conference is a glowing testimony of African achievement. By the end of this year, more flags of new African independent States will adorn our State mansions, our international Conference Halls, and the United Nations Organisation itself.

'I am not a prophet, but I daresay that in the next few years the recalcitrant and decadent powers of dictatorial Portugal, and the fascist apartheid regime of South Africa, will definitely come tumbling down. We cannot rest, and we shall not rest, until every corner and every soul of this Continent of ours is free.

'Complete liberation of Mother Africa should be viewed not as the end of our struggle, but as the beginning of a new and challenging task: the removal of territorial, political and economic balkanisation. The well-known policy of "divide-and-rule" was put into full operation during the so-called scramble for Africa, breaking up our Continent

into numerous small territorial units. The imperialist
powers are still playing this game. Our one and only
weapon to beat them in the game is African solidarity
through dynamic pan-Africanism.

'Let me say this: as we strongly believe in pan-
Africanism, we must not entertain territorial expansionist
aims, which some pan-African brothers wish to pursue. Pan-
Africanism means bringing together into closer union our
various countries, so that the artificial boundaries between
us created by imperialist powers are of little consequence.

'This Conference of the Heads of independent African
States will have accomplished a great deal, if territorial
claims and boundary disputes between African brothers are
declared to be contrary to the spirit of pan-Africanism. I
have examined many of these claims, and my conclusion
is that they are based on some form of tribalism or imperialist plot, trying to put African nationalists at each other's
throats, and thus to kill the pan-African movement.

'We must be categorical on this matter. We cannot on the
one hand have African solidarity, and on the other hand
have disruptive boundary disputes. If we were to try and
reorganise territorial boundaries in the Africa of today, we
should succeed only in starting a chain of reactions that
would break up African solidarity, with the shedding of
blood. How long must we tolerate the imperialist game of
divide-and-rule? This game must die and be buried.

'Addis Ababa is the Headquarters of the Economic Commission for Africa, whose activities and agencies could be
greatly utilised to interpret pan-Africanism in a concrete
form. I am a great supporter of the steps being taken to
create an African Common Market, with the harmonisation
of monetary zones in Africa, and the co-ordination of
economic development plans, so that Africa may move
forward in unity and in a spirit of brotherly fellowship.

'I would have liked very much to be with you at this
Conference, but this has proved impossible. At present, we
are holding our General Election, leading us into full
internal self-government, to be followed shortly by

complete independence. It is a most crucial election. As I
have led the struggle for freedom here in Kenya throughout my entire life, it is imperative that I witness the
fruition of our long struggle. But my spirit is with you, and
I am sure that success will attend all your deliberations.'

(It may be recalled here that on May 25, 1963, while
results of the poll were being awaited in Kenya, the 32
Heads of African States meeting in Addis Ababa signed a
Charter which established the Organisation of African
Unity.)

Chronologically, inside Kenya, the next event of note was
a message to the people from Kenyatta — May 17, 1963 —
just before voting began:

> On the eve of the most crucial election in the history
> of our country, I appeal to every one of you to behave
> with calm and dignity. In particular, I ask you to co-
> operate with the officers of the Administration and of
> the Police, while carrying out their difficult tasks at this
> time. Remember that, as a result of this election, they
> will become our Administrators and our Police. They
> will be responsible to a truly representative African
> Government. Any acts of hooliganism, any disorderliness
> will thus be directed against your own Government. It
> will be no use if the election goes off calmly in 99
> constituencies, but in the hundredth there is trouble.
> Any single outbreak of disturbances will harm the good
> name of Kenya and of the incoming Government. Let us
> show to the world that we are a responsible nation.

By May 27, counting had progressed to the stage when
it was evident that a KANU majority in the Lower House
would be assured. Mzee Kenyatta at once issued a statement, which said in part: "We shall build a country where
every citizen may develop his talent to the full, restricted
only by the larger aim we have of building a fair society.
The rights of all, and of their property, will be fully
protected. There will be no privilege for any minority.
Equally, we shall see that no member of any group under-

goes discrimination or oppression at the hands of the majority. Only by creating a sense of national unity will it be possible to harness the efforts of all the people to make a success of independence."

The following official release then emerged from the Press Office in Nairobi on May 28, 1963:

In view of the results to date in the general election, the Governor of Kenya, Mr. Malcolm MacDonald, today invited Mr. Jomo Kenyatta, the leader of KANU — the majority Party in the House of Representatives — to make preparations for the formation of a new Government under himself as Prime Minister.

Mr. Kenyatta expects to present proposals for his Cabinet in the course of the next few days.

It is expected that the new Government will be ready to assume office on Saturday, June 1, and that the new Constitution will come into effect on that day.

The wheel had come full circle in eleven years — the arrest on contrived charges; the suprious trial and verdict; in the wilderness at Lokitaung; isolation at Lodwar; the farcical sojourn in Maralal; homecoming; assumption of leadership and triumph at the polls. Mzee Kenyatta was now elected to the duty that had always been his destiny.

That night — May 28 — he delivered a message to the people:

'On this momentous day, which sets Kenya on the final stages before independence, I ask for the co-operation of every man and woman in this land to help build the new nation.

'In the past, we have known racial hatred in this country. Let it be forgotten. We have experienced the setting of one tribe against another, one community against another. Let us not remember it now. Rather let us build together, in unity.

'The Government which is in the process of formation will be committed to a path of democratic African Socialism. We aim to create a fair society, where no citizen need suffer in sickness because he cannot pay for treatment. We believe that no child should go without education, merely because his family is poor.

'It will be the Government's intention to do away with the terrible poverty of so many of our people. In particular, we must see that the backward areas of our country catch up and keep pace with the more prosperous parts. Special attention will be given to the needs of the Masai, the Somali, the Suk, the Turkana, and other pastoral groups.

'We do not expect to do all this from foreign charity. We are not going to compromise our independence by begging for assistance. The Government will make it quite clear that our progress, our hopes, our ambitions, will only be fulfilled if we have hard work from every citizen.

'The Government will draw up a plan for our economic and social development. We shall see that experts, technicians and advisers are available in the field to explain to our people what they themselves can achieve. We intend to lead this country to prosperity by inspiring everyone to work hard and with efficiency.

'I have been impressed by the way in which Kenyans of all communities have worked together during the election campaign. I have been heartened by the friendliness and good humour which marked the elections in nearly every area. I hope this will be a pointer to the future.'

THE END AND THE BEGINNING

On June 1, 1963, Kenya duly attained internal self-government. In a brief speech following the public ceremony in Nairobi at which he was sworn in as Prime Minister, Mzee Jomo Kenyatta declared:

This is one of the happiest moments of my life. We are now embarking on the final brief stage which will lead this country to independence. It is not a celebration by one Party as its election victory. Rather must it be a rejoicing of all the people of this land at the progress towards the goal of independence.

But as we celebrate, let us remember that constitutional advance is not the greatest end in itself. Many of
our people suffer in sickness. Many are poor beyond
endurance. Too many live out narrow lives beneath a
burden of ignorance. As we participate in pomp and
circumstance, and as we make merry at this time,
remember this: we are relaxing before the toil that is
to come. We must work harder to fight our enemies —
ignorance, sickness and poverty.

I therefore give you the call: HARAMBEE! Let us all
work hard together for our country, Kenya.

Thereafter — for the record — Kenya became fully
independent on December 12, 1963, at glittering outdoor
ceremonies in Nairobi graced by the presence of the Duke
of Edinburgh and attended by the then Colonial Secretary,
Mr. Duncan Sandys. On December 12, 1964, Kenya adopted
the status of Republic. The addresses delivered by Jomo
Kenyatta on both these occasions are reproduced in full
within the Appendix section of this volume.

This is not the place, and it is not yet the time, to
attempt any historical account of the work and achievements of successive Governments headed by President
Kenyatta since 1963. Data is still organic, not yet malleable.
The perspective is too near.

But there is challenge here, to be met in due course by a
student of politics, a student of Africa, a student of the
strivings of mankind.

The fashioning and significance of national unity; constitutional and parliamentary shaping; the contribution of
Kenya to pan-Africanism, to Commonwealth counsels and
to world affairs; the key factors of stability and order; the
whole approach to economic planning and social development; maintenance of high administrative standards; the
assembly and constructive allocation of capital; the
modernisation of agriculture and scientific conservation of
natural resources; the provision and impact of new educational opportunities; the build-up of security forces, community development structures and information services . . .
all these and many other matters will repay study and

interpretation, and public narrative, not solely for their nature or result, but also for the inspiration of underlying philosophies and the bold realism of executive undertaking.

Meanwhile, however, the epoch stretching ahead from the moment — June 1, 1963 — when Mzee Kenyatta became Prime Minister cannot be ignored. It is for this reason, to satisfy a purpose of broad enlightenment, that the Appendix section which follows has been designed. The selected verbatim speeches by Jomo Kenyatta up until October 1967, with the stage merely set for each one, can achieve far more than narrative, at this juncture, to complete a political portrayal, and to serve as prologue to the saga that is nation building . . .

There is little more to say now on Kenyatta himself. This work will have spoken for him, and on his behalf. It is a picture of a man of constancy, a man of dedication and resilience, whose principles could never be undermined by injustice or calamity, the bruising of indifference, or the burden of power.

The content of this volume is an answer to his heartfelt hope, expressed at Kapenguria, that one day the truth should be known.

And now his life goes on. His work is not yet finished. Many tasks still beckon him ahead.

APPENDIX

Speeches by His Excellency, Mzee Jomo Kenyatta, President of the Republic of Kenya

These selected speeches are reproduced verbatim, following introductory comment. They span the period between September 1963 and October 1967, and appear in chronological sequence.

CONSTITUTIONAL CONFERENCE — 1963

During the little more than six months that separated Internal Self-government from Independence, there was the final Constitutional Conference convened by the British Government in London. On the eve of his departure from Nairobi at the head of the Kenya Government's delegation — September 21, 1963 — Prime Minister Jomo Kenyatta used these words:

Since the Election and the formation of an African Government, I and my Ministers have spared no effort in our endeavours to create unity and understanding throughout the country. The Government appreciates the response of the people to this call, and we have been very impressed with the way the ordinary man in Kenya has been keen to serve his country, and is not committed to tribalism or secession.

At the same time, the Government understands the fears and anxieties of some communities, and hopes that — by its example during these few months in office — such fears will be seen to be unfounded. The KANU Government is concerned with the welfare of all the people, regardless of their race or tribe, and this will be the policy of the Government in the future.

The final talks on the Constitution are to be held in London next week. The Government is pleased to see that the Opposition has at last decided to attend the talks.

In presenting its case, the Government will be guided by the wishes of the people, which have been so clearly demonstrated in the General Election, as well as in the County Council and Municipal elections. Our purpose is to establish a strong and effective Government, and to promote unity rather than encourage disintegration.

The Kenya Government delegation will urge on the British Government the need for a Constitution for Kenya that is both realistic and workable. It will press for a Constitution that is based not on fear and suspicion, but on faith and confidence in Kenya. The assumption of faith and good intentions on the part of all groups and communities within Kenya, rather than of hostility and conflict of interests, must be the starting-point for a peaceful and united Kenya.

Before our departure for London, I wish to take this opportunity to appeal to all the people of Kenya to keep calm and maintain the peace. The new era that Kenya will enter as an Independent nation — in the spirit of 'Harambee' — in December, is one which will call for dedication, hard work and unity. This is the challenge of the future.

Just a month later — October 20, 1963 — the Prime Minister arrived back in Nairobi, and reported to the country on the outcome of this constitutional mission:

Four weeks ago, we went to London for the final Constitutional Conference before Kenya's Independence. It has been four weeks of hard bargaining, but I am glad to say that all has ended well. I can now confirm that the date for our Independence will definitely be December 12. This is only 51 days ahead.

I hope that, now that we are back with confirmation, anxieties will disappear, and all our people will instead concentrate on readiness for Uhuru celebrations. Uhuru has been long awaited, both at home and abroad, and will attract a lot of interest. I am determined that it shall be a day to remember for all our people for all time.

In addition to confirming the date for Independence, we have been able to secure a number of significant changes to the Constitution. These include amendments to create one Public

Service Commission of Kenya instead of eight; a unified control and command of the entire Police force; and a change in the amendment machinery to enable changes to take place on a two-thirds national referendum.

The whole purpose of the Government was to secure a flexible and workable Constitution for Kenya. I assure the country that the new Constitution now provides a strong base for a united Kenya nation, within which everyone — regardless of tribe or race — shall feel safe and secure. Within this State there will be no room for domination, but there will be ample room for everyone to participate and contribute towards our efforts for nation building.

There is no room for autonomy or secession. Such talk is idle, and will lead nowhere. Why should anyone deny the Kalenjin, Masai or Coastal tribes the right to be part of the new Kenya nation? Why should anyone try to deny these tribes the right to participate in and contribute towards the exciting task of creating a new nation? These are questions which I am sure the people will soon ask of their leaders. I have no hesitation in saying that the people will reject petty and negative leadership.

I know that one of the most sensitive questions in our country is land. This has been played on by some people. I now give a categorical assurance that, under the Constitution, all tribal land is entrenched in the tribal authority, and no one can take away land belonging to another tribe.

I do not regard our mission to London as a victory for KANU. This is a victory for Kenya, and for responsible and sensible policies aimed at the welfare of all our people. Let us not talk of opposition and Government. Let us talk of Kenya and our people's need. I invite the Opposition leaders to forget the past, and come together with us to form a united front to fight our real enemies — poverty, ignorance and disease.

All of us want to fight these three evils. So why do we not join together now — in the spirit of 'Harambee' — and move forward? I see no shame in forgetting the past. To do this is an act of wisdom and courage that goes with genuine leadership. Here is our opportunity: let it never be said that we refused to take it.

INDEPENDENCE DAY — 1963

Although the Uhuru Day speeches of December 12, 1963, are accessible elsewhere, no work of this kind would be complete without their reproduction here for reference purposes. Jomo Kenyatta, who was convicted and imprisoned ten years earlier, reviled and banished thereafter, stood on this Day — as Kenya's Prime Minister — to receive the instruments of his country's Independence, hailed by Princes and Premiers as an elder Statesman, a noble patriot, a world leader. Any lesser man might have enjoyed drawing cynical comparisons, or have indulged in spite. In fact, his words matched the hour:

*

It is with great pride and pleasure that I receive these constitutional instruments today as the embodiment of Kenya's freedom. This is the greatest day in Kenya's history, and the happiest day of my life.

Our march to freedom has been long and difficult. There have been times of despair, when only the burning conviction of the rightness of our cause has sustained us. Today, the tragedies and misunderstandings of the past are behind us. Today, we start on the great adventure of building the Kenya nation.

As we start on this great task, it is right that we who are assembled at this historic ceremony here today, and all the people of Kenya, should remember and pay tribute to those people of all races, tribes and colours who — over the years — have made their contribution to Kenya's rich heritage: administrators, farmers, missionaries, traders and others, and above all the people of Kenya themselves. All have laboured to make this fair land of Kenya the thriving country it is today. It behoves each one of us to vow that, in the days ahead, we shall be worthy of our great inheritance.

Your Royal Highness, your presence here today as the personal representative of Her Majesty the Queen is for us a great honour, and one which gives the highest pleasure to all the people of Kenya.

We thank Her Majesty for her message of good wishes, and would request you, Sir to convey to the Queen the warm greetings of all our people.

We welcome also today Her Majesty's Secretary of State for Commonwealth Relations, who has been so closely concerned with us in the final stages of our march to Independence. With Britain, which has watched over our destinies for so long, we now enter a new relationship. The close ties which have bound our two countries are not severed today. Rather, they will now grow in strength as we work together as two sovereign nations within the Commonwealth, that unique association of free and independent States to whose counsels we look forward to making our contribution.

To all our honoured guests, I extend — on behalf of the people of Kenya — a warm and fraternal welcome to our country on this great occasion. Your presence here today brings added pleasure to our rejoicings.

Today is rightly a day of great rejoicing. But it must also be a day of dedication. Freedom is a right, and without it the dignity of man is violated. But freedom by itself is not enough. At home, we have a duty to ensure that all our citizens are delivered from the afflictions of poverty, ignorance and disease, otherwise freedom for many of our people will be neither complete nor meaningful. We shall count as our friends, and welcome as fellow-citizens, every man, woman and child, in Kenya — regardless of race, tribe, colour or creed — who is ready to help us in this great task of advancing the social wellbeing of all our people.

Freedom also means that we are now a member of the international community, and that we have a duty to work for the peace of the world. Abroad, we shall count as our friends all those who strive for peace.

My friends, we are now an independent nation, and our destiny is henceforward in our own hands. I call on every Kenyan to join me today in this great adventure of nation building. In the spirit of HARAMBEE, let us all work together so to mould our country that it will set an example to the world in progress, toleration and high endeavour.

Mzee Kenyatta then paused for a moment, gazed around at the huge crowds thronging the Uhuru Stadium, and — remembering that this was their moment of history as well as his — spoke to his people in Kiswahili. Such is his magnetism that the people did not simply listen; he held them in his hand, and they became part

of the image he created. Now it is not possible, whatever
the scholars may say, to translate the glowing idiom of
the Swahili which he employed into English of comparable fluency and impact. There are nuances that have no
parallel. This, then, is simply an English-language version of his unscripted address:

We are grateful for the greetings from Her Majesty the Queen
which the Duke of Edinburgh has read to us today. We ask him —
when he returns to Britain — to convey our greetings to the Queen:
Tell her that, although we have become independent, we shall
remain her friends. I think, my brothers, that our friendship with
the Queen and the Government of the United Kingdom will now
be of greater value. Before, this was not of our choice; it was being
forced upon us. But now, although we have broken all chains, this
friendship can be real and of great importance.

I also want to thank the Duke of Edinburgh for having brought
us an important book, different from any other. This book says
that all the people of Kenya are free, that the people of Kenya
are upholding their own Government, whether anyone else likes
it or not. We thank the Duke of Edinburgh again, and we shall
never forget that it was he who brought us this important book.

I am grateful that distinguished guests from all over the world
have joined us in celebrating the achievement of Independence
for our country. I greet you on behalf of the people of Kenya. We
all wish you a happy and enjoyable stay in our country. But, as
you know, mistakes and imperfections can be found here and
there and should you encounter such things — be you black,
white or brown — we ask you to excuse us and accept that this
is unintentional. We are all human, and human beings are sometimes bound to make mistakes.

What I have to say now is for the people of this country, but
first let me say a word to our brothers in Africa who broke the
chains of Colonialism before us. I say to them: we are now
independent after you. You have already tasted the honey of
Uhuru, and now that we are with you, I know that this is sweet.

But to all who have Independence, I say: this would be meaningless if in our Africa, some of our brothers are still under the
yoke of Colonialism. We therefore face a great challenge to help
those of our brothers who are left behind, still dominated by
foreign rule. If we look at South Africa, and if we look at
Mozambique and Angola, we find our brothers still being exploited.

It is thus our duty to fight, by all means available to us, so that our brothers can achieve their Independence.

African unity is very important. If there is no unity in the whole of Africa, we shall still be slaves: we shall have entered into a new type of slavery, the slavery of divide-and-rule by more powerful countries which have tasted the sweetness of ruling, and which — whether waking or sleeping — only think of ruling Africa. And when they sleep, a dream comes to them urging them to divide Africa, divide and then rule. It is our duty to stop this, and the only means is unity.

If we achieve unity, the whole world will respect us. We shall be the foundation and the shield of mother Africa. Our Africa has been milked until she is almost dry. Now we want to restore and sustain mother Africa, so we can enjoy the little milk that is left. If we do not do this, we will be finished. I want to emphasise that our salvation must come from unity.

Some people may say that — alas! — Kenyatta now is advocating a colour-bar. This is not so; I have no colour feeling at all. What I want is for us to be united, so we can go forward and co-operate with the rest of the world. This is our goal.

And there is another matter: some people are saying — 'Kenyatta, you and your brothers are now independent, so which side will your independence take you to; will you be pro-West or pro-East, on the side of the devils or the angels?' I therefore declare to you now that the aim of my Government which starts today is not to be pro-Left or pro-Right. We shall pursue the task of nation building, in friendship with the rest of the world. Nobody will ever be allowed to tell us, to tell me: you must be friendly to so-and-so. We shall remain free, and whoever wants friendship with us must be a real friend.

We shall never agree to friendship through any form of bribery. And I want all those nations who are present today — whether from West or from East — to understand our aim. We want to befriend all, and we want aid from everyone. But we do not want assistance from any person or country who will say: Kenyatta, if you want aid, you must agree to this or that. I believe, my brothers, and I tell you now, that it is better to be poor and remain free, than be technically free but still be kept on a string. A horse cannot choose: reins can be put on him so he can be led around as his owner desires. We will not be prepared to accept any aid that will tie us like a horse by its reins.

Now my words to the people of Kenya: many people may think that, now there is Uhuru, now I can see the sun of Freedom shining, richness will pour down like manna from Heaven. I tell you there will be nothing from Heaven. We must all work hard, with our hands, to save ourselves from poverty, ignorance and disease.

We ourselves can save us, but nobody else. When the Children of Israel were crying, saying: 'God, why did you bring us to this wilderness, where there is no water or sustenance?' God said He would bring them something called manna. This cannot happen again. He said He had closed the door, and anyone who wanted manna had to work for it. These are not the words of Kenyatta. God Himself told the human race. He said He had closed the door with a lock, and had thrown the key into the ocean; that the door would never open again and there would be no more manna in the world.

Therefore, my brothers, we have got to work hard and be faithful, to make our Independence mean all that we want and hope. If we do nothing but sleep, there will be many difficulties. All types of work must be done.

Many people in the world have despised us. I remember one time when I was travelling in Europe, a man told me: 'Kenyatta, the people in your country are very lazy'. When I asked him why, he quoted a story that, since our country was very hot, all we did was sleep under a mango or coconut tree, praying to God that a fruit would fall down while we slept, and then — when it did — waking up to eat it.

From today onwards, I want our Uhuru to mean: 'Uhuru na Kazi ... Freedom and Work'. This will help us greatly.

Another point, my brothers, is this: do not think that, because there is no longer a Colonial Government, there will no longer be need to respect the country's laws The laws of the country will remain; the Police and Prisons will remain. Do not think that, because the other day I freed about 8,000 people from prison, all prison doors will now be closed and no more people will be sent in. This is not so. Anyone who breaks the laws of the country will be dealt with firmly.

An African Government wants faithfulness. It wants the laws to be obeyed. This is what Government is for, and what it should be. I do not want to burden you. But I do want those who will help me in building our nation, and making it a worthwhile place to live in, to be faithful. Those present who are prepared to help me in this vital task should raise their hands ... I thank you all.

I thank you as well for electing me to lead you into a new phase in the progress of our country. In the past, we used to blame the

Europeans for everything that went wrong. When things went wrong, we used to say the Europeans are bad, they are sucking our blood. When we lacked education, we said the Europeans were only educating their children, and the Asians were only educating their children, so when will ours be educated?

Now the Government is ours. Maybe you will now be blaming Kenyatta, saying: 'Kenyatta, we elected you, but where is this or that?' But you must know that Kenyatta alone cannot give you everything. All things we must do together. You and I must work together to develop our country, to get education for our children, to have doctors, to build roads, to improve or provide all day-to-day essentials. This should be our work, in the spirit that I am going to ask you to echo, to shout aloud, to shatter the foundations of the past with the strength of our new purpose....HARAMBEE!

O.A.U. DAY — 1964

May 25, 1964, was a day of significance, to the concepts and practical purposes of African unity that Mzee Jomo Kenyatta had championed for so long. To mark this occasion, he issued in Nairobi a short but revealing statement on this theme:

*

For the first time in an independent Kenya, we celebrate the first anniversary of the OAU by a public holiday. A year ago on this day, 32 Heads of African States signed a Charter in Addis Ababa which established the Organisation of African Unity. It is therefore with great pride that I look forward to the visit next month of my friend, His Imperial Majesty, Haile Selassie I, the Emperor of Ethiopia, who played such a major part in convening the Conference.

I also remember that the setting up of OAU was a fulfilment of 44 years of sustained struggle for the independence of Africa, which started in Paris in 1919 when the Pan-African Movement gained an organised form. I have myself actively participated in this movement since its inception, but would like here to recall the names of my colleagues and founders of the Pan-African Movement: the late Dr. William E. B. Du Bois and the late George Padmore.

Countrymen, I want to remind you that we fought for independence to free ourselves from foreign rule. Having done so, we must also liberate our minds and souls from foreign ideas and thought. In our own country here, Colonial mentality persists. I should like you to be vigilant, and to re-dedicate yourselves today to building a nation deeply rooted in our own thoughts and ideas. This may mean rewriting school textbooks, evolving new architecture, and preserving in many arts the African traditional forms and culture.

The OAU exists not only to promote a new culture, but also to strive for the consolidation of African independence and unity.

We must defend our sovereignty and territorial integrity. We must eradicate Colonialism, and promote genuine international co-operation and friendship. Guided by the Charter of OAU, Africans are resolved to play a prominent role in the affairs of the United Nations.

My Government believes strongly in African unity, and will strive to broaden the basis of this unity in a manner that reflects realism. We shall uphold the principle of equality of States, negotiate disputes peacefully, enhance personal liberty and freedom of expression.

STATE VISIT TO KENYA — 1964

In mid-1964, Emperor Haile Selassie of Ethiopia paid a State Visit to Kenya, undertaking many formal engagements in Nairobi, but travelling widely as well — and receiving a tumultuous welcome — throughout the country. The Emperor delivered an address to both Houses of the Kenya Parliament on June 9, 1964 and Mzee Jomo Kenyatta (as Prime Minister) spoke in reply:

*

On behalf of myself and of all Members of the National Assembly, I thank Your Majesty for visiting our Parliament and for addressing us so graciously. Your visit is all the more welcome on account of the disappointment which we experienced when you were unavoidably prevented from attending our Independence Day celebrations last December. We are glad that our hopes of offering you the hospitality of Kenya have now been realized.

This has indeed been a great occasion for all of us. As His Excellency the Governor-General has already said, you are the first Head of State to pay a visit here since Kenya became independent. More than this, it is the first time that we have had the opportunity of listening to one of the foremost elder statesmen of our time. Let me assure Your Majesty that the people of Kenya rejoice at being able to pay our humble respects to you. Your Imperial Majesty's presence has enkindled a new sense of pride and elevated our hearts and minds to new dignity.

Ethiopia and Kenya have much in common; we have a common boundary, our economies are primarily agricultural and pastoral; we need to develop our industries and strengthen commerce. We need to improve the basic living standards of our peoples. Above all, we must resist our common enemies, not only those who wage war against us with guns and other weapons, but also the more insidious opponents of disease, ignorance, poverty and illiteracy.

Our problems are those of many other of the developing countries of Africa. They can only be solved by hard and patient toil, by the utilization of all available resources and by mutual co-operation between the countries of Africa and the world. With these objects in view, our two countries have denounced those possessed with unholy ideas of territorial expansion.

We attach great importance to understanding each other. To this end, I know Your Imperial Majesty is keenly interested. Our hope is that by the time you leave Kenya you will have gained a first-hand knowledge of our country and of our people, and that you will carry with you back to Ethiopia happy memories of our new State.

It will always be a matter of regret that I personally was not qualified, on account of Kenya not having achieved independence, to attend as an official representative of my country the Conference of the Heads of African States when the Organization of African Unity was born in Addis Ababa last year. The whole world knows that the birth of the Organization was a great personal triumph of Your Imperial Majesty. In subscribing to it, this country would like to pay tribute to your vision and statesmanship. Through the Organization the hopes of creating a strong United Nations Organization have come nearer to reality; so are hopes of liberating from racial domination our brothers in South Africa, Rhodesia, Angola and Mozambique.

I hope that this visit will be a prelude to many other visits to Kenya by members of your Government and other citizens of Ethiopia, and that I myself and my Ministers and officials of my Government will be privileged to visit Addis Ababa and other parts of Ethiopia so that there may be a constant exchange of ideas and experience from which both our countries may mutually benefit.

I am glad to be able to tell the House that Kenya has completed a defence treaty with Ethiopia which will provide for mutual assistance should this be necessary. Furthermore, the Ethiopian Government has agreed to make training facilities available to the Kenya Armed Forces, and it has been agreed that there will be co-operation between our Governments to protect those of our peoples who live on our frontiers. It is also with great satisfaction that we have noted Your Majesty's personal effort in making a start to build a highway to make road communications easier between our two capitals.

I am also happy to be able to report that at long last agreement has been reached on the delineation of the Ethiopian and Kenya frontier. This has been the result of many years of patient survey.

The work, however, has proved well worth while. A line of demarcation acceptable to both our Governments has now emerged.

Before closing, I would like to introduce a personal note. From the time I met Your Imperial Majesty about thirty years ago we have remained good friends. During this time my esteem and affection for Your Majesty have continued to grow unceasingly. May I say that at the time we met none of us knew that the Lord of Nature had planned for us to meet again in Nairobi in such a joyous atmosphere. We know that much has happened since our first meeting. Ethiopia fought and won her freedom and then joined the world to free mankind from fascism. We in Kenya have also struggled and have won our independence. I must assure Your Majesty that it is a great joy to the people of Kenya and myself personally to be able to welcome you to this Parliament in your rightful capacity as Emperor of one of the oldest free nations of the world.

Your Imperial Majesty, on behalf of both Houses of the National Assembly of Kenya, I wish you a long and prosperous reign. All happiness in the future for you and your people.

Long live brotherhood between Ethiopia and Kenya. Long live African Unity.

SOUTH AFRICA — 1964

In many of his public speeches, both at home and at Conferences overseas, Mzee Jomo Kenyatta made reference to apartheid and the whole intractable problem of South Africa. Following the outcome of the Mandela trial, a major protest rally was held in Nairobi on June 21, 1964. Here, the Prime Minister spoke of freedom, and then threw out a challenge to mankind by placing the issue of South Africa in the whole context of world stability. In this further warning, Jomo Kenyatta sought yet again to ward off the horrors of a conflict based on race:

*

This is the first major political rally to be held in Nairobi since we achieved our Independence. That we should choose on this occasion to demonstrate our feelings over the situation in South Africa, shows the over-riding importance we attach to the struggle for freedom throughout our Continent. I hope that the significance of this will be apparent to the whole world. I know that our oppressed brothers in South Africa will hear of it; I would like to think that even the fascist minority rulers of that unhappy country will take note.

True, we have our own freedom. But we cannot fully rejoice in this while other parts of the Continent are still gripped by Colonialism and minority rule. The Portuguese and Spanish colonies must be freed. Southern Rhodesia must have genuine independence under a popularly-elected Government. We want to see Bechuanaland, Basutoland and Swaziland move swiftly to independence. South Africa and South-West Africa must be rid of their tyrannical regimes.

The desires we have had for so many years to see Africa free and united will not be dimmed because we in Kenya, in one part of our Continent, have our own Independence. Rather, the fact that we have thrown off Colonialism means that our will and our resources can be devoted to aiding the struggle of our brothers. Moreover, we cannot feel secure in our own Independence while we are threatened to the south by a State ruled by racialists.

So long as the current undemocratic system prevails there, South Africa represents a threat to the peace of the whole Continent, and indeed to the stability of the whole world.

I have said before — and I will say it again — that we shall do everything within our power to bring democracy to South Africa. The people of South Africa have made it clear that they are not going to be fobbed off with Bantustans in place of democracy. They want to build a country where race is not of importance, and where all will have equal rights.

I like to think that, in a small way, we in Kenya and in East Africa are already demonstrating that peoples of different races and tribes can live together harmoniously in one State. I hope that we are showing that white racialism need not be replaced by black racialism.

There are still signs in South Africa itself that the Africans are prepared to accept the Europeans as brothers. Many Europeans and Asians and other non-Africans are still prepared to work alongside the African leaders. Many of them are suffering for sticking to their principles. Some were tried and sentenced as colleagues of Nelson Mandela.

I pray that Verwoerd and his fellow-racialists will not goad and goad the Africans, to a point where the nationalist movement is driven to oppose the white man as such. I have enough faith in humanity to believe that this will not happen, however much Verwoerd may be leading to it by his actions.

As I have said, it is not only the security of Africa, but the peace of the whole world, which is threatened by the continuance of apartheid. That is another reason which makes it so important that the system should be ended as quickly as possible. The longer it continues, the more likely does it become that the situation could erupt into a world explosion.

We of Africa, and many countries of Asia, and some elsewhere in the world, have already given support to the people of South Africa by means of the trade boycott, sanctions, and in other direct ways. We have been given support — and have been promised more direct aid — by a number of States outside Africa.

Yet the countries of the West, and Britain and the United States in particular, pay lip-service to our cause, while they go on underpinning the South African economy by their investments, their buying, and their sales. And it is critics from these countries who are stupid enough to accuse us of bringing the Cold War to Africa, when we declare our readiness to accept aid in our struggle from other sources. We do not want the South African issue to become part of the Cold War. We want all the nations of the world to help us in our struggle for freedom in South Africa.

By refusing to participate in workable sanctions against South Africa, the countries of the West are creating a situation in which violence becomes the only answer. If, by their neglect to take non-violent measures, there is fighting and bloodshed, where will the countries of the West stand then? Will they be with us or against us?

For more than half a century, the African nationalist movement in South Africa, supported by many individual non-Africans, based itself upon the principles of non-violence.

In a most moving address during his trial a few weeks ago, Nelson Mandela explained why he and his colleagues were driven to a position where sabotage had to be embarked upon, in the struggle for their rights. How much more bitterness will the white racialists who rule South Africa stir up before they are finished? The recent history of Africa shows well enough that violence will only beget violence, and that the forces of freedom and justice will prevail.

Let us remain in silence for one minute in honour of Nelson Mandela and his colleagues sentenced to life imprisonment. Let us pray that the South African Government, and the evil philosophy which guides it, can be removed without great bloodshed and human misery.

A ONE-PARTY SYSTEM — 1964

In his capacity as President of KANU, Jomo Kenyatta issued a full statement on August 13, 1964, about Kenya's progress towards becoming a one-Party State... (three months later, on November 10, 1964, the Opposition Party — KADU — was voluntarily dissolved; the KADU leader — Ronald Ngala — said it had become clear that the country had chosen to enter the Republic under the one political leadership of Mzee Kenyatta, so the Opposition would bow to the popular will and join the Government to work for future development in a spirit of national unity) ... In this August statement, the KANU President was less concerned with pronouncement or decree than with the philosophy underlying Party systems, especially in Africa. He sought to introduce the perspective of historical reason into a process often dismissed as merely ominous. And from his long experience, he expelled the misconception that multi-Party systems alone could give expression to democracy. This argument by Mzee Jomo Kenyatta will for long be consulted by all students of politics:

*

On my return from the recent London and Cairo Conferences, I said that from now on we will work towards a one-Party State. Events have shown not only that a one-Party system was inevitable, but also that it was the most prudent method of attaining those aims and objects which our people hold so dear.

The evils of Colonialism and Imperialism left mass poverty, illiteracy, disease and ignorance in our midst. As we embark on the historic task of eradicating these evils today, neo-Colonialism in its many manifestations has already reared its ugly head in our motherland.

Thus we have a two-fold job to do: to secure our people from aggression emanating from our enemies, and from subversion originating from some of our self-appointed friends both within and without.

Our aim in Kenya is to cultivate a social and political order which is consistent with our needs and our conditions. We will borrow what is relevant, and compatible with our aspirations, from any country of the East or West.

Africanism — which continues to gain momentum — will thereby become a powerful instrument for elevating our Continent and accelerating development. Nevertheless, we must be quite clear about what we mean by Africanism before we can associate it with a one-Party State.

To some, Africanism means negritude. To others, it connotes the pursuit of those ideals that are inherently African, while to yet others it implies the mixture of the African tradition with what is right, modern and progressive.

I submit that the Africanism to which we aspire in this country is the Africanism which combines the best from the past, present and future: the Africanism which seeks to fulfil what our people want to be, to do and to have.

Indeed, this is the Africanism to which I dedicated my book.... ("Facing Mount Kenya").... in my early days in the political field, when I said that: 'The dead, the living and the unborn will unite to rebuild the destroyed shrines'. It is this Africanism — as opposed to chauvinistic nationalism and economic autarchy — which is becoming increasingly manifest in most one-Party States in Africa.

Why, the Western democrat asks, does the African not adopt the Western type of democracy? Why, comes the rejoinder from the other camp, does the African not go Communist and adopt our system?

We reject a blueprint of the Western model of a two-Party system of Government because we do not subscribe to the notion of the Government and the governed being in opposition to one another, the one clamouring for duties and the other crying out for rights.

The Westminster model of Government has evolved from the traditions of the people of Britain, over many hundreds of years. The irritating aspects of British traditions, to be discerned on some occasions in the House of Commons, have been translated into unwritten rules which embody the emotions of the Anglo-Saxon.

Yet those who are today harping on the Westminster model, trying to say that we are aspiring to a one-Party State in too much of a hurry, are themselves conscience-smitten, for they know that

— having been poisoned by Imperialism and Colonialism — they are in an unenviable position.

We have only just seen the leader of the so-called Opposition, our beloved brother Ronald Ngala, tearing up a copy of the country's Development Plan. Instead of being constructive from within, he prefers to be destructive from without.

These gentlemen have lately gone to the extent of courting what they lavishly call detention, in their alleged opposition to my recent hint about a one-Party State. In the first place, this is a cowardly reaction to a bold approach to our country's post-independence need for political stability. Secondly, everyone knows that — when some of us were tucked into detention and imprisonment — some of those who are today literally applying to be detained were warming their bellies under imperialist wings.

Nor are we prepared to justify our predilection for a one-Party system of Government by using the fragile perennial argument that Parties are the expression of social classes, and that therefore there must be only one Party. The theory of class struggle has no relevance to our particular situation here.

One of the chief gladiators of this thesis of class struggle had this to say, at the end of the last century: 'the modern labourer ... instead of rising with the progress of industry ... sinks deeper and deeper below the conditions of his own class ... there was an ever increasing mass poverty, oppression, enslavement, degeneration and exploitation ...'

Now there was nothing inherently foolish in these statements during the period of the Chartist movement in Britain. Laissez-faire was the catch-phrase of the times. Governments regarded capital outlay and incomes as given, and held that employment and investment were dependent only on the decisions of the entrepreneurs.

The latter thus had powers to exploit the working classes. Politics, therefore, was a superstructure erected on an economic base, and the practice of politics was therefore impotent. But in a one-Party State such as we envisage, we hold that politics is a potent instrument; it is through our political institutions that we influence economic trends, and not the other way round.

For instance, taking the total growth in the average earnings per worker here, the indices show a rise from 100 in 1946 to 565 in 1963. This is partial proof that trade unionists through collective bargaining, and freedom fighters through their struggle for equality of opportunity, were able to improve their lot against considerable barriers and denial of opportunity by the Colonialists.

If they could improve their lot against Colonial domination, how much more can they do so under a free Kenya Government!

The necessity for a one-Party system in most parts of Africa — including Kenya — stems from two predominant factors. First, African society traditionally revolves around the family tree, the wider pattern of blood brotherhood, and the wider network of clans and tribes. At no time did the African tribes, or groups of tribes, see the State in the same way as the Greek City States. At no time did African tribes see themselves as tinpot 'nations'.

Rather, at any rate before the advent of Imperialism, they regarded themselves as responsible semi-autonomous local governments who regulated the conduct of life of the people. They continued to act independently insofar as — and to the extent to which — there was no overwhelming danger or natural catastrophe seriously threatening the existence of one or all.

When catastrophes and calamities occurred, there was no doubt that many tribes acted in concert and demonstrated their community of interest. An instance is, of course, the advent of Colonialism. When the Colonisers first came to Kenya towards the end of the last century, which single tribe did not oppose them? The whole country — from the Coast to Kisumu, Masailand to Kikuyuland, and the NFD to Abaluhya areas — is scattered with graves of our dead men and women who died at the hands of adventurous Colonialists.

Secondly, tribes in this country united in times of famine, when there was considerable movement of population from one tribe to another. By the time Imperialism, armed with all modern weapons of destruction, set upon our defenceless people and took our freedom by devious methods, inter-tribal integration had advanced so much that inter-marriage and barter trade, and other forms of co-operation between tribes, were accepted as a valuable routine.

What answer did the African have to the important question of: 'what is the State and why should I obey it?' To him, the traditional Tribal Council — which occasionally met other Tribal Councils through nominated representatives, or in times of war through intermediaries — was at once a Government and an expression of the very personality of each and every citizen.

It may be argued by some scholars that the African took no part at all in self-government, and that government was run solely by autocratic leaders who imposed their will on their subjects. But people with such qualities of leadership are to be found in many parts of the world, and there is nothing inherently African in this.

The main point is that African leaders invariably had a number of advisers, who were selected by virtue of their logic and reasoning. They in turn elected their spokesmen by popular acclaim. The Elders thus elected were constantly in touch with families, blood brothers, clans and tribes. In this context, the rulers were to the people what the people were to them. By obeying the Tribal Councils, the people maintained that they obeyed themselves and their true will. The State — and its geographical areas were immaterial — was justified on the grounds that only therein could people find peace and security.

The idea of 'constructive opposition from within' is therefore not an alien thing, so far as traditional African society is concerned. But we did not have to create Leaders of the Opposition, maintain them from public funds, and tolerate their insatiable desire for agitation, merely because they wanted to oppose for the sake of opposition.

This unity, coherence and homogeneity — although subjected to terrific pressure from close Imperialist and Colonialist rule — remained throughout most of the period of Colonial domination. In 1960, after the Constitutional Conference in London, all the Members of Parliament recognised the need for and reaffirmed their faith in unity and solidarity, in keeping with this traditional African way of life.

The vanguard of the nationalist struggle for Uhuru was launched. It was only after this Party — KANU — was formed that several dissidents formed a splinter club which was later called KADU. It would be a sham to imagine that these self-conceited grasshopper politicians formed their new club because of their belief in majority rule, democracy and the rule of law. Had that been the case, the present leader of the cabal known as KADU would not have connived with a Colonial Governor in an unholy alliance to coerce the majority and delay independence.

Granted that these are valid reasons in favour of a one-Party system — either as a transient device or a permanent institution — what are the prospects for democracy in Kenya?

This depends to a large extent on the nature of the relationship between the State and the individual. It was once argued that the socialist world placed the State above the individual, and that the capitalist system placed the individual above the State. The difference between a socialist and a capitalist is that each represents a fusion of these two underlying principles in varying proportions.

Be that as it may, my Government is pledged to uphold the traditional freedoms of association, speech and assembly, and to respect the rule of law and human dignity. In case of genuine complaints, citizens have recourse to independent Courts of Law. In addition, as provided in the Constitution, machinery already exists for a change of Government through free elections when the time comes.

One question which is usually raised about one-Party States is that they do not offer a conclusive explanation about means of controlling political power. But to assume that the intrinsic desire for power will one day be eradicated is to show a very mistaken view of human nature. The desire and competition for power is a healthy thing, so long as there are effective machineries to restrain dictatorial tendencies.

It was never possible — and it never will be possible — for the human race to exist in a vacuum. In fact, progress in all walks of life has come about as the result of a conflict of ideas.

It is my considered opinion that the greatest innovation in the political institutions of the world is not the one-Party State or the authoritarian regime. Dictatorships are as old as the hills. The fascinating innovation in our time is the mass Party, and the mass Party is to be found under both one-Party and two-Party systems.

It is the nature of the organisation of mass political Parties — outside the scope of this Paper — that is the real threat to the rule of law and democracy. Consequently, there are two-Party States which are tyrannical and dictatorial, and one-Party States which can be said to be democratic and liberal. In other words, all two-Party States are not necessarily democratic, and all one-Party States are not necessarily authoritarian.

Secondly, those who talk about democracy and individual freedoms must think critically about the position of democracy in the light of scientific and technological advancement, and especially in the light of the advent of mass media in communications and propaganda.

At this stage, however, we have no choice to make. Through the historical processes of the past century, we find ourselves with myriad relevant grounds and conditions for a one-Party State. It is inevitable. In our particular situation, practice will have to precede theory. But should relevant grounds for a multi-Party State evolve in the future, it is not the intention of my Government to block such a trend through any prohibitive legislation.

"BACK TO THE LAND" — 1964

Mzee Jomo Kenyatta has always been a farmer by instinct and inclination. From his Gatundu home, he looks out on soil that he worked and trees that he planted when he was young. His attachment to the land of Kenya was never assumed as a political weapon; it is part of the enduring personality of the man. As Prime Minister of Kenya, he became increasingly impatient with those of rural stock whose thoughts and footsteps turned to urban living and white-collar employment. While fully understanding the need — through industry and commerce — to diversify the economy in modern urban communities, Jomo Kenyatta believed passionately that Kenya's future must be rooted in sound agricultural practice. And so, in a television broadcast on September 11, 1964, he exhorted the country to go back to the land. This was one of his sterner feats of leadership:

*

In the past few weeks, I have spoken at public meetings and called on our people to recognise the value of land. I also called on our people to begin to dirty their hands in the effort of nation building.

Since independence, the Government has kept constantly in mind the need for rapid economic growth, and for short term measures to secure relief of unemployment. All along, the Government has been aware that its first task — in endeavours to fulfil the aspirations of the people — would be to accelerate the pace of economic expansion.

So far we have made an impressive start, but today I would like to discuss the part that the people themselves must play. It is not possible for our economic plans to succeed merely through Government measures, and investment from overseas. Our greatest asset in Kenya is our land. This is the heritage we received from our forefathers. In land lies our survival and salvation. It was in this knowledge that we fought for the freedom of our country. Whatever our plans for the future, they must spring from a resolve to put our land to maximum production, however small the acreage we may possess.

Our Party manifesto contains proclamations and pledges which must guide all our actions and decisions. A reference to it will show the importance attached to accelerating our agrarian revolution. It recognised that production of cash crops for the market constitutes the backbone of our economy. It called for a dynamic breakthrough in farming methods, if we are to be able to finance the Welfare State we intend to build.

In order to use our land efficiently and effectively, we must ensure that each farmer is certain of his land rights. We must also ensure that each farmer has the kind of security to give him access to necessary credits and loans from Banks or other Government and private agencies.

Our manifesto called for encouragement of land consolidation, and registration of land titles, in order to facilitate these measures. I believe that by now all our farmers appreciate fully the need for such things.

Anyone who has gone about our country will not have failed to see the difference in development and production, as between areas where consolidation and new farming methods have been introduced, and those areas where the old peasant methods are still in existence.

Kenya has become a country governed by the normal pressures of a modern monetary economy. Land or cattle which do not yield enough income must be regarded as a liability and a drain on our resources.

Many of our people have been attracted to the towns, and some believe that the only way of earning money is by working for wages and then returning to the land for brief visits. They leave their land unattended, or in the care of old mothers, wives, or young brothers. This attitude is not only negative, but it promotes the biggest waste in Kenya today.

Many able-bodied people come to town and spend many months living on relatives and friends, and being generally a nuisance. Such people distort the purchasing-power of their relatives and friends, making them poorer and miserable, and also interfere with the social plans and provisions for the genuine residents of the towns. This is a clear waste of manpower, and a definite obstacle to proper farming for the future. Any able-bodied man who exploits his relatives and friends in this manner is a disgrace to his manhood and to our society. Their friends and relatives must get rid of these people and stop feeding them.

Whereas we believe in African socialism, we do not believe in loitering and laziness. We believe in co-operatives, but not in promoting a state of affairs in which some people try and live on the sweat of others.

The time for slogans and empty words has come to an end. We cannot cry for more land, and yet fail to develop that which we have. The Government has shown its determination to fulfil its tasks. It has created political stability. It has introduced unemployment relief measures. It has stimulated and encouraged foreign investments. It has appealed to friends, and received technical and financial and other help. It has produced a Development Plan, and thus defined the steps to be taken on the road towards prosperity.

It is now time for every citizen to make his contribution. We all agreed that Uhuru would mean hard work. We also agreed that progress would require sacrifice and discipline. Now, then, is the time to take the first step. We must begin from the base of our culture, the land. We must return to the land that we love. This is our greatest asset, and I now call on our people to complement the efforts and achievements recorded by the Government in the past eight months, by exploiting to the full the soil of Kenya.

My Ministers and Government officials, Members of Parliament and Party officials, will from now on be required to assist directly, by showing people in the villages that hard work cannot do anyone harm. We must all be prepared to dirty our hands in promoting our return to the land.

ECONOMIC POLICY — 1964

During his tenure of office as Prime Minister of Kenya, Jomo Kenyatta spoke many times — in Parliament or at industrial ceremonies or during broadcasts — on different aspects of economic policy. But in one major speech, reproduced below, he covered almost the whole ground: the spread of trade links in conformity with foreign policy; tariff systems: unemployment; the need for skilled manpower; definition of a mixed economy; contribution of the State in commerce; an assurance on nationalisation; investment guarantees. This was an address on September 29, 1964, to a large gathering of businessmen in the Nairobi City Hall:

*

When we became a sovereign nation last year, we dedicated ourselves to develop the economy of this country as fast as we could, so as to promote the welfare of our people.

Further, my Government gave an assurance that the conditions necessary for accelerated growth would continue to be maintained and improved. This assurance was addressed as much to the business community as to the agricultural community, because we recognised that these are but separate branches of the same nation.

In order to achieve our aim, we decided to spread our commercial and trade contacts to countries with whom these activities had hitherto been either non-existent or negligible. Apart from the need to spread marketing risks, this step also suited our approach to international problems. We believe in a policy of non-alignment in foreign affairs.

We are faced with the difficult task of building a nation based on greater welfare for all citizens. In this resolve, we will resist pressure from any quarter which seeks to divert our energies into commitments of Cold War politics. We will adopt ideas or schemes which fit our requirements, irrespective of their origin, being guided strictly by what is best for Kenya.

When we choose some techniques from the East, it is not because we approve the conduct of their domestic or foreign policies; nor should we be accused of being pro-West if we adopt or perpetuate some Western ideas. We are African socialists, and are determined to develop Kenya as a democratic African socialist country.

Following these principles, we have therefore established trade links with the socialist countries of Europe and Asia. As a result of the trade agreements concluded with many of these countries, we have increased the volume of our external trade considerably. At the same time, we have maintained and increased trade in our traditional markets.

Mindful of this need, we have been anxious, together with other like-minded nations, to stress the importance of a more liberal attitude towards the importation of primary products from developing countries. In this connection, the immediate results of the Geneva Conference were disappointing; but I would like to express the hope that, in the long term, tariff walls and quota systems will be brought to a more reasonable level.

At home, one of the very pressing problems is that of unemployment. I wish to take this opportunity to assure you of how much my Government appreciates the co-operation given by private employers in our endeavour to find a solution. I refer to the Tripartite Agreement, under which private employers agreed to take on additional labour. I regard this as a true manifestation of the spirit of Harambee.

But we fully realise that a long-term solution can only be found by achieving more rapid economic development, which would create increased employment opportunities.

While I am on this theme, I should like to remind you of one of your important responsibilities. I refer to the need to maintain low prices of scheduled products mainly consumed by our labour. Indeed, I should like to appeal to you to reduce your profit margins wherever possible, in order to to spread the benefits of development to those with low incomes.

In the past, we have been more fortunate than most African countries in possessing a reservoir of skilled manpower, which has been an important factor in attracting investment. But I am advised that, if the economy continues to expand as fast as it is doing, we shall be running into a shortage of skilled personnel. We shall need people not only to tighten nuts and bolts, but also to make precision instruments. To fill this gap, Government has placed high priority on secondary school education, particularly in its technical and scientific field, in the six-year Development Plan.

I know that the private businessman is already playing a major role in the development of our nation, but I appeal to you to consider all possible schemes for training your staff, to enable us to meet our future needs for skilled men.

I have stated before, and wish to repeat, that our aim here is to establish a mixed economy. And I would like to dispel the confusion which seems to surround this objective. By a mixed economy, we mean that we shall work towards a situation in which the roles of private enterprise and of Government are complementary to each other.

The Government realises that Africans must be integrated into the commercial and industrial life of the nation. We are therefore instituting measures which will enable Africans to take an ever-increasing part in these fields.

But we are determined that the development of African business and industry should be carried out without damaging the existing fabric of the economy. A simple transfer of a business from one man to another does not necessarily expand business or develop a country. Some machinery already exists in this whole context, but we propose to set up additional organisations. I am thinking of the Industrial and Commercial Development Corporation, and the Development Finance Company of Kenya, through which Government will directly participate in industrial projects in partnership with private capital.

One of the greatest weaknesses in our commerce is that, in the distributive trade, it is not always easy for the small retailers to get reliable service from wholesalers. In this sector, we need the commercial equivalent of land consolidation. We consider that the most efficient way of achieving commercial consolidation is by developing a State-owned Company, to act as a focal point for reorganising and expanding the distributive trade.

We also consider that, in order to derive maximum benefits from our agreements for mutual trade with the socialist countries, it is necessary to establish a single State-controlled agency. I must emphasise here that it is not the intention to swamp the distributive trade by a monolithic Government organisation, and there must remain a very large section of the economy under private enterprise.

A similar approach will be adopted for industrial projects which the Government may find it necessary to initiate. You know that, up till now, industrial development has been sponsored by private enterprise. But we have reached a stage where certain enterprises can only be launched if they are financially backed by Government You must not interpret my remarks as implying nationalisation. We consider that nationalisation will not serve to advance the cause of African socialism.

You will appreciate that we have gone to greater pains to guarantee private investments than most countries have done. The Constitution provides safeguards for private property; and in addition to these, the Government has provided further safeguards in the proposed Foreign Investments (Protection) Bill. Our taxation system, including investment allowances, provides a further testimony of our determination to assist. I urge you, therefore, to study this Act, and reassure your associates overseas that it is Government's intention, not only to continue to work together with private enterprise, but also to promote conditions in which private enterprise can thrive. In this connection, the Government will continue the policy of tariff protection for pioneer and infant industries, including refunds of customs duty for imported raw materials.

I have talked about our resolve to integrate Africans into the commercial and industrial life of the country. For this purpose, the Government attaches the greatest importance to the development of the co-operative movement. The ideals of the co-operative movement are, in essence, those of African socialism. Mutual help is an inherent African tradition, and we expect the co-operative movement to play a major part in the expansion of the whole economy.

In the course of my address this afternoon, I have referred to the need for the Government to reorganise its machinery to meet new challenges. This need for reorganisation may apply to you as well. And while I will not try and tell you precisely how to meet your particular challenge — which is a matter for you yourselves to decide — there are one or two points which I hope you will keep in mind.

One of these is that racial identities in business are not in keeping with the spirit of building one nation.

Secondly, you may have to adjust your organisation so that the newcomers to commerce and industry can be seen to be taking part in your activities. This may be difficult, but it has got to be done. We shall only add to our difficulties if we do not make it clear to everyone that opportunities in the business sphere must be open to all.

It is true that newcomers will not have sufficient resources and know-how, but some way must be found of getting everyone to pull together. It is probable that an effective way would appear irrational, or even unique, but our circumstances are peculiar, and we should not be afraid of new experiments. Whatever the method finally adopted, it must be one which is acceptable to all of you, and which does not allow any one group — still less any one person — to dominate the business field.

I know that if we have confidence in each other, if the business community understands the Government's problems and Government understands your problems, then we can develop and build up this country to become a real force in Africa and in the world.

KENYATTA DAY — 1964

Jomo Kenyatta was arrested when the Emergency was proclaimed on October 20, 1952. Since then — through an impetus described in the text — this date has come to be commemorated each year as Kenyatta Day. In Kenya's first full year of Independence, the Prime Minister (as he then was) delivered a special message to the nation over the radio and television services. He employed this opportunity, not only to review the progress of the country, but also to portray the philosophy which had marked with such constancy his long career as political leader and elder statesman. This speech by Mzee Kenyatta (October 20, 1964) is reproduced in full below:

*

On this Day that bears my name, I want to speak to you all without formality, in your homes or in community centres or wherever you might be. And I want to speak to all, today, not just as a Prime Minister, but as a man. For although — by your wish — I am the leader of my country, the recollection of this Day in all your hearts and minds means more than just a tribute to a title. It reaches back in time. And it reminds me very vividly of all the phases and milestones of more than forty years of work and service, dedicated to the freedom and the dignity of Africa, and to pan-African ideals.

This is the first celebration of Kenyatta Day since, here in Kenya, our struggle for Uhuru was ended, and we became an independent sovereign State. I am proud to think back on the part that I played in this struggle. Much was direct contribution. But it gladdened me to know, through a long period of anxieties and sufferings, that my conception of duty — to this country and its people — inspired and upheld others, when I could not be there.

Our struggle was a just one. All the noble Charters and Declarations of history, and all the Constitutions that enshrine human rights, have sprung from one paramount truth: that men in their spirit and in their striving, under the law, have the right to be free. The world in these past years has moved rapidly forward, from the Colonial age. Peoples in many countries have been freed, and not just from political bondage. Their talents and their ambitions and their cultures have all been released. Their productive energies have altered the old pattern of economic privilege. Their philosophies have made impact on the thinking of mankind, bringing fresh hope to the cause of world peace.

All this is what we sought for ourselves. And on this Day, I share your joy that we in Kenya have the rights and the responsibilities of free men. To me, this is a monument to years of service.

What I want to say to you now is what these years have taught me. Triumph in a struggle of this kind cannot be achieved without a long history of setbacks and sufferings, of failure and humiliation. But all this is worthwhile, and all can be forgotten, when its outcome is the foundation on which a future can be built. It is the future, my friends, that is living, and the past that is dead. In all that I have seen, in many countries and at many periods of my life, never has there seemed any purpose in arguments about the past, or any nobility in motives of revenge.

There have been murmurs here in Kenya about the part played by one set of people, or another set of people, in the struggle for Uhuru. There has been talk of the contribution made, or refused, by this group or that. There has been — at times — vindictive comment, and a finger of scorn has been pointed at some selected race, or group, or tribe. All this is unworthy of our future here.

I want this celebration of Kenyatta Day to mean more to you all than just some particular Tuesday in the calendar. Let this be the day on which all of us commit ourselves to erase from our minds all the hatreds and the difficulties of those years which now belong to history. Let us agree that we shall never refer to the past. Let us instead unite, in all our utterances and activities, in concern for the reconstruction of our country and the vitality of Kenya's future.

How our future must be built here was outlined to you first in the KANU Election Manifesto. This was our blueprint, still valid today. And whenever I consult this Party statement, I am struck afresh by the vision of its approach, and the wisdom of its declarations, on the issues that mean everything to you all.

As this Manifesto made clear, achievement of sovereign status and the urge for reform must have a fundamental purpose that is never set aside. This is to remove from our people the burden

16 Kenyatta, Nation

of poverty, the scourge of malnutrition and ill-health, the frustration of illiteracy, and the demoralising lack of economic
opportunity. Here is our motive, in all that we are working on
now. Some of you have wondered if I and the Party had forgotten
all these fundamental needs. But let me assure you today that I
and my Government will never rest until victory over all these
evils and injustices is finally won.

I know that all of you — the unemployed; farmers and businessmen; workers and students and public servants; the parents of
our children — had high expectations on our Independence Day.
This feeling serves the country well. We need to maintain the
sense and the spirit of ambition and urgency, in all our social
and economic affairs. But if you perhaps have been feeling that
we might have moved faster than we have, just remember certain
things.

Kenya has been an independent sovereign State for only ten
months of one year. However hard we worked in this opening
stage of nation building, and even with the assistance of miracles,
it would be impossible to eliminate all past imperfections and injustices, and to meet all modern aspirations and needs, in such
a short time. But a great deal has in fact been done.

Through our programme of Africanisation, we have done much
to augment the status and security of our country. Nearly all the
high appointments in the Civil Service are now held by Africans.
In the Police force, this process will shortly extend to the rank
in Inspector-General. The Kenya Army will soon be commanded
by an African, and many other African Officers — up to the rank
of Lieutenant Colonel — have successfully completed training to
take their rightful place. We have founded the Kenya Air Force,
and a Kenya Navy will be formally established before long.

While on this subject, I want to emphasise here one point that
I have made before. The purpose of our Africanisation programme
is simple enough: to maintain an efficient and effective machine
of Government by and for Kenya's people. Any breakdown in the
machinery of Government, at any level, would not carry the
country forward, but would cast us back. For this reason, Africanisation has not been, and cannot be, an automatic programme
based on colour or race. We need at many levels not only talent
and loyalty, but also experience. This is why training schemes
have been instituted, and must be continued, to equip our people
for posts of high responsibility, and give them opportunity to
gain the maturity that comes from experience.

I have made it clear many times that our Government will not discriminate against any citizens on matters of employment opportunity, recruitment and promotion. All citizens of Kenya, regardless of their race or colour or country of origin, have equal opportunities and duties in the building of our Public Service. I expect all civil servants — including those who have become Kenya citizens — to work loyally for the country.

At present, the loyalty and experience of many expatriate Officers are serving a critical need. We shall have to recruit more expatriate Officers, technicians and professional men, if the country is to progress rapidly in fulfilment of the Development Plan. It is most important that these Officers be made to feel welcome here, and be assured that the job they are doing for Kenya is appreciated. I must, therefore, urge some political leaders, and some Members of our National Assembly, to bear this in mind. They should refrain from making any statements likely to undermine the spirit and confidence of these expatriate Officers, now and for some time ahead.

Within this short period of ten months, our six-year Development Plan has been prepared and published, and work has already started to build a new economic and social fabric to meet the hopes and serve the wellbeing of all Kenya's people. We have in fact recorded economic progress — actual and pending — on a very significant scale, aided in many cases by investment in concrete projects, or development loans, from overseas. The oil refinery, and new textile factories, and new industries of many kinds, are there for all to see. In addition, some massive agricultural developments have been introduced or planned, involving — for example — the greatly increased production of sugar, and of cotton on irrigation schemes, and of tea. Experts are now studying ways to expand our livestock industries. We are welcoming visitors from many countries of the world, and have developed tourism, through the conservation of natural resources, as a major enterprise.

The Education Commission, appointed early this year, will be reporting soon, as a vital step on the road towards our eventual goal of free, compulsory education for all. The Development Plan itself provided that priority should be given to secondary education, as a means of serving our future needs for skilled manpower in fields of science and technology.

As the background to all this, more than sixty thousand of our people have now been accommodated on the settlement schemes. We already have in being more than a hundred co-operative farms. Jobs have been found for tens of thousands of the unemployed, through the Tripartite Agreement and on Government-sponsored projects. Thousands of our young men have been taken into the security forces, or been given new hope by means of training schemes, within the whole inspiration of the National Youth Service.

In the political field, we have decided and arranged that Kenya shall become a Republic on December the 12th. During this week full details of the new Republican Constitution will be placed before Parliament and the country. We have actively pursued the cause of greater unity within East Africa, and I am proud to reaffirm here and now that Kenya has played a prominent part throughout this year in the purposes and active work of the Organisation of African Unity. In foreign affairs, and in all our dealings with the countries of the world, our policy has been that of non-alignment, and this we have maintained without any of the damage to our sovereignty or dignity or economic interests that some observers had predicted.

We are grateful to our friends — both in the West and in the East — for their generous response to requests for assistance and proposals for co-operation. In this vital initial year of Independence, this has helped to fulfil our commitments and launch our new plans.

But I must warn the country now that, in the long-term, the prosperity and development of Kenya will depend on the efforts of the people themselves. We must work hard and constantly towards the greatest possible degree of self-reliance. We cannot and must not always rely on outside aid. It is not good for the economy, or for the morale of a country, to be greatly dependent on overseas assistance, which itself may be influenced by changes in policy or personnel. We have accepted the kind of foreign aid that is without strings. But at the same time, there are always subtle obligations. Kenya must develop her own strength. And we must be in a position as well to help others, our brothers elsewhere in Africa, with continuing struggles for freedom and economic independence.

I have told you enough, I think, to show that the attainment of our Independence has been followed by the dynamic and properly-planned activity of your Government. But just before I close, let me re-emphasis some important ideas and beliefs:

What is in my mind now — and what should be in the minds of all of you — is to look forward, not to look back. Our children may learn about heroes of the past. Our task is to make ourselves architects of their future. And in this, we must think beyond self.

I would be satisfied now, with my life, simply through knowing that I had made some contribution to a free and better life for Kenya's people. I would be satisfied even if I were not Prime Minister, with many grave tasks and responsibilities still lying ahead.

The fruits of life, my friends, are there, for as long as one has the strength to seek them. I say to you now that service to one's fellow-men can never be confined by a price or a reward. Its true satisfaction comes in the nature of dedication. In my long life, this has been dedication to my country and its people, to the cause of freedom and pan-African ideals, to progress through unity and the bounty of our land.

Not all of you can be leaders. But all of you have your families, your farms or businesses, your daily tasks. By applying all that you are and all that you do to the cause of national unity and the progress of our country, then this dedication which I have known and enjoyed will be something we all can share.

UNITED NATIONS DAY — 1964

A special parade, mounted by contingents of the National Youth Service, was held outside the Prime Minister's Office on October 24, 1964, to commemorate United Nations Day. In an address to a distinguished political and diplomatic company, Jomo Kenyatta paid tribute to the world forum, and called for saner counsels in international affairs. These were his words:

*

It is with great pleasure — shared by the Government and people of Kenya — that I take part today in this ceremony, marking the 19th anniversary of the founding of the United Nations.

This is a well-chosen day for celebration in our Continent, since our good wishes go out to the newly-independent Republic of Zambia, now able to make a full and sovereign contribution to world affairs.

A principal motive for the foundation of the United Nations, at the end of the Second World War, was to save future generations of mankind from the sufferings and wastage of global conflict. But motive without vision is seldom enough. The effectiveness of this world forum was found in its Charter. Its provisions and purposes had the simplicity of greatness: to enshrine the dignity of man; to codify and preserve human rights; to recognise the equality and respect the integrity of member nations; to champion justice under international law, to instil respect for freely-entered obligations; and to use world resources in science and technology to combat poverty, illiteracy, sickness and malnutrition.

The world today, although beset by problems and suspicions, knows more stability than would have been possible without United Nations efforts. Its achievements have, therefore, been critical. And the success of this world body has reflected the sum total of selfless goodwill and contribution from all member States.

Among the 46 countries represented at the foundation meeting, at San Francisco in 1945, only two — Ethiopia and Liberia — were African States. Since then, many more African countries have achieved their independence, releasing their talents and energies and philosophies for the service of the family of nations. Today, 34 member States from Africa have seats at the United Nations, and more will follow shortly.

My Ministers and I have said many times that Kenya will not feel free until the last traces of Colonialism and racial domination have been finally wiped out. We have in mind here the racial discrimination and brutalities of the South African regime. We deplore the oppressive measures of the Portuguese in Angola and Mozambique. And we are appalled by the contempt for democracy shown by the minority Government of Southern Rhodesia, which is approaching tyrannical seizure of power by suppressing the will of the people.

In these matters, we look forward with confidence to more realistic support from the new Government in the United Kingdom. We especially anticipate that, in the case of Southern Rhodesia, a solution based on human equality will be found. Indeed, this will have to be found.

The future of Africa depends less on complex ideologies than on simple human values. Here, Kenya is a lesson for all. We are ourselves a kind of United Nations in miniature. And here, all our citizens have equal respect; all have equal rights and responsibilities, and equal obligations, under the law.

Beyond its great purpose in political philosophy and adjustment, we in Kenya appreciate very greatly the practical efforts and aid of the United Nations, through its specialised agencies in the field. I well recall, in July last year, opening the Nairobi office of the Technical Assistance Board and Special Fund. And I must assure Dr. Chidzero today how grateful we are for many forms of technical assistance offered by these bodies.

The foundation of Kenya's foreign policy is the principle of non-alignment. Our judgment is an independent judgment, not subject to power-bloc pressure or appeal. We have been working closely with the other member States of the Organisation of African Unity. We have contributed to the activities and recommendations of the Afro-Asian bloc. In all our work and attitudes, we have sought to bring to our support for the United Nations a real commitment for peace and the social advancement of all mankind.

One great imbalance within the United Nations structure springs from the exclusion of the People's Republic of China. The participation of China in the exchanges and activities of the United Nations is vital for lasting world peace. There is no other world forum in

which conflicts, suspicions and injustices can be dissolved, by those
dedicated through a Charter to the brotherhood of man.

In our domestic concerns, and in our views on international
disputes, we have deplored the argument of force. Kenya believes
that the best way of resolving differences is by frank negotiation
and discussion.

Human will in the context of world understanding must be
rooted in a love of peace and an urge for human progress. We
are, therefore, alarmed and discouraged, at times, when the so-
called Great Powers pour out their treasure in fashioning greater
and more horrifying weapons of destruction, while more and more
other Powers seek to join the nuclear race.

Within the United Nations, we must work for the elimination of
all these engines of destruction. We must seek the harnessing
of nuclear energy for the peaceful purposes of mankind. And we
must seek the allocation of all this astronomical finance to meet
the real human challenge of hunger and ill-health and economic
frustration.

Let the United Nations rule and secure that, on the threshold
of the Space Age, our own shrinking planet should become a place
of dignity and hope for all the human race.

Africa will be proud — Kenya will be proud — to make a contribution to this purpose. Let the twentieth year of this world
body herald for all people a new era: absence of discrimination,
opportunity for social progress, and freedom from fear.

REPUBLIC CELEBRATIONS — 1964

Mzee Jomo Kenyatta was sworn in as President of the Republic of Kenya on December 12, 1964. Following an eighteen-month term of office as Kenya's first and only Prime Minister this event marked a new climax in his career. Celebrations and ceremonies were held almost without respite throughout Jamhuri Week, but the period of most intensive pageantry and dedication extended from December 11 to December 14. In this time, President Kenyatta delivered four major speeches, which are reproduced fully below. It seems doubtful whether any other world leader can have outlined — in such a short span — so comprehensive a review of national policies and aspirations in their international perspective. His words and sentiments injected fresh hope and inspiration into the hearts of men, within and far beyond the borders of Kenya. Distinguished comment held that, through his wisdom and farsightedness, Jomo Kenyatta here had placed both the emergence and the potential of Africa on a whole new plane of maturity.

1. Farewell to the Governor-General

The Right Honourable Malcolm John MacDonald arrived in Kenya on January the third of 1963. At the time, the relationship of the Government and people of Kenya with the high office which represented Colonial administration was far from happy. There had been disharmony of thought, which clouded normal contacts. And so, in people's minds, any change could only be from one human symbol to another of continuing oppression.

It was on this discouraging stage that His Excellency first appeared as Kenya's Governor.

The newspapers had made it common knowledge that this man, a son of one of the great Labour leaders, Ramsay MacDonald, had

held high office in some British Governments before the war. He
had served, at various times, as Secretary of State for the Colonies,
and for Dominion Affairs. Subsequently, and for a span of twenty
years, he had served with great distinction in many important
parts of the Commonweatlh.

But apart from the splendour of this record, little was known
of him in this country as a person, at first.

Happily, it soon became apparent that Kenya's year of destiny
had produced an enlightened man, with warm and vivid mind,
to assist us both as counsellor and friend. Malcolm MacDonald
took unalloyed pleasure in Kenya's attainment of Internal Self-
Government, six months after we watched him arrive. And six
months after that, on our Uhuru Day, Kenya took pleasure, in
turn, when he was sworn in, not just as Governor-General, but as
trusted ally and servant of our new nation.

Kenya now has adopted the status of Republic, and Governor-
Generals must therefore depart. But here let me distinguish between the office and the man. We have no apologies to make, and
no regrets, that our own status and structure of Government has
been fashioned in accord with Kenya's needs.

While there have been no shackles to our independence for these
past twelve months, we are about to break the last links which
chained us to a longer past. For even where a system is practised
with supreme grace and propriety which so distinguishes Her
Majesty the Queen, yet the ultimate hand of Monarchy is foreign
to the evolution of our thinking here and to the freely-created
fabric of social and economic progress to which our country is
committed.

Returning from the office to the man, thoughts must now turn
to the massive contribution made by Malcolm MacDonald, throughout nearly two years of constitutional design, nation building and
social change. He has spared himself nothing, in friendship and
strain. Whenever I or any of my Ministers have needed advice,
we have found him both helpful and sympathetic.

We shall remember the Governor-General as a man who understood both the fine arts and the basic simplicities of humanity,
and the struggles of mankind against economic and social frustration. And whenever doubts were cast upon stability or purpose in
Kenya, throughout his term of office, he came forward to demonstrate the underlying threads of justice, wisdom and strength.

Kenya salutes his warmth and courage. As the last expatriate occupant of what once was called Government House, His Excellency brought both to his task and its setting an informality that lost nothing in dignity, but won friendship in depth. He imparted to this hitherto foreign building the attributes of home. And we are glad that he found here, amid the scenery and wildlife of Kenya, unique opportunities for the happy recreation of watching birds.

To the office, we say farewell. To the man, as well as to Mrs. MacDonald and their family, my people and I say: God speed your return. We hope to see you again before long. Speaking personally, and on behalf of the people and Government of Kenya, let me assure you that we await this day, both for the arrival of a High Commissioner and for the return of a friend.

One final charge remains. We ask you to convey the greetings and respects of Kenya to Her Majesty the Queen, and to His Royal Highness the Duke of Edinburgh, of whom we have such happy recollections on our Independence Day.

2. Broadcast to the Nation

The Republic of Kenya will be born at midnight tonight. It is fitting that we should greet this moment with festivity and with rejoicing. But in step with celebrations, let there also be reflection. With the sunrise tomorrow, there will be no sudden fulfilment of all our ambitions and needs. Many tasks and many challenges still lie ahead.

The foundation of Kenya's foreign policy is the principle of started with our Independence. Throughout this past year, we have had absolute freedom to conduct our Government and parliamentary institutions, and to take all decisions affecting the security and progress of Kenya. With the status of Republic, we shall be a sovereign nation, not only in fact, but also in appearance.

With the unique and historic decision of the former Opposition Party to join the Government, all manifestations of Colonialism have been left behind. What remains, without any distraction, is our obligation and purpose: to build one strong Kenya nation for the benefit of all, with leeway still for constructive self-criticism amongst ourselves.

The manner in which we have achieved our Republic is of the utmost importance to our national image. We have not thrust and bullied our way into Republican status. There has been no force and no coercion. The Government stated its policy. The people then freely elected to support what was necessary and to do what was right.

Such an outcome has not threatened our stability, but has greatly enhanced it. And far from damaging the environment of confidence in which we must progress, this confidence has been reinforced.

There were some a year ago, fainthearts or false prophets, who professed that our Uhuru would prove to be only a novelty, intoxicating at first, but quickly followed by internal strife.

These critics did not understand the maturity of Kenya's people. They did not appreciate the elements of wisdom and resolution that underlie African culture. They could not foresee the energy and self-reliance that would emerge, when once the talents and ambitions of the African people were unshackled. They could not imagine the desire, which has so abundantly appeared, to create and to contribute. They could therefore form no picture of the steadfast and unified foundation which our Republic has symbolised today.

The Republican Constitution is firmly based on the principle of national unity. The document does not recognise or burden the country with division. There are no complex clauses related to artificial differences, that in the past were based on fear, in fields of tribe or race or economic privilege. This is a Constitution, made stronger by its simplicity, founded on a structure of national leadership and national duty that the people themselves can understand, and in which full confidence can be reposed.

With this Constitution, we have made great progress towards the centralisation of all vital tasks and concerns. The Government of the Republic of Kenya will have full control of our economic development in all its branches. There will be central responsibility for all policy matters in spheres of education and health. And all Local Authorities will themselves be directly responsible to the Central Government.

By the unanimous agreement of the people, a system that was cumbersome, expensive, and bound by its nature to frustrate the whole national purpose, has now been set aside. But let me just reaffirm here that we have nowhere abolished or even amended those entrenched constitutional provisions which provide safeguards for land and for property, and which ensure human rights.

I tell you all, my countrymen, that the new Republican Government will embark on its task, concerned more for its obligations to the country and the people than with an assessment of its power.

We have retained in our Constitution two essential provisions. One is the collective responsibility of the President and the Cabinet. The other is the supremacy of Parliament. If we think at all of power, it is here, in our National Assembly, that power lies, springing from and at all times reinforced by the people.

Over this past year, Kenya has made significant contributions to the work of the Organisation of African Unity. Henceforth, with our new status, we can and must do even more. And we shall continue to warn mankind, through the OAU and the United Nations, that the apartheid dogma of the South African dictatorship is both an affront to human dignity and a threat to world peace.

The kind of unity that we have built in Kenya, expressed as brotherhood and understanding between all the African States, could do much for the peace and progress of our Continent. It could also offer a new philosophy, and a new practical challenge, to a world wrapped in deadlock between two massive systems whose proudest boast is their capacity to annihilate mankind.

On Monday next there will be a ceremonial occasion, on which it will be fitting for me to refer to the economic and social foundations we have laid in this past year. Many practical structures and achievements have, indeed, already sprung from these foundations, and these are plain for all to see.

My Ministers and I have been guided by a single inspiration: to raise the living standards of the people. Our task has been, and will be, to attack as fiercely as we can the enemies of malnutrition and sickness, illiteracy and economic frustration. Then we can thrust wide open the gateways of new hope, looking out towards frontiers of new economic and social opportunity for every man, woman and child. This is our commitment.

But let me say, countrymen, that the Government cannot fulfil this commitment alone. We need the understanding and the contribution of you all. This past year has signalled a triumph for the spirit of Harambee. This spirit must carry us on.

And I must say to you now that, above all else, we must continue to preserve our national integrity and freedom. This, too, is a duty in which everyone must join. It may be that, within or beyond the boundaries of our nation, enemies will arise to challenge our national leadership and purpose. Vigilance against such enemies must never be relaxed.

Each one of us is both guardian and custodian of the security and integrity of the State, to an extent that if called upon to lay down our lives we shall do so. This is a solemn obligation. But if we are seen ever to hesitate in this resolve, we may be pulled down, our integrity devoured, by the jackals who await some sign of lethargy or weakness.

And let us remember, while thinking of external threat, our sons and brothers in north-eastern Kenya, fighting those who now challenge the State with the physical weapons of bullets and guns. To them I send a special word of tribute to their steadfastness and courage. We will support and reinforce them in their task, until the causes of sanity and justice again prevail.

Never in Kenya has the need been more vital for the slogan we adopted last year: Uhuru na Kazi. And never have the rewards of hard work been greater or more accessible than now.

But it is the spirit in which we work and plan for the Republic's future that is so critical today. From the grass-roots of African culture, we must discipline ourselves with thoughts of duty and morality.

The Republic of Kenya will be what we make it to be. We have ensured our national dignity and freedom. I tell you now that we must go on to ensure, amongst ourselves, greater human respect. We are charged with nation building, on a foundation of stability, to fashion here a new society. This must emerge not only from what we create but from how we behave.

We must gear ourselves to a fundamental belief in individual human rights, as the basis of respect. And this respect must be extended, beyond what a man is or what he does, to what he owns and cherishes. Without respect for property, security of property, chaos can swiftly come to any State.

We shall enforce law and order through the Police and the Judiciary. But our purpose should be made so strong as to sweep from our society those crimes that are rooted in jealousy and greed. We have achieved unity. We are all moving now towards a common goal. We need, therefore, respect for a new social conscience, in which the criminal is not just a candidate for punishment or pity, but a traitor to our purpose and an object of scorn.

We need complete morality in every walk of life. There must be no corruption in our Civil Service, for selfish or subversive ends. We must justify our trust in all who have some charge of public funds. We must guard against temptation, or even thoughtless action, in a new environment where self-respect can flourish.

We do not have to be so pious and so careful as to obliterate the character and boldness of the human personality. But whether you are a public servant faced with important judgments, or an employee entrusted with valuable machinery, or the treasurer of a Co-operative Society, or maybe a teacher with a large class of children, or a forest guard, or a medical orderly, or a shop assistant, or the driver of a passenger vehicle carrying many precious lives, I say to you this: you are part of our society. What you do matters to us all. Do your work honestly and well. For the State's obligation to you is no greater than your obligation to your fellow-men.

The Republic is the people. And just as I called on you all to enter the Republic in the spirit of Harambee, so I call on you now to enrich the Republic with the spirit of community.

Commencing with this coming year, let every man who is educated teach a man to read and write. Let every man who is healthy help, in whatever way he can, a man who is sick. Let every man who has work and position find some prospect for a man who is unemployed and poor. Let service be the inspiration of our future, so our future can be made worthwhile.

3. The Inauguration Ceremony

Today, on the first birthday of our Independence, the Republic of Kenya is born. This is another great moment for us all. For twelve months we have commanded our destiny, and have had our own voice. The Government and all the people have been free. But we lived and worked in what is called Dominion status, so that men could look at us and say: 'Kenya has Uhuru, but Kenya is still tied, Kenyatta is still tied, to some Mfalme in a foreign land'. It is not true in fact that we were tied. But now we have the title of freedom, which no one can misunderstand.

Today we have freedom and unity, as the pillars of the State. This is what Republic means. The Republic is the people of Kenya. All through the Colonial days, for the purpose of divide-and-rule, we were constantly reminded that we were Kikuyu or Wakamba, or Giriama or Kipsigis or Masai, or English or Hindu or Somali. But now, the Republic has embodied those features of equality and respect which cut through any differences of race or tribe.

None of the ceremonies of these past few days mean that we are no longer friendly with Britain. We send our greetings and good wishes, from this Jamhuri Park, to Her Majesty the Queen. But what this occasion does mean is that we no longer have any ceremonial links with or any kind of obligations to, any other State. We are able to create, and to go forward by way of, true African socialism. And from the heart of such a community, founded on co-operation and service, we may offer our unhampered friendship to all.

It has often been stated that Kenya must spring from the roots of our African culture. Many times, my Ministers and I have declared that we want the fullest African participation in the Civil Service, in commerce and industry, and in proper usage of the land. All this is described as the African image, in building an African State.

But it is not enough to have simply an image in our minds. We cannot be satisfied just with a design, or take refuge in dreams. The Republic is the people. And from all citizens of Kenya we need the vigour of practical initiative, the fire of a new patriotism, to turn image into reality.

I say to you this: in freedom and with unity, there is nothing that we cannot accomplish. An approach to our future, in this spirit, is something else that the Republic means.

We have much cause for rejoicing at this moment. We can reaffirm here our dedication to the tasks that lie ahead. But let us spare some thought as well for those, our brothers in Africa, who are still in bondage and despair. And let us resolve that, within this coming year, racialism and bigotry must be finally conquered, not through the blood and the evil that come of setting one community against another, race against race, but through the forces of enlightenment, service and dignity that can be harnessed by all decent men.

I have warned the world before how the tragedy of South Africa could lead to a breach of world peace. Not only the security of humanity, but every worthwhile principle of humanity is here at stake. Proposals before the United Nations call for the commercial and social isolation of South Africa, by means that on a universal scale would be quickly effective. We shall see in the event how countries of the Western world, of all parts of Europe, and of the Far East, may smother the effectiveness of moral protest with the crude realities of investment and trade.

Our objective here in Africa is justice, after long years of desolation, exploitation and neglect. Africa is fast awakening, not for conquest or disruption or revenge, but to contribute to the world a new philosophy. All men are equal. All men are equally entitled to respect. The talents and resources of the world are enough to banish squalor, and to bridge the gap between the richer nations and those where poverty has stifled man's creativeness.

All that is needed is a new social conscience in human relations. There must be the will, underlying declarations, to banish the arguments of nuclear power, the parading of destructive strength, the confining of man's intellect behind bleak walls of ideology, the advancement of self-interest as an escape clause in all testaments of morality.

The world is a small place. All men are close neighbours today. Distance is defeated by the aircraft and the telephone. But technology, in some ways, has advanced beyond ideas. Man himself is still a prisoner of traditional selfishness and fears. The world needs the purpose of justice. And in this, the philosophy of life that places emphasis on humanity can launch a new crusade.

Each State of Africa must make its contribution. Let our Republic give a resounding lead. For our unfaltering concern must be to rid poverty and hunger, all economic and social frustration, from the lives of men.

All my life, I have told you that in unity lies our salvation. Disunity is a false trail, leading men into the desert of conflict and suspicion. Unity will lead us to rich pastures and the waters of life. We have won freedom, and have acquired a national unity. These are precious things.

We must cherish our unity, and be vigilant against challenge. There are those ill-served by peaceful progress, jealous of good order, and contemptuous of law. As we go forward, we must always maintain stability. All of us must safeguard the integrity of our State. And we must look on law and order not just as an institution of society, or a code of behaviour, but as the outward image of our self-respect.

Let me tell you what I mean by progress, and by nation building. These are things that must be clear in all our minds. The fact of the Republic has removed all traces of Colonialism from this land. And with it can go all sense of exploitation, the feeling we once had of being used. In all our progress and our striving now, we can know that we are working for ourselves.

But this working for our country is not simply a new opportunity. It is also a new challenge. We have nobody else to rely on. Therefore, every contribution counts. It is everything you do that matters. The efforts and the attitudes of all the people add up to nation building and the progress of the State.

We must build with our sweat and with our brains. A Minister who negotiates an important economic agreement is contributing to nation building. So is the parent who scrapes and saves that his children may be well educated. The Director of a Public Corporation who designs a new marketing system is contributing to nation building. Even so is the smallholder who builds up productivity and determines to have a clean farm. A senior surgeon working tirelessly on his hospital rounds, and saving valuable lives, is contributing to nation building. But so is the long-distance bus-driver who is always careful and courteous on the road. The businessman who invests large sums in a new factory is contributing to nation building. But so is the man in a village who organises self-help schemes, to build a community centre or a water pipeline or a local bridge. The University teacher equipping our scientific and professional manpower is contributing to nation building. But so is the man faithfully guarding some lonely forest from destruction by trespass or fire. The backbench Member of Parliament who does his job well is contributing to nation building. But so is the lowest official of the smallest Area Council, who works honestly and hard. The man who represents the interests of Kenya in Washington or Moscow is contributing to nation building. But so is the labourer whose sweat and muscles can build a new dam. The Secretary of a Trade Union who works responsibly is contributing to nation building. But so is the woman who studies hygiene and nutrition and provides for the family a happy home, or the nurse who brings comfort to the sick.

I tell you this: nation building is not a matter of having money to employ, or of having authority to wield. It is a matter of patriotism and pride. In your work, whatever this is, and in your homes and in your districts, the smallest efforts to build and to improve are most important. Progress is created by the people.

At this moment in our history, I want to thank you all, my people, for having called me into service as first President of the Kenya Republic. This is an expression of confidence which no words can measure, and no feelings can surround. I do not regard this as reward, but look upon this office rather as an opportunity for redoubled effort in your service. By electing me to be your President, my faith in the people of Kenya has not been enhanced. For more than forty years now, this faith has never changed.

We all have obligations to the State. Mine must be exercised now in daily collaboration with my Ministers, and in deference to our Parliament.

I shall be working always as one of you, in your cause. But I ask you to understand that the complex machinery of a modern State is completely demanding. As Head of State and Head of Government, there are constant duties that I must perform in your service. But together with my Ministers, upheld by your co-operation and confidence, I will do everything possible to meet you in your homes and your districts whenever I can.

The Republic is the people. Your dedication and faith is the source of my strength.

And now, countrymen, I ask you to join me in the inspiration which has brought us unity and has launched us on our purpose. Let the nation rejoice on the birth of our Republic....HARAMBEE!

4. State opening of Parliament

This Parliament gives form and expression to the heart and mind of Kenya's people. My first and pleasurable duty, therefore, is formally to advise this House that the Republic of Kenya has been inaugurated in accordance with our Constitution as approved by the requisite majorities.

I have also to report that, through legal testimony and public witness, I am empowered and bound to address you today as President of the Kenya Republic. Such distinction was conferred upon me on the first anniversary of our Uhuru, by the terms of the present Constitution.

This is a very significant day in the history of our country. There is only one such day in the lifetime of any nation. The people of Kenya have been holding celebrations and attending ceremonies to mark the birth of the Republic. But only now, through the opening of this Parliament, can they feel that this birth has been certified by their own representatives.

My presence here as Head of State symbolises the departure from Kenya, a few days ago, of the first and last holder of the office of Governor-General. The work and personality of the Right Honourable Malcolm MacDonald have drawn from Honourable Members, on an earlier occasion, sentiments of tribute and regard.

But I am sure the House would wish now to join in expression of thanks for the untiring effort, the wise counsel, and the spirit of friendship, which so distinguished his association with the

Government and people of Kenya. We owe much to a man, who arrived as a Colonial Governor, but who departed as a steadfast and trusted advocate of the Kenya nation.

The second attendant event is the formation of a new Government, the members of which have been duly sworn in. This Government will serve as vanguard of the people, united now in their resolve, for the continuing battle against poverty, illiteracy and social injustice.

The Constitution under which this Republic has been created included provisions to make the powers of scrutiny and sanction, and all the rights and duties of the Kenya Parliament the supreme instrument of the State. My purpose at this ceremony is to outline to the House the Government's overall intentions. But I wish first to continue to place this occasion in perspective, and to say something more directly about its setting.

The Constitution has provided, as a matter of vital consequence, that the Head of State should also be the Head of Government. In addressing this Parliament, therefore, I am addressing an institution of which I am also a part. The whole apparatus of the State becomes personalised when I step down to join you. And this process of so stepping down is not only a valuable personal right, but also a significant Presidential obligation.

What this House must contribute to the Republic is something far more than just machinery which can give the plans or requirements of the Government their lawful status. This must be our forum, for discussion and proposal, for question, objection or advice. It must give full modern expression to the traditional African custom, by serving as the place where the Elders and the spokesmen of the people are expected and enabled to confer.

To carry out this task requires the discipline that is normally described as the dignity of Parliament. And while we will be giving further thought to the symbols and the procedures of this House, which must conform to the needs and the understanding of our society, a foundation of dignity is something we will always preserve.

There are a few other general observations that I feel bound to make at this time.

While the obligations of Parliament emerge from the Republican Constitution, those of individual Honourable Members are not quite so firmly defined. Let me emphasise to the Members of this House that theirs is a two-way obligation: to represent fairly to the Government the views of their constituents, and then to interpret fairly to their people the policies and decisions of the Government.

Members of Parliament must serve as a bridge between Government and people. They stand astride the national stream of activity and thought. And unless this bridge is well maintained then the national wellbeing suffers, through lack of access to, or lack of contribution from, some portion of our land.

Perhaps above all, the Republic demands from every Member an absolute loyalty, to the House, to the Party and to the country. It happens in many young countries that Members of Parliament may become, in particular, the target of some foreign Government or some subversive institution. Forces may become unleashed, spurred on by external pressures. I must make it very clear that the Government of Kenya will meet any threat of subversion with the fullest rigours of the law. But I feel confident, in fact, that each Member of this House will act as a guardian of our national integrity and will assist the Government in stamping out any hint of such threat, before it has time to develop.

And there is yet a further way in which Honourable Members may greatly assist with nation building. In political and economic contexts, we have already recorded significant achievements. It may fairly be stated that, at the end of the first year of Independence, Kenya has acquired a national maturity. But now, on to this foundation, we need to erect greater human respect.

I have spoken elsewhere of a sterner moral integrity and do not wish now to labour this point. But each of you will know of instances of exploitation within our society, or lack of compassion, or denial to a man of respect for what he is and how he strives.

Crime is one affront to our society, rooted as it is in jealousy or brutality or greed. Corruption is an evil, which we must never invite or condone. But so, too, are many matters that are technically within the law: the overcharging of a man who needs some food or service, but who, through ignorance, cannot tell the proper cost ... or the public operation, for a profit, of vehicles so dangerous that they really should be scrapped ... or the offer of starvation wages to a man who must work or else starve.

So many practices, criminal or evilly-designed, can increase for our people the burdens of poverty or hazard or despair. These must be eradicated. We must work together here, for the creation of a new social conscience.

Let the Republic be rooted in human respect.

The forthcoming programme of the Government will be submitted to the House, in its component forms, through the publication and presentation of effective Bills. I do not propose today to embark on a catalogue of pending measures, or to stipulate priorities. My association with this House, in the constitutional manner that we have designed, will ensure that a legislative structure emerges from the function of Government and Parliament, working as a team.

But I must now outline to the House the manner in which our initial achievements and approaches will be carried forward, and something of the Government's objectives in more general terms.

The overall intention of the Government is to move further towards African Socialism, by placing fuller emphasis on those duties and social obligations which reflect, in their rewards, effective pulling together of the State and the community.

Now that the country has been swept clear of Party discord, the Colonial image of division created by suspicions and fears, all energies may be harnessed to the purpose of evolving here a Welfare State.

To achieve this aim will require the full co-operation of all citizens and other residents of Kenya. It will require the maximum and deliberate exploitation of all our resources, both human and material. In this regard, the Government is urgently aware of the need to speed up the educational advance and training of our people, including the need to improve health facilities.

Already, steps have been taken to carry through a rapid programme of Africanisation, and to help our own farmers and businessmen to participate more effectively in the economic life of the country. I must express my satisfaction with the young Kenyans who have recently had to take over senior responsibilities in the public service of our country.

Inherent in our policy of 'back to the land' is the awareness that our economy is founded on the land, its use and its resources. We are also lucky to have so much that we can offer to world tourists. All these areas will receive special attention, and will be the subject of discussion and debate in our Parliament.

The Government is actively engaged in deciding the new policies that will guide us in these matters. I need not stress the important role which must be played by the workers and youth of Kenya in this task of nation building. They have been the vanguard in our struggle for Independence, and we shall rely upon their energy and enthusiasm in the future.

I should also like to make reference to the work being done in expanding, training, modernising and equipping our Armed Forces. I am glad to be able to say that our Army and Police have already given a good account of themselves in the North Eastern Region, and in the all-important task of preserving law and order in Kenya. Our new Air Force is already moving to operational point, and the inauguration of our Navy will complete our Service trinity this month.

Our Government continues to stand firmly for unity and freedom within our nation. The Press and the citizens of our country will enjoy every freedom, and all we require from them is a keen awareness of the responsibilities and duties which they, on their part, must have towards this nation and its people. Here I must mention the steps taken by the Government to develop our own Press, radio, television and news services. This step will greatly help us in promoting unity in the country, and also in projecting our image abroad.

During our first year of Independence, we have established friendship with many nations. I would like to take this opportunity to thank all those nations whose friendly and active co-operation we have enjoyed in this past year. But while we express appreciation of their assistance and co-operation, and the hope that this co-operation will continue, I am bound to reiterate that the success of our effort to build a Kenya nation lies entirely in the hands of the Kenya people.

It is upon this approach that we must proceed to face the task of nation building, determined that our country's future shall be on the basis of our own policies, and as a result of our efforts and sweat. Here then is the true meaning of our motto HARAMBEE!

Many advantages to the East African countries have accrued from working together within the framework of the Common Services Organisation. We shall continue to work closely with our neighbours in East Africa, in order to retain and expand the benefits of mutual planning and economic endeavour, together with the various research and technical services administered by EACSO.

The Republic of Kenya will subscribe faithfully to the Charter of the Organisation of African Unity. We shall continue to work for the solution of African problems by the Africans themselves, and to achieve a Continent marked by brotherhood and understanding between States, which could lead so rapidly to the greater enlightenment and prosperity of all people.

In foreign affairs, the Republic of Kenya will steadfastly adhere to the policy of positive non-alignment. We shall not be aligned with, or regard ourselves as beholden to, any ideological group or power bloc. We shall permit no incursions into Kenya, by philosophy and practical example, in normal diplomatic exchanges, and within the Commonwealth, and through the United Nations, Kenya will seek to contribute to world peace and a new economic order for mankind.

Our Republic has come into being at a moment when the dying embers of Colonialism have brought into vivid focus the economic and social injustices of half a century. The world now is experiencing the shock waves of change. Men are rising from the bondage of domination and frustration, to demand their rightful places and their rightful shares in the pattern of human society.

This is not a moment, Honourable Members, for Kenya to be bitter, or to seek retaliation or revenge. The role of our Republic must be to make a contribution, and to build, so that out of the ashes of discredit, and the larceny of human souls, we may fashion for our children and those of other nations a world that enshrines what is right.

Let us march forward in the spirit of HARAMBEE!

Long live the Republic of Kenya!

ECONOMIC HORIZONS — 1965

Delegates from many countries were assembled in Nairobi on February 9, 1965, for a meeting of the Economic Commission for Africa. The meeting was opened by Mzee Kenyatta, who delivered a general review of the background to these supra-national economic deliberations:

*

It gives me much pleasure to welcome to Kenya distinguished delegates from so many African States, for the seventh annual session of the Economic Commission for Africa. This is the first time that Nairobi has been honoured as the venue for a full meeting of this Commission. I extend to you all a warm welcome on behalf of my Government and the people of Kenya, and trust that during your stay here you will come to know us and our country better. Let me assure you that no door to any aspect of our life or recreation will be closed to you.

In this twentieth year of the United Nations, it is fitting that I should reaffirm Kenya's support for its Charter and objectives, and the readiness of this Republic to work with all other member States in securing better distribution of economic and social justice among mankind. We are proud of the fact that the current Chairman of the U.N. General Assembly is an African. It is fit and proper that Africa's impact on the United Nations should be intensified.

Apart from its high principles, and its service as a forum for political understanding, the United Nations has increasingly expanded the range and purpose of its specialised agencies. We recall with appreciation that this Commission was the first of the United Nations agencies to take root in our African soil.

At the moment, the United Nations is faced with a financial crisis, as a result of disagreement within the organisation. We look on this dispute with grave concern and increasing disappointment. With all its imperfections, the United Nations is the only hope for world peace. In common with other developing countries, we in Kenya are most anxious for a speedy settlement of the current crisis, in order that the practical objectives and functions of this great organisation may forge ahead without hindrance. Our humble advice to all parties is that concern for the future of humanity is more important than desire to save face.

This Economic Commission has had to spend its first few years in settling down in Africa, and gathering statistical information of various kinds. At the end of this inescapable period, the Commission has a more operational role to play in African affairs. It can promote economic co-operation. It can serve as a clearing-house for field experience, planning techniques, and the impact of technological skills. We in Kenya acknowledge and appreciate the benefits we have received from study and projects initiated by the Commission.

Nearly two years ago, in Addis Ababa, the Organisation of African Unity was formed. It has wisely been recognised that there must be a disciplined harmony between the initiative of Africa represented in OAU, and the advisory functions of the ECA. These two bodies have given, and must continue to give, mutual support to each other in a common task.

In one important field now, the assembly of knowledge within the ECA can greatly assist the African States. This is in planning and pursuit of common strategy to secure liberal and rational policies in all fields of international trade. My country supports the stands taken by developing countries during the last Trade and Development Conference at Geneva. Indeed, developing countries like ours must continue to press for stabilisation of agricultural prices and fuller access to world markets for their produce.

Last year registered an increase in trade between African States. But we are alarmed to note — as one instance — the importation of meat and dairy products to Africa when there exists a surplus of these commodities within this Continent.

The agenda for your Conference illustrates both the broad interest of the Commission, and the great potential of Africa's latent strength. In seeking to harness that strength, many of Africa's developing countries are faced with common problems. These spring from the rising population and the age-group imbalance; the need to survey and conserve natural resources; the need to intensify agriculture and stabilise markets; the task of balancing industrial growth with the essential needs of the land; the allocation of scarce capital resources; the immediate issue of unemployment; and priorities to be given to education and other services in development planning.

Solutions to such problems cannot all be advanced within the scope of economics alone. They affect people, with traditions and tastes and ambitions that must be taken into account. While I have nothing but respect for the economists, I would suggest that many of the sociological effects of economic actions might often call for closer study.

All those countries of Africa which have won their independence have agreed on one thing: that true economic independence should follow political freedom. Here, it seems to me, this Commission has a part to play in two important fields. First, it must provide the assistance and stimulus of an expert body to all those member States of Africa now striving for their self-reliance. All of us can benefit from such advice. And all of us can look to this institution as a source of information and experience, ideas and data, having application to Africa as a whole.

Secondly, the Commission must gear itself to African objectives, adopting practices and seeking solutions that meet the needs of Africa. The purpose of the awakening Africa must be to redress all the economic injustices of centuries past. And we must never, through sense of obligation or through lethargy, permit ourselves to be harnessed to some foreign ideological system. We welcome unfettered aid from any source, recognising the sovereign right of every individual country to decide the source and terms of any aid it might accept. In all this, the ECA may give advice on the respective economic advantages of alternative courses of action. Such a function presents this Commission with a noble task.

I will take up no more of the time that should be devoted to your agenda. I will merely re-emphasise that the purpose of all our work is to build a better life for our people, ensuring for them a future of prosperity and peace. I wish you all success in your deliberations, and a sense of real achievement when you finally disperse.

UNIVERSITY CEREMONY — 1965

Mzee Kenyatta had been elected an Honorary Fellow of the Royal College (now the University College, Nairobi) in the course of an Academic Ceremony during the Uhuru celebrations of December 1963. As President of Kenya fifteen months later, he visited Kampala to be vested as Honorary Doctor of Laws by the University of East Africa as a whole. This ceremony was held in the Makerere University College on March 26, 1965. In his speech, Jomo Kenyatta ranged over a wide field of outlook and recollection:

*

In such honourable and distinguished company, it is with real feeling that I thank the University of East Africa for conferring distinction upon me today. To share this honour with an eminent scholar such as Dr. Lamont makes it a double tribute.

When this College was first founded, I was already actively engaged in political work, agitating for more and higher education. For this, I needed no academic Degree; indeed, one has never seemed necessary in political life. All that time ago, it was impossible to forecast how things would work out in Africa. There were so many obstacles to overcome, so much power to uproot, so much bigotry to sweep away. And although the work went on, we saw only darkly the shape of things to come.

For instance, you would have been regarded as a madman, or at best a visionary, to suggest the establishment of a self-governing African State, let alone the setting up of a University institution like this. Now this College has become a part of a University community, and there are 36 independent African States.

The struggle is not over, but these reflections are a source of great pleasure to me. It is inevitable that imperialism will be wiped out of Africa. But the greatest need now is to build viable sovereign nations. Others have longer experience on how to go about this most exciting task, but I would like to make my own contribution in this field.

In my country, we started with a divided people, and it was essential to get them moving in the direction of nation building as one cohesive force. The struggle for independence had brought Africans on the one hand, and Asians and Europeans on the other, into open conflict. When I came out of prison, I stated that the various races in Kenya could live together in peace and harmony. Very few people believed me, and — as a result — our independence Constitution contained every imaginable safeguard to protect the interests of non Africans. It even went further, and created tribal and regional groupings.

With such discordant forces in our Constitution, it was impossible to build a nation, and I was determined to do all I could to eliminate them. I am fully aware that complete integration of these races into the life of the nation will take time. Contacts on a cultural level are few and superficial, and any suggestion in the Press that — say — a Hindu girl can marry an African boy produces a most acrimonious debate. I have also noted that non-Africans have been very slow in taking advantage of early registration as citizens.

The second child of the regional Constitution — namely Government by tribes — received shock treatment when our Republican Constitution came into being. But we are still faced with tribal jealousies awakened during the period of regionalism. Nevertheless, I believe this is a temporary phase. Proper education on what the Government is doing must in time bring more informed understanding and mutual respect.

For Government to be effective, there must be sub-division, with acceptable relationships between Government and Parliament, the Cabinet, Departments of State, and the Public Service. A great deal of confusion arises from lack of understanding of the roles of political institutions. These institutions grew from compromises forced upon the Colonial authority, and they are not necessarily suited to our situation. To give maximum service, they presuppose a somewhat sophisticated community, people who can communicate properly by letter and by telephone. The vast majority cannot do these things, and regard such facilities as either amusing toys or as trouble to be avoided at all costs. New adjustments to allow for this must constantly be made.

But it would always be unwise to start by demolishing the whole structure created by the Colonial Government, in favour of some untried experiment. A careful appraisal of each institution and its relationships is necessary. We have found, for instance, that location Headmen or Chiefs cannot just be swept away. They fulfill necessary functions in serving the people.

There are thousands of people whose abilities were of great value in the struggle for Uhuru. They were prominent in their Districts, or in some particular task. Suddenly, they found that the nation building phase called for different talents, and training was needed. They themselves were unqualified in administration, or in science and technology, or in any of the arts and professions.

Any undergraduate could tell you that, to develop a country, it is necessary to increase education and expand welfare and economic services. And this is not a superficial truth, since it is the basic objective of all our striving.

But it is often forgotten that military strength is also part of political design. It has proved tragically true that, as each new nation is born in Africa, it becomes a pawn or a target in the Cold War. And in those nations that prove unresponsive, experience has been that certain elements will go to any length of subversion, in order to bring a Government and a people into their ideological orbit or under their strategic command.

Here lies the foundation of our policy of non-alignment in world affairs. We do not wish to be influenced, and we will not be driven, by the ideologies of foreign powers. We are seeking to fashion an African image to bring about rapid improvement in the living standards of our people. We want to offer to humanity new concepts of economic justice and social objective, as alternative to the sterile divisions of mankind.

Along with like-minded nations, we in Kenya see no point in having freed ourselves from the shackles of Colonialism, only to find ourselves in economic or political bondage of some more subtle kind. And it is unfortunate indeed that hard-pressed resources must be diverted towards military preparedness, in the cause of vigilance.

It is quite fundamental that economic development must reflect and be built around the life of the people. Alien and unwanted systems cannot be imposed and will not last. We have not yet found all the answers. Uhuru opens up a whole new universe, composed of those reactions and ambitions that for so long were locked away in people's minds. Everybody wants such things as hospitals, new sources of employment, or improved roads. But we have to deal with many prophets who appear to know all the answers, but who gloss over the difficulties or the means of putting answers into effect.

Our purpose is to produce the substance underlying the ideals of our new society. But this can only be translated and pursued through the constructive application of our hands and minds. We are doing all we can to expand opportunities for vocational training. We are giving the highest priority to education at secondary level. And we are offering our utmost support to the growing Faculties of the East African University.

This is the first occasion on which this University as such has awarded honorary Degrees. I am sharing distinction today with Doctor William Lamont of Glasgow, who came here as Principal some twenty years ago, and prepared plans for the special association of this College with the University of London. Now there is a separate institution, with a status and challenge in which, through this ceremony, we may proudly share. I know that Doctor Lamont will join me in expressing my thanks to the University of East Africa.

Now let me conclude in this way: the need to allot due respect to the principle of academic independence is understood. But is there any danger, in this University, of aloofness from the problems and realities of the surrounding society? Is there enough flexibility in motives and initial standards, and in seizing opportunities in the light of East Africa's pressures and needs?

Here is a unique assembly of talent and facility. It would surely be wasteful, were such an institution to adopt the role of a spectator, neglecting a potential contribution of objective example and influence. I am aware, as a member of your Common Services Authority, that you are making every effort to dispel doubts in these respects, and I want to wish you every success.

I am honoured now to feel a part of all that this University can offer and inspire: the bounty of knowledge, the zest of research, the faculty of judgment, the gift of humility. All these attributes we need, so that in building our nation we may create a society that is vigorous by nature, strong in faith, and eternal in the arts of peace.

AFRICAN SOCIALISM — 1965

Sessional Paper No. 10 entitled "African Socialism and its Application to Planning in Kenya" was published on May 4, 1965, and a reference to the vital significance of this document was made in the narrative portion of this present work. The Paper was introduced to the people of Kenya through a Foreword written by President Kenyatta:

*

Since attainment of our independence just over eighteen months ago, the Government has been deciding on the measures that will ensure rapid economic development and social progress for all our citizens. Apart from the Budget statement last year the Government produced a Development Plan covering the years 1964-70. This Plan was prepared at very short notice and was intended to be flexible to enable Government to adjust any of its provisions on the basis of experience and new ideas. Already much has been accomplished in the short space of time since Independence, but a lot remains to be done if we are to achieve our declared goals.

In a recent statement the Minister for Finance has promised the country a balanced Budget in 1965 and also stated that for the first time since 1952 Kenya will meet all her recurrent expenditure from her own resources. It is also good to note that our foreign exchange and balance of payments positions have shown considerable improvements since Independence. There have been numerous delegations and inquiries about investment in Kenya in addition to the actual investments that have taken place. We have gone out to find new markets and new areas of technical and trade cooperation in the world. From the recently published Economic Quarterly Report it will be seen that our own small farmers increased the value of their gross marketed produce from £11.6 million in 1963 to £14 million in 1964, or an increase of nearly 21 per cent. In education, while we await the final report of the Education Commission, primary school enrolment has been increased from 891,553 in 1963 to 1,028,000 in 1965, and secondary school education is being vigorously expanded.

In economic terms eighteen months is a short period in which to attain decisive accomplishments, but it is obvious that everything points to rapid progress.

All along the Government has been guided in its approach to developmental matters by the declarations contained in the KANU Manifesto. In this we declared that our country would develop on the basis of the concepts and philosophy of Democratic African Socialism. We rejected both Western Capitalism and Eastern Communism and chose for ourselves a policy of positive non-alignment.

Our entire approach has been dominated by a desire to ensure Africanization of the economy and the public service. Our task remains to try to achieve these two goals without doing harm to the economy itself and within the declared aims of our society.

The Government has produced this Sessional Paper which discusses in detail both the theory of Democratic African Socialism and its practical application to planning in Kenya. There has been much debate on this subject and the Government's aim is to show very clearly our policies and also explain our programme. This should bring to an end all the conflicting, theoretical and academic arguments that have been going on.

The Minister for Economic Planning and Development and his Cabinet colleagues will help explain and interpret this paper to Parliament and to the public so as to ensure that it is fully understood. I thank him and his colleagues for the time and effort they have devoted to the preparation of this paper, which has received the unanimous support of my Cabinet.

To the nation I have but one message. When all is said and done we must settle down to the job of building the Kenya nation. To do this we need political stability and an atmosphere of confidence and faith at home. We cannot establish these if we continue with debates on theories and doubts about the aims of our society. Let this paper be used from now as the unifying voice of our people and let us all settle down to build our nation. Let all the people of our country roll up their sleeves in a spirit of self-help to create the true fruits of UHURU. THIS IS WHAT WE MEAN BY HARAMBEE.

MADARAKA DAY — 1965

Parades and ceremonies were held in Nairobi on June 1, 1965, exactly two years after Mzee Jomo Kenyatta was first sworn in as Prime Minister. Now as President, on this day of Madaraka .... (Swahili for " assumption of responsibility", i.e. internal self-government) .... he delivered a special message to the people of Kenya. His principal theme was that of safeguarding the country's integrity against any forms of political subversion or physical challenge:

Two years ago today, the people of Kenya assumed authority for the governmental affairs of this country. For me, this was a happy and proud occasion, and I am pleased to celebrate the second anniversary of Madaraka with you. In future, 'Madaraka Day' will be a public holiday.

When we celebrated this day last year, we were happy then to inaugurate the Kenya Air Force. At that same time, we promised to establish a Kenya Navy. This promise was fulfilled in December last year. I am therefore able to report to you now that our Armed Forces include all three Services: the Army, the Air Force and the Navy. The modernisation, training and Africanisation of these forces is proceeding with all speed, and today we can truly be proud of our men under arms.

The safety and security of our people, and the integrity of our country, comprise the first responsibility of this Government. Today, I would like to congratulate the men of our Army and Police Force for their work in the North Eastern Province. The disturbances there have been a challenge to our determination and strength. Relative peace now exists in the area, but I want to ask the people there to give greater co-operation to the Government, so that normal conditions can be restored, allowing for fuller and speedier development of water facilities, education and communications.

My Government is aware that there are forces outside Kenya which have encouraged shifta activities. Without these forces, the shifta gangs would all have been eliminated by now. I therefore now repeat the pledge of my Government to the people of Kenya. We shall not surrender a single inch of our territory, nor shall we abdicate our responsibility to our people in the area.

The voluntary dissolution of the Opposition was a historic achievement for Kenya's people. It was the people who called for unity. It was the people who rejected tribalism and tribalists. It was you who refused to compromise on unity, and who forced the leaders to hear your voice.

But unity cannot be taken for granted. There are many forces that do not want to see us remain united. There are some people who remain tribalists at heart, and who regard unity as their enemy. There are others whose personal ambitions drive them to forget the people and the nation. And there are those people and nations outside Kenya who do not want the African Government to succeed: instead, they want our nation to serve their interests and work to their dictation. To remain united, we must ever be vigilant.

For over forty years, I fought and sacrificed my active life so that this country could get rid of the yoke of colonialism and imperialism. Many sons and daughters of our land suffered and shed blood, so that our children might be born free. You can therefore understand my personal feelings about the future. How can I tolerate anything that could compromise or jeopardise the promise to our children? Let me declare once more that, as Head of your Government, I shall combat with all my strength anyone, or any group, or any country, that may be tempted to try and undermine our independence. This pledge holds true whether such forces operate from inside Kenya or from without.

I am confident that my faith is shared by all true nationalists in our country. What is more, it is supported by every worker, peasant, farmer and soldier here. I am equally confident that all the youth of Kenya would not hesitate for one moment to join me in fighting against forces of disunity, subversion, external intrigue and personal greed. Let me remind you that the defence of this country will depend on the loyalty and devotion of all our people, just as much as on the uniformed Services. Love for your country is the most effective weapon in fighting against subversion.

It is in this knowledge that I am able to say to you — and to the world — that Kenya will remain firm and resolute in her declared stand for positive non-alignment. Indeed, I feel that I should speak bluntly on this subject today. We do not want this to become a slogan. We must make it a practical and working policy. Otherwise, it could be exploited or used as a cover by those who do not care for non-alignment.

In the Party Manifesto, we made it quite clear that non-alignment did not mean non-commitment. We cannot stand aside when important issues confront Africa or the world. We have definite views on Rhodesia, Angola, South Africa, Vietnam, Malaysia, and of course disarmament. We do not hesitate to express these views when the situation demands.

But let me say quite plainly today that Kenya shall not exchange one master for a new master. We intend to remain our own master forever. Let every nation in the East or West take heed of this warning. We welcome genuine friendship, but we detest flattery. We welcome co-operation and assistance, but we will not be bought or blackmailed. We may be under-developed, and our people may walk barefoot, but we are a proud people: proud of our heritage, our traditions and ancestry. What is more, we will not betray our children.

I must warn those in our country who seek to create confusion. It is true that we have passed through many years of Western imperialism. It is natural that we should detest Western colonialism, and associate the word imperialism with the West. But if we are truly non-aligned, we must not shrink from making friends with those Western countries which extend an honest hand of co-operation and trade. To do so would prove that we are not free and we are unable to separate good from bad. It would prove that we still suffer from a Colonial mentality.

Some people deliberately try to exploit a Colonial hangover for their own selfish purposes, or in order to serve some external force. We must reject such people publicly.

It is naive to think that there is no danger of imperialism from the East. In world power politics, the East has as much designs upon us as the West, and would like us to serve their own interests. This is why we reject Communism. It is in fact the reason why we have chosen for ourselves the policy of non-alignment and African Socialism. To us, Communism is as bad as imperialism. What we want is to develop the Kenya Nationalism which helped us to win the struggle against imperialism. We do not want somebody else's nationalism. It is a sad mistake to think that you can get more food, more hospitals or schools, simply by crying

Communism. I am amused by those who suggest that we cannot condemn something that we have not seen or tasted, or who proclaim that our only threat is neo-colonialism from the West.

I speak plainly on this subject today because the time has come for us to do so, in order to leave no room for confusion. I am happy that we have our Constitution, a document on African Socialism, and a Party Manifesto. These three documents have been endorsed by our people and Parliament, and must be a guide to our new society. It is now for the public to judge the actions of the Government, and the utterances of all our leaders, according to what is laid down in these documents. The world is looking to see if we shall be able to live according to these policies and ideals.

On this day in 1963, we all responded to the call of 'Harambee'. By this call, we said to the world that we would build a new Kenya through co-operation and hard work. We knew and accepted that the aspirations of our people would be realised only through hard work and discipline. There is no room here for the lazy and idle. There is no room for those who wait for things to be given for nothing. There is no place for leaders who hope to build a nation of slogans.

I will have nothing to do with those who seek to play upon the fears, anxieties and present problems of our people or country. We must tell our people the truth.

It is true now, for instance, that in 1964 we had over a million children in primary schools, and that this number increased by 100,000 in 1965. But to continue to enrol more and more children, we shall need more teachers and more money from taxation.

Let me end on a happy note. In accordance with our promise to provide free medical services for the people, I am pleased to announce today that Government has decided — as a first step — to introduce free medical services for all children at Government clinics and hospitals. Our nation has an urgent responsibility towards the children. This is in keeping with our traditions. And I hope that in coming months we can announce further measures in fulfilment of our welfare programmes.

DIPLOMACY IN AFRICA — 1965

On July 29, 1965, Mzee Kenyatta was Guest of Honour at a Luncheon given in Nairobi by members of the Diplomatic Corps. He took this opportunity to reaffirm Kenya's position on the world stage, and the Republic's attitude to some immediate crises or problems:

*

This Luncheon started life as an arrangement for a Dinner. So perhaps I should first apologise for circumstances which brought about this transformation. I have been looking forward to this meeting for some time. A social gathering in this company is one of the most pleasant duties on my working diary. It is a meeting of minds representing worldwide society, with their resources and contributions. And for enjoying all this, my wife and I make no apology at all.

Let me assure Your Excellencies that I and my Government welcome you here as friends. I hope that, on this foundation, we will build a rewarding relationship. Your task here can be more meaningful than the preparation of despatches for your Governments, and the routine of consular administration. We ask you not just to observe, but to get to know our country and its people, and to make friends of us all.

Diplomats of many countries find themselves in Kenya at a time when the challenge of nation building is being firmly met. As you are aware, from the Sessional Paper reflecting the views of KANU, we are committed here to the principles of African Socialism. Our fundamental task has therefore become the translation of these principles into practice.

The essential of our African Socialism can be defined as inspiration. We are seeking to inspire dedication, not in pursuit of an ideology or in search for power, but for the welfare of mankind.

I believe this can be done. We invite you to accept and understand these policies, as being more than a political strategy for an economic programme. In your interpretations, and in your concern for Kenya, we invite you to believe both in our sincerity, and in our ability to triumph as we move along towards our objectives.

As I have said many times, our external policy is firmly based on non-alignment. We take no sides, and will not be dragged into intrigues between rival groups and power blocs. This is our position on the world stage. In this we have no monopoly of wisdom. But mankind even in this twentieth century is still struggling for the order and new purpose which alone will enable mankind to survive. And let me add that this is our position on the stage of Africa as well. We adhere to the Charter of the O.A.U., and have devoted our resources to fostering friendship between all African States.

You are here today because you are, in effect, colleagues in a chosen service. You have duties and loyalties to your respective Governments, whose policies and purposes may differ. But your responsibility, I would suggest, is wider than this. You have opportunity to explore and express the community of interest that must exist as between yourselves and between your countries. Your task, in fact, is to set a noble example of a pattern of behaviour that should serve mankind.

Of course, on occasion, one has to leave principle and come down to particular problems. Two of these are problems which perhaps I should mention today. At the recent Commonwealth Conference in London, views were offered on the issue of Rhodesia. I would like it to be clearly understood that time in Rhodesia is running out. No solution which is not based on majority rule can succeed. As in Kenya, an accepted Constitution can enshrine all safeguards for minorities and stability for economic growth. But the will of the majority must prevail.

There have been extremist attitudes, threatening to force Rhodesia towards minority seizure of power. There has been protracted negotiation, in the apparent hope of finding some compromise solution.

But the issue is basically simple. It is said that peace is indivisible; I am certain that justice is indivisible. This is a question bearing directly on human rights and human dignity, which no political calculations can set aside.

The other dominant issue today is that of Vietnam. We made it clear again, at the London Conference, that while Commonwealth initiative was welcome, such initiative could not be properly expressed if led by a Commonwealth member committed to one point of view.

But some way must be found to break through the web of diplomacy and tactical assessments. Some way must be found for those involved to talk, and to clarify and compromise. The world must not be forced, on this issue of Vietnam, beyond brinkmanship into active war.

This morning, I understand, President Johnson of the United States has addressed another call to the United Nations, seeking its intervention and good offices in the dispute. Some such forum of goodwill must sponsor a new approach to a lasting solution. No one should fear or avoid discussion. Silence or uncertainty can breed despair.

Gentlemen, I have spoken of your position here, and of your wider purpose. I have spoken of principles and problems. Let me conclude with just one simple observation. The investive genius of man can casually place our whole planet in mortal peril. Disaster can no longer be selective, and power is no longer a key.

I submit to Your Excellencies that the world is now one. There is inspiration enough, in decades that lie ahead, in meeting the challenge of social injustices and economic frustrations. If we devote ourselves, all of us, to the cause of humanity and the service of our people, the whole world may then rise to a nobler purpose.

DEVELOPMENT PLANNING — 1965

When the Government promoted an initial Seminar — at the Kenya Institute of Administration — for Officers engaged in implementation of Development Plans, President Kenyatta elected to deliver the opening address. This was on August 19, 1965. Mzee Kenyatta spoke of the background to fresh development opportunities in Kenya, and the new thinking which must henceforth inspire modernity and progress:

*

I am glad to have this opportunity of opening the first of two important Seminars for senior Officers of my Government. The Provincial Commissioners and their technical colleagues serve as a vital link in the chain of Administration. I except such Officers to absorb the inspiration of our principles and planning and carry them to the people. At the same time, you must faithfully transmit the problems and prospects encountered in the field back to the Central Government.

In this whole context, there are certain things that you must understand.

We in the Republic of Kenya fought hard, in years gone by, to free ourselves from foreign rule. The principles of human rights and human dignity were involved in this struggle. But we believed, as well, in our own talents and ambitions. We believed that we could do things better than the Colonialists. So now we must face the judgment, of our own people and of coming generations, on the reality that we make of this belief.

We have to welcome this opportunity for judgment. It is a challenge which we all sought, and to which we all belong. You hold posts of high responsibility in the Republic, of which you can be proud. The Government must not only rely on your devotion. It must gather strength from your initiative, your constant search for improvements and ideas.

I have emphasised many times a point clearly stated in our KANU Manifesto, and expanded in our recent Paper on African Socialism. In the field of nation building, there is no substitute for hard work and national dedication. Whether this age of African opportunity becomes in fact the age of African achievement, depends on how we move, as one united team, towards a common goal. I tell you gentlemen, that we are not simply passing through a phase of history. We have our own history to make.

You will all have made close study of our Development Plan and its purposes, and the ways in which it is to be applied. This Seminar will give ample opportunity to increase your understanding of such matters, and to discuss such queries or problems as must always arise. I merely wish to draw your attention to one or two points.

It is often said that the key to our development lies in a healthy and thriving agriculture. Certainly, our land and our people are the primary resources on which we must build.

Here in Kenya, one farmer barely produces enough food for six of his fellow-men. In some advanced countries, a farmer can produce food for himself and thirty other people. Our salvation and our progress greatly depend on the movement that I have often described as 'back to the land'. But we cannot be satisfied today with the fruits of traditional techniques. We must raise the whole level of our agriculture, by means of capital, machinery, modern methods of cultivation, better seed and better stock, and harder work. The Government can and will continue to provide opportunities and facilities. As the Government's sense of touch, yours is the critical duty of inspiring and implementing on the ground a revolution in technology and business management, so that our farming becomes a scientific enterprise able to hold its own in a scientific age.

My second point springs from modern science. Especially outside the high potential areas, you must consider always the vital question of proper land-use. There is the paramount need to conserve the soils and water reserves and protective vegetation on which the physical future of our people must depend. And there is need to consider how modern techniques of resource management, including wildlife management, might be adapted to produce the optimum yields of revenue, employment and trade.

Urban growth and the development of manufacturing industries should improve our external economic position, and help build up a wage economy for our skilled labour. But our real economic and social strength lies in the land, and the use we make of the range of our resources.

Against this background, all our economic plans and education programmes have one motive: to wipe out the miseries of the past and build a new life for our people.

This Seminar has yet another value. There is more to progress than can be achieved by enthusiasm and discipline and dedication. We must develop international standards of skill in all fields and professions. So there is still room for all of us to work just as hard at learning as at doing. In more developed countries, as many of you may have seen, professional men and administrators are constantly seeking ways to improve their performance. They read books and technical Papers. They seek special instruction in advanced technology. And they welcome a guided discussion in study-groups and seminars.

My Government is devoting considerable funds and effort to this same end, in order that civil servants may be taught what we know to be needed for efficiency. I expect such training facilities to be well utilised. Against the sum total of human knowledge, we are all ignorant, and there is no loss of dignity in recognising such a simple fact. I want to make it clear that you should welcome and encourage the continuous process of training. For the Government and the country must be concerned with your personal productivity as well. If we are going to master the techniques of producing nuclear energy and electronics, it is because we have faith in the ability of our children to learn and train.

This Seminar is one symbol of the end of an initial planning phase, and the beginning of action for development. I feel sure it will inspire you with a new sense of urgency, and will refresh your determination in the part you have to play.

A programme for development can be compared to the planting of trees. Some saplings grow quickly, and within a few years will provide us with firewood and fences and fruit. Others are slower, but we know that our children will enjoy the shade of these greater and longer-living trees, and think kindly of those whose effort and foresight provided this bounty.

So it is with development projects. Some programmes we must have to produce quick results, and produce the necessities of life. Others more deply-rooted must lay now the foundation of the future prosperity of our country. A sound Development Plan has to balance the calls of the present with the needs of the future.

It is our privilege, gentlemen, to administer the present in the context of building Kenya's future. I have complete faith in our ability, and in our people. I am confident that we shall build a State that will not only win the respect of other nations, but will ensure new happiness and dignity for those we serve.

I urge you now to commit yourself anew to your vital responsibilities. In the spirit of 'Harambee', great challenge will confront you and the fulfilment of many hopes now lies in your hands.

THE REPUBLICAN PARLIAMENT — 1965

There follows now the memorable Address delivered by His Excellency the President, Mzee Jomo Kenyatta, at the State Opening of Parliament on November 2, 1965. In the presence of many Heads of State, distinguished visitors, and diplomatic representatives of many countries, Mzee Kenyatta painted in a constitutional background against which he could announce or describe, in all their detail and promise, the practical endeavours and objectives of his Government in all the many fields of nation building. These were his words:

*

This is the first State Opening of Parliament since Kenya became a Republic. It is also the first sitting of the National Assembly in this new Chamber. Our business here, in accordance with the manifesto of our Party, is to fulfil the aspirations of our people. The Parliament of Kenya is elected by the people, as a law-making body to administer the affairs of the State. Today I address you as the Head of State. But our people have the right to elect a Parliament to serve them not only as a forum, or as a Council of Elders, but also as an executive instrument. We therefore believe that no part of the Republic's Government should lie outside our Parliament. Our Constitution provided that all Members of the Government, including the President in his capacity as Head of Government, should be Members of the Lower House.

The Republic is the people. So we feel it proper that the right of final sanction for all our country's laws should reside in the representatives of the people. Moreover, as honourable Members are aware, final control over the conduct of the Government is exercised by Parliament through the allocation of public funds. I mention such matters today because only a strong and fully representative Government could thrive in such a system. The Republic needs a strong Government. The whole process of nation-building rests upon the service and dedication of such a Government.

But it is equally true that the Government must be able to count on the maturity and vigour of our Parliament. The Members of Parliament do not simply have a narrow responsibility to their constituencies. They have an over-riding duty to the State. Each Member is a link, binding the Republic to the people. And in each direction there is an obligation both to guide and to lead.

It must be the purpose of this Parliament to wield supreme power in a truly national spirit. This means not only that each Member must understand the true meaning of each item in the Government's legislative programme. It means also that each Member must understand the position of the Government, and strengthen the whole institution of Parliament in the eyes of the people.

I now wish to say a word about the position of Kenya as a one-party State. The Government does not intend to submit legislation to Parliament on this matter.

In other independent States of Africa, there exist a number of other constitutional experiments or practices. We shall continue to watch these developments with brotherly interest and goodwill.

We can both learn and benefit from our own approaches to this matter, and our own achievements. Kenya has no need to copy some alien ideas. We have our own concept of Ujamaa, springing from our own culture here. Our whole constitutional structure is rooted in our African traditions. These give our people the right to select and to strengthen our Council of Elders, that is today called the Kenya Parliament. And by these traditions, national unity may endure as something we have fought for and won.

Our Party must always be the instrument of the people, guiding and guarding their interests. It must never come to be manipulated by a few. And while I need not elaborate the point today, the whole strength of our Party must be based on non-alignment.

At this point, I should outline to the House something of the Government's forward programme in the most important fields. I shall deal first with those social services which figure in our advance towards a Welfare State. Then we may come to the means of increasing our national wealth to support our welfare policies.

But I must remind honourable Members that our revised Development Plan is about to be published. This will contain all the

Government's policies and projects, in the fullest detail. Today, therefore, I can touch only briefly on each item.

My Government will be increasingly concerned with housing, as a basis of family welfare and self-respect. The provision of proper homes is now a most critical need. Apart from creating a new company to finance house purchase, and encouraging housing co-operatives, the Government will introduce legislation to set up a National Housing Authority. This new body will be empowered to lend money to local authorities for housing schemes, and also to build and administer its own housing estates.

The Government recognizes that the health of every citizen is of immediate importance, and that on the health of the nation will depend the outcome of our resolve for development. Further announcements can be expected on the abolition of in-patient fees for all those admitted to general hospital wards, and our Development Plan will give details of new hospital construction. Legislation is shortly to be introduced for comprehensive hospital insurance schemes. My Government has now agreed to the establishment of a full undergraduate medical school in Nairobi in 1967, and medical students from Kampala are already attending the Kenyatta National Hospital for their fifth year of clinical teaching. New training schools for nurses are also to be built.

Education is perhaps the greatest single foundation of effective nation-building. Today, on the road to our African socialism and true prosperity, we have well over a million pupils attending primary schools in Kenya, with curriculum common to all. To stabilize this position, and with further expansion in mind, a commission will shortly examine matters relating to the whole primary education structure. Secondary education will be seen to have the highest priority in the amended Development Plan. The Government will keep progress in this field under constant review, and seize any opportunity of stepping up the intake of pupils. It has already been announced that there will henceforth be free secondary education for all pupils within Forms 5 and 6. By 1970, we shall have more than 6,000 primary school teachers in training, and as from next year 200 prospective secondary school teachers will be enrolled annually for training. The Government has decided to reorganize and improve trade schools, and we shall continue to expand and encourage all possible higher education opportunities for our people. The enrolment of Kenya students in the East African University will increase by 50 per cent in the coming session, and today over 4,000 Kenya students are engaged on post-secondary studies in nearly twenty countries overseas. Parliament has been asked to approve the setting up of an Adult

Education Board, and we shall be receiving further assistance from Unesco with our programme of adult literacy work.

One of the most heartening features of today is the still growing enthusiasm from self-help schemes. Construction of more than a hundred Harambee schools is but a single example, alongside water schemes, road development, and hospitals. But a problem for the Government is co-ordination of individual projects with the overall Development Plan. To meet this, seminars are now being held in every province, seeking to direct the enthusiasm of the people into schemes which will best speed up development in every district or location. Community development staff are now hard at work in twenty-six districts of the Republic, and further officers will be engaged. Under the national plan for community development, we propose also to set up multi-purpose training centres in every district.

By 1970, it is estimated that the co-operative sector of Kenya's economy will be responsible for up to 20 per cent of our gross national product. At present, the co-operative movement is concentrated on agricultural marketing, but the Government recognizes the need to enlarge the number and scope of co-operative enterprises. Societies at village level are now being consolidated into more soundly based organizations, and the first of a number of district co-operative unions has now been established at Nyeri. The Government has decided that provincial co-operative training will be undertaken at six farmers' training centres, in addition to the Central Co-operative College.

My Government is totally committed to serving the people, by increasing the initiative and improving the living standards of every family. Such an aim greatly depends on the effective operation of local government. In this regard, we deplore a position in which people in many areas are blaming their local authorities for inefficiency, while the councils blame the local people for not paying taxes that are due. All this means in effect that thousands of families are unable to enjoy all the services they need. We shall therefore continue to examine the whole local government position, and see how present difficulties can best be met and put right.

The conservation and development of natural resources is a long-term process, having equal standing with all other developments and services as a key to Kenya's future. In the coming year, my Government will announce a new policy for a more effective programme of water development. We have recently noted a change of attitude by Kenya's people, who now increasingly support the Government's efforts to create and develop forest areas. The Government has allocated funds to expand and develop the fishing industry in three major lakes and at the Coast. We shall increase our efforts to educate our people in the importance of wildlife conservation and management. In parts of many districts, complete wildlife management projects may represent the highest form of land-use, and bring the maximum benefits in revenue, employment and trade.

Tourism is an industry which may rapidly help Kenya to diversify the whole economic pattern. We confidently estimate that, by 1970, Tourism will be employing more than sixty thousand people directly. We shall be spending nearly two million pounds over the next four years, on the development of lodges and of access roads. The new Tourist Development Corporation will participate in various projects, either alone or in association with local or overseas companies.

It is vital to our future economic strength and employment potential that we supplement agricultural effort now by every possible kind of commercial and industrial enterprise. To this end, the Government is preparing an industrial development plan for every province. I can reveal that, in the private sector, some twenty important industries are expected to begin production in the coming year and expansion is planned in many others. This Development Finance Company is now investigating the part it can best play in the promotion of twenty-five new and major industries. The Industrial and Commercial Development Corporation, which has already approved industrial loans to the extent of more than fifty thousand pounds since July, will be concerned henceforth both with promotion and training. Apart from work at the Industrial Training Centre in Nakuru, the Government is preparing further schemes for educating African businessmen in technical and managerial skills. The National Trading Corporation has made useful progress, and will increasingly direct its operations towards the benefit of small African traders, even in remote rural areas. Reorganization of the scheme for traders' loans has almost been completed, and a number of newly-employed Trade Development Officers will be posted to the districts. It has been decided to establish five industrial estates during the period of the development programme, on which fully serviced plots and buildings may be taken up, enabling the less experienced man with relatively small capital resources to start some profitable enterprise. A necessary Bill will be submitted to re-introduce a form of traders' licensing, and arbitration machinery under the Landlord and Tenant Act will henceforth ensure that businessmen are not exploited by unscrupulous landlords.

Roads may be regarded as among the prime movers of industrial and commercial activity. Within the present development period,

Kenya will have a full tarmac road between Nairobi and Mombasa. Other vital stretches brought to tarmac standard will be between Lesuru and Tororo, to complete the link with Uganda, and between Athi River and Namanga, to complete the link with Tanzania. Apart from these major trunk routes, the programme will include new tarmac roads in Western Kenya, and the improvement or reconstruction of many others. The Government will pay particular attention to roads which serve tea development, expansion of the sugar industry, and tourism. It is also proposed to extend facilities at Nairobi Airport, and to expand Mombasa for use by jet aircraft on international services.

Nothing is more important than that all Government policies should be executed by a loyal and effective civil service. The House and the country may be assured that my Government will continue to pursue Africanization of our whole administrative structure. But we cannot now move more rapidly than the supply of Africans with suitable qualifications and training will permit. The position today is that, out of a total of 51,000 civil servants, about 44,000 are Africans. We have allotted more than half a million pounds for the running of four training institutes and the provision of bursaries for in-service training. This is a symbol of our determination to proceed, but always on the basis of necessary standards and improved efficiency.

The security and welfare of all our people is uppermost in the mind of the Government. Ever since my speech in the House in February 1964, on the whole issue of Somali aggression and Shifta unrest in Northern Kenya, we have pursued a policy based on defence of our rights and our territory, human tolerance and understanding, and belief that justice and patience would together bring about a return to normal conditions. But appeals are no longer enough. My Government can and will no longer tolerate a position whereby almost one-third of Kenya's land area exists virtually under a state of siege. We can no longer permit the complete frustration of economic and social development in this huge area. My Government now requires and expects the co-operation of all the people of the North-Eastern Province to bring about a full development of this area in a climate of peace. And if such co-operation is not forthcoming, then whatever measures are required to subdue or remove the remaining criminal elements will be initiated and enforced.

Honourable Members must clearly understand that further rapid Africanization of our economy can only spring from more domestic savings. And in our own independent Republic, everything we budget for must be paid for with our own money. In the period since Independence, the Government has effected a remarkable restoration of business and financial confidence. This year, we have been able to budget for the largest annual development expenditure in the history of Kenya. The Government has also succeeded in financing without subsidy an expanding recurrent budget. But climatic conditions this year will reduce Government revenue and call for a strict control of expenditure. Any growth in recurrent budgetary expenditure henceforth will have to be related to the growth in the National Income. The principal financial highway to future development must lie along the route of restraining consumption and increasing savings for investment. To step up the capacity for domestic savings, a number of provisions have been or will be introduced.

Following the announcement of the East African Currency break-up, Kenya instituted a sound and flexible system of exchange control, which has already played its part in the restoration of financial confidence. We have every confidence in our ability henceforth to maintain the stability of Kenya currency, to assist in the promotion of further development. As the House is aware, the three East African Governments have set up a working party to look into existing common market problems and recommend ways of strengthening East African co-operation.

Finally, I wish to turn again to a call that has sometimes quite suitably been described as "Back to the Land". Full development of the bounty of our land is the basic issue in Kenya today. We seek by this means not only to reduce urban unemployment, but to work the land as the springboard of national welfare. We understand our land. It is not like complicated machinery, and it has always been our way of life.

All Government policies in this field are directed towards serving the individual farmer, by increasing his initiative and capacity. My Government will seek by every means to sustain and encourage the farming family. But honourable Members and the country should clearly understand that there must be determined response from the people.

The share of smallholders in Kenya's total agricultural production has been growing rapidly, and will continue to expand. The vigour and prosperity of small farmers must and will give agriculture in the Republic a whole new shape, with the African becoming dominant in the production, marketing and processing of output. But this policy must be matched by a constant effort to raise productivity. And quality production will always be of critical importance.

Members of this Parliament have a most important duty in the rural areas, to urge their people to follow the advice of technicians.

19*

Modern methods and techniques of husbandry, and careful selection of equipment and materials, could treble productivity on small farms almost overnight. And it is particularly vital for younger people to realize that agriculture in Kenya is now a modern industry. We must all work together to capture their imagination, and to see that they are interested and trained.

The Government will be expanding the agrarian loans scheme, to give the hard-working small farmer access to better seed, improved stock, new implements and fertilizers, or to help with building bomas or dips. Already we are seeing the early fruits of a revolution in the use of fertilizers in many districts. Another major advance in the efficiency of agriculture will come through proposed large-scale mechanization schemes.

It was unfortunate that, when our preparations for self-sufficiency in staple foodstuffs were all but complete, the country was stricken by drought. This created immediate problems, and threw an ordered programme out of balance.

A crash programme for the planting of Gathano maize in suitable areas should result in the planting of 33,000 acres in the current short rains. If professional advice is followed, we then expect to be self-sufficient in maize next year, and a review of maize prices has already started.

In the longer term, apart from improvements in cultivation techniques and higher yields through the use of fertilizers, our programme will be based on supplies of better and selected seed for maize production in three main areas. For commercial maize production west of the Rift, a high-yielding hybrid maize is now freely available. We shall be setting up a research station at Embu to produce improved seed for use in areas of customary shortage east of the Rift. And for the difficult and marginal areas, seed of Katumani maize is already being bulked.

My Government will promote further schemes to diversify the cash crop economy, to supplement traditional and still important foundations of coffee, sisal and pyrethrum. The tea acreage in Kenya will be doubled within the next five years. Major developments are pending in sugar production, and cotton is rapidly expanding to become a major crop. A new scheme will now justify the doubling of smallholder production of pineapples for an assured market. The passion fruit crop can now be expanded to six times its present level of output. The cashew nut crop is being successfully extended and developed at the Coast. The Mwea-Tebere rice irrigation scheme is to be enlarged even further. We shall continue to encourage horticultural production to serve overseas luxury markets.

But I wish to emphasize one thing to the House and the country: everything that is marketable is in effect a cash crop. Farmers can grow such varied products as bananas, wheat, chillies, coconuts, tobacco, castor seed, groundnuts, onions, potatoes, tomatoes, millet. All these products are valuable and saleable. They add to our total supply of national wealth.

Apart from crops, we shall continue as well to expand and diversify our livestock industries. We need high-quality cattle for milk and dairy produce, and for beef, built from stock improvement schemes assisted by expanding A.I. services. We aim at a great increase in sheep production for meat and wool. And there is great scope for controlled expansion of our pig and poultry enterprises. Our home economic extension programme is now served by a network of instructors and field workers throughout the country. Their task is to show the people how best to exploit the results of harder work. They will also show how to improve family diets through such products as vegetables, milk and poultry. And I cannot urge more strongly the importance of keeping back enough of the produce of the farm to improve the living standards of the family.

The Government's settlement programme will continue next year. More and more emphasis will be placed on agricultural development, to build up the ordered flow of high-quality produce from all these schemes.

There continues to be in Kenya an ever-growing demand for land consolidation. This is widely regarded as the fundamental basis of modern agricultural development. I shall tell honourable Members now that the Government has set a target period to complete this work, in respect of land considered suitable for registration.

It will be of the greatest importance to pursue all pending developments in the context of a proper land-use policy. The Government has a fundamental duty to conserve our natural resources in land and water reserves and protective vegetation, so as to ensure that a rapidly growing population in our country can do more than just survive. Our children will expect as a heritage far more from us than the heritage with which we began. And we have a further duty, in our economic planning, to adjust where necessary all inherited ideas, and so bring into use scientifically and fruitfully all the resources and capacities of Africa.

Speakers and honourable Members, I commend the programme of my Government to the National Assembly and to the country. Much will now depend on the vitality and character of our people, in whom I have much faith. Let us all now devote ourselves to our tasks and to our challenges, in the spirit of Harambee.

UHURU/JAMHURI DAY — 1965

Mzee Jomo Kenyatta delivered a special broadcast Address to the Nation for December 12, 1965, two years after his appearance in the Independence Arena, and exactly one year after Republican status was attained. On this occasion, the President elected to combine some encouragement — "real progress is visible" — with the statesmanship of realism:

*

Tomorrow will mark the second anniversary of our *Uhuru*. The two years that now lie behind us were our own years, lived as free men. We have travelled far, on a road of our own choosing. As we celebrate this occasion with joy, let us remember all those of our countrymen and friends by whose sacrifices freedom was won. Let us dedicate ourselves anew to the cause of freedom and nation building. Let us tell ourselves and our children, with words and songs, the significance of this occasion. But whatever we do, let us do it without bitterness of the past but with happiness and maturity of a free and proud nation.

Our Republic is stronger today than ever before. We are united under one Kanu Party; the numbers and units of our Armed Forces have increased and their fire power improved; the economy continues to expand despite the drought, and we have built a Civil Service composed mainly of our own people.

What matters most in a country like Kenya is the positive commitment of all the people to progress. *Uhuru* released the energy that for so many years was frustrated. As Kenyans we now know who we are, and what we stand for, and along what path of human progress we are determined to move. I therefore welcome all those persons who demonstrated faith in our future and have registered as Kenya citizens.

As I said on *Madaraka* Day two and half years ago, progress will not fall to this country like manna from Heaven. Since then, I have been greatly heartened and encouraged by the response to the call of *Harambee*. All over the country *Harambee* projects have sprung up through the people's own initiative. The spirit

shown by those 25,000 landless families who have been settled on
a million acres of farming land has given me much pride. So also
has the response for voluntary famine relief contributions, which
now amount to about £90,000. With this money, and the expected
good crops of this season, we now hope to overcome the famine
challenge. I wish to take this opportunity to express my thanks
most sincerely to the people who have generously contributed
to this worthy cause.

I say to you today that Kenya's real progress is visible. All my
long experience of public life, and of travels to many countries,
has taught me that real progress is not just a matter of figures.
It lies in the spirit of the people, and there are many signs. As
I travel to all parts of the Republic, I see more and more of our
ordinary men and women looking fresh and vigorous and modern.
Athletes like Kipchoge have put Kenya on the map. As one person
expressed it, "Our people look straight, not downwards as in the
colonial times." Increasingly now, we feel the benefit of self-
respect and pride in ourselves as human beings.

So important is this kind of progress that nothing must stand
in its way. And to this end, I am most encouraged to see that
crime in the Republic has gone down. Countrymen, we struggled
for *Uhuru* in order to build a society in which each one of us can
feel free and secure. Those responsible for criminal acts should no
longer feel that they have friends among us.

At the State Opening of Parliament last month, I outlined to
the country the range of policies and programmes within which
we shall now advance. Our revised Development Plan will provide
the full detail of our objectives and will bring out fresh concepts
of practical development. But until we have secured universal
literacy in our Republic, there remains the problem of conveying
the content of all these speeches and documents to all our people.

Those of us who can read and write appreciate how enjoyment of
life is extended by quiet reading in one's home. Indeed, an illiterate
man cannot be truly free; he is a slave to other people's thought
and understanding. I therefore attach great importance to the
literacy campaign.

The Government accepts its own duty. But in this field we
come back yet again to personal initiative. I tell you today that,
between these annual celebrations, our joy and pride in our
country will be enhanced by the number of our fellow men who
have acquired the light of reading and writing.

The Republic in these past two years has created its character
by building on the dynamic force of nationalism. We have ad-

vanced on the sure foundations of a sense of unity and a single purpose.

In this advance, the Republic very much depends on the labour and initiative of countless men and women, some of whose names are not known to the public. I have in mind, for instance, the headmaster who, year in and year out, has continued to improve the organization of his school; the chairman of a co-operative who has continued to serve his members; the doctors, nurses, policemen and soldiers who remain on duty long after most of us have gone to bed. I should like to pay real tribute to these people.

But in the early days of nation building, there are always some people who remain slaves of the past. There are those who still occupy their little worlds of doubt. There are those who find some comfort in the spreading of suspicion. There are those who cannot rise above envy and continue to speak as if *Uhuru* meant the abolition of work and demolition of other people's property. There are those who cling to the barren past of tribalism and instead of leading people to new areas of progress, continue to speak as if other people are the authors of their misfortunes. I am happy to say that already these negative minds are disappearing. These people are being by-passed by the national stream of progress and of thought.

The truth is simple. For the man today who wants to travel or to move his produce, new roads are there. For a man who wants a farm, there is the settlement programme. For the family seeking education, there are new schools and training facilities. For the producer needing loans, there is machinery for this. For people in sickness, there are new hospitals and health services. For the man who needs justice, there is our own Parliament and a law of the people. For those seeking outlets for skills, there are new factories and enterprises.

On so many of these anniversaries, or occasions which call for ceremony throughout the year, a great contribution is made by the men of the armed forces and the police. I wish to pay tribute today to the manner in which all security forces carry out their duties on State and other social occasions, and in the sphere of many nation-building activities. Many dangers and difficulties have been surmounted by these men, within and beyond the North-Eastern Province of Kenya.

You will expect me to say just a word about Rhodesia. As you know, the three East African Governments, together with the Government of Zambia, have together decided on measures that should be taken in the circumstances. Work to implement all the agreed measures is now continuing. My Government is prepared, with the approval of Parliament, to support Zambia to maintain her territorial integrity. The position of Kenya is to give full support to our brothers in Rhodesia, to secure their just rights and to become fully independent of all foreign domination. We will adhere to O.A.U. and United Nations resolutions on Rhodesia.

It is fitting that on this anniversary, our National Social Security Fund should be launched. Starting within Government and other large employers of labour, this scheme will expand to cover 15,000 employers and 400,000 men and women in employment.

In accordance with the Kanu Manifesto and the principles of our African Socialism, this social security programme will have as its main objective the provision of benefits for old age. It will also bring increased security for workers or their families in the event of sickness or death.

Nation building must not only meet the problems of today, but also look towards the future. I am happy to reflect that so many of those who have done so much to make Kenya's future possible may henceforth contemplate an age of retirement free from anxiety and want.

And now let us move together into our third year, with all its tasks and aspirations, strong in our *Harambee* spirit and committed to nation building.

THE PARTY DYNAMIC — 1966

An important KANU Delegates' Conference was held at Limuru on March 13, 1966, to hold new elections for principal office-bearers and to thrash out new formulae for the dynamic and the functioning of the Party. In his Presidential Address to the Conference, Mzee Kenyatta — quite typically — made no attempt to pretend that the mechanics of the Party at all levels, or the relationships between KANU and the Government or Parliament, were always satisfactory. But through a keynote speech — and by his very presence — he sowed the seeds of measures calculated to strengthen and revitalise the Party:

*

In multi-party states the machinery of political parties is largely concerned with defeating opponents at the polls. To this end they are organized throughout the country to keep the headquarters informed of the pulse of the electorate, and to advise what policies and personalities are likely to win votes from the opponents. Between elections there tends to be a lull in party activities throughout the country.

In a one-party state it is necessary to find a completely different role for the party and its machinery. Such a role has not been clearly defined yet for the party since the *de facto* emergence of a one-party state in Kenya. Possibly partly for this reason the party machinery both at the centre and at the branch level has been weakened, discipline from the centre is poor and the mutual exchange of information on policies and reactions between the centre and the branches is inadequate.

The situation has led to much confusion and frustration which if allowed to continue could seriously damage the image of the party and the Government in the country. In seeking a role for themselves, for example, elected politicians have pressed to take over the executive control of civil servants in districts. Because of the absence of a forum within the party there have been embarrassing attacks in Parliament on individual Ministers, and on Government policies.

The situation is likely to continue until—

(a) the party organization is strengthened at the centre and in the branches by the appointment of full-time officials chosen as much for their organizing ability and administrative competence as for their political strength and reliability; and

(b) the role of the party in the national endeavour is clearly defined in a new constitution, and efficient administrative machinery is established for its operation.

I make these points because I believe that the unsatisfactory relationship which is in danger of developing between the party and the various organs of the Government is due largely to the failure to define the role of the party on the emergence of a one-party State. This state of affairs is avoidable and is not due to inherent flaws in the Constitution of the Republic.

It is not my function to suggest what the Constitution of KANU should be, but since good relations between KANU and the Government depend on an efficient party organization which speaks with one voice throughout the country, I venture to make the following tentative suggestions for administrative reorganization:-

(a) The Central Executive should be established and served by the full-time officials of high calibre who are given status and pay commensurate with their qualifications and experience and comparable with what they would enjoy in Government or commercial employment.

(b) Serious consideration should be given to making Branch Secretaries full-time employees *appointed and paid from Headquarters.* This might contribute towards getting Central Executive control of the district units of the party. It would also enable civil servants in the districts to be sure whom to liaise and co-operate with without getting involved in factional wrangles and disputes.

There needs to be a clear distinction between the executive and decision-making functions of the Cabinet and the Ministers and the role of the Central Executive as a political body formulating the broad framework of policy objectives within which the

Government might work. If the executive is strengthened by appointment of competent full-time staff, these people could carry out basic research and investigation necessary for them to prepare memoranda on broad political policy for the Central Executive to consider. In this way the party might be able to pronounce on such issues of policy.

In the absence of a well-organized party machinery which is able to inspire and influence the government, the KANU Parliamentary Group has assumed the role of the party watchdog on the Government. A well-organized party should clearly have the role of dealing with matters of general political policy and Members of Parliament themselves should be guided by the general framework of policy laid down by the party, which should be in a position to discipline a Member of Parliament who consistently refuses to toe the party line. The Parliamentary Group would then concern itself exclusively with Parliamentary business and the welfare of Members.

There has been some argument that civil servants should be allowed and encouraged to become active members of KANU. The argument is based on the quite tenable ground that in a one-party State the intellectual expertise of civil servants should properly be made available to help in the formulation of party principles and policies and that closer links between the Civil Service and the party would bring closer understanding of each other and a greater commitment on the part of the Civil Service to the achievement of the party programmes. But there are dangers in this path which should not be ignored. The Government requires the Civil Service to develop the high degree of professionalism which is necessary to cope with the complexities of modern Government. If civil servants were to become active members of the party, there is a danger that in the division of interest between politics and professionalism the efficiency of the Service would suffer. It would be only too easy for the situation to develop where civil servants are promoted and appointed on the ground of political zeal rather than professional competence. This would lead to a rapid run-down of the morale and competence of the Civil Service.

There is also the embarrassment that could easily arise if a civil servant used his official knowledge in the councils of the party to attack or discomfit a Minister. If Ministers are to be able to discharge their responsibilities effectively, it is essential that the processes by which they reach their decisions should remain confidential even from the party. If it were to be otherwise, the party might give the appearance of taking over the functions of the Government.

Lastly, it should be noted that there is a one-party State in Kenya by agreement only. There is nothing in the law of the land to prevent new parties being formed. Should this happen, the need for party neutrality of civil servants would become obvious. But consultations at the level of officials of the party and Government should be developed.

The need to bring a closer understanding between the party and the civil servants is real but it can be met in other ways. Already there are District and Provincial Development Committees on which civil servants and party leaders could sit together. This could, with advantage, be extended in other fields. For example, there might be district public relations committees on which party leaders and civil servants would sit together for briefing on the Government's programmes and policies for the district, to consider the best means of communicating these to the people and to review the impact of these programmes on the image of the Government and the party in the district.

There might also be extended use of the system of Parliamentary Committees for a number of subjects covering the portfolios of Ministers and arrangements made for professional officers of the Ministries to attend meetings of these committees to explain the technicalities of Ministry programmes and to answer questions on progress.

If these arrangements could be pursued, it is suggested that for the present at least, civil servants should not be allowed to become members of the party.

A decision has recently been taken to appoint a commission of inquiry into the Local Government system and opportunity may be taken to prepare ways and means of linking the party machinery with Local Government machinery. It is at that level that much co-operation can be achieved to the interest of national development.

"DISSIDENT ACTIVITY" — 1966

On April 26, 1966, Mzee Jomo Kenyatta delivered a special broadcast address to the Nation, which came to be known as the Presidential "speech on dissident activity". This followed the breakaway from KANU of a handful of Elected Members — some senior, some junior — and announcement of the formation of the Kenya Peoples' Union. The President placed the whole matter in perspective, in these words:

*

For nearly half a century my life and work in politics has sprung from my faith in the vitality and character of Kenya's people.

I have not felt it necessary, over these past two weeks, to make any personal appeals for stability and calm. I was certain that the understanding and maturity of the people would preserve the living truth of our national unity, and that no threat to public order would occur. My confidence has been fully justified.

I believe you would wish to hear my views on recent events. These happenings must be seen in their perspective. They have never constituted any crisis. I express these views, therefore, not in response to any challenge. This would be too strong a word for describing the political significance of recent movements. I shall merely advance certain comments on ill-considered activities and statements, which many of those responsible may already have come to regret. Sometimes in public life there is a change of outlook, when the heat of ill-advised passion is reviewed in the cold light of day.

Public attention has become distracted by a small number of dissident members of our society. In a kind of emotional spasm, these men have suddenly abandoned their past loyalty to Kenya nationalism. They have also denounced the nation-building policies which, within the Government or as Members of Parliament, they formerly supported or helped to design. All this is clearly on record. It is not a matter for denial or debate. Members of the dissident group have thereby flouted the whole institution of our

Parliament, and have placed self-interest above their duty to the nation and the people.

This is all that has occurred. There are no high moral principles involved. The situation is, of course, regrettable. It is a grave matter at these individual levels. Apart from any question of conscience, the men concerned cannot for too long avoid facing their constituents. And they will know that they have earned the condemnation of our country.

Seldom is there any completely strange element in human behaviour. In this instance, no new factor has been introduced by the immature action of a few frustrated individuals. Their motives were ordinary enough. In some cases, these men had become disappointed in their personal ambitions, or unable to meet their external commitments. They saw no profit for themselves, or for the causes they served, in progress and stability. Some others, among the younger men, were the pitiful victims of flattery allied to purchase.

The older men in this dissident group, in their bitter vanity, and the younger men in their tiny arrogance, have isolated themselves from the national stream of political and social advance. This is a time demanding patience and mature judgement. After so many national foundations have been laid, new structures are now rapidly taking shape. The dissidents have emphasized at this time, in word and deed, the futility of breakaways and wrangling. In withdrawing their talents and loyalties from the national effort, they revealed the emptiness of disunity. They have nothing to offer our staunch, hardworking men and women except false and disruptive propaganda.

I want to tell you now that there is no change in the policy of your Government, and no change is contemplated. We are totally committed to national sovereignty, economic progress, and social justice for all. And let me emphasize as well that there has been no lessening of the strength of your Government, through the forces it commands, in support of this determination.

Over these past three years, I have visited so many of you in your districts and your homes. This was mainly to inform you of our nation-building progress and also to discuss local problems and plans. I have been heartened always by the awareness and the zest of people everywhere. I have found a ready understanding of priorities, and a solid recognition of our practical advance.

All our achievements, you know, are not hidden from the people of the Republic. They are there for all to see. But now this dissident group has been claiming that two years of national effort have accomplished nothing. They must evidently assume that the people are blind, or are fools. Obsessed with their own ambitions, they have entirely misjudged the character of Kenya's people. And from the depths of my long experience, I can tell each one of them that this was their greatest mistake.

All of you will know, because it has been happening around you, the detail of the progress we have made and that which is pending. It is not for me to answer futile charges by repeating the review I gave only five months ago, at the State opening of Parliament. But let me just explain some things, especially to the younger and impulsive group, in your name. I address you now as Head of State and as a leader who was elected by the people. Our Republic is the people and not the President.

Universal education, for example, can never be provided until enough schools have been built, until teachers have been trained in sufficient numbers, until administrative machinery has been set up, and until ways have been found to allocate finance. No rational and thinking man would question such facts. Wherever you may live, you will no doubt find that new schools and educational institutions have been established since Independence. At the same time you will see that many more children are today attending school in your own district. The efforts of the past three years have brought the goal of universal education nearer. All of you know that we have taken many important steps in the desired direction.

All the members of the dissident group applauded, or were associated with this work for educational expansion until two weeks ago. It seems remarkable that doubts should so suddenly have arisen in their minds only after suffering defeat at the Limuru Conference.

Agriculture may be taken as one other example. The country is already witnessing major steps in the modernization of agriculture and a huge advance in productivity. Many critical preparations have had to be made. The Government has been concerned with creating the necessary financial, technical and marketing facilities, in support of the 35,000 African families now settled in the former European areas. Then, on a national scale, we have launched schemes permitting registration of titles, and increased mechanization and widespread access to fertilizers. We have given more assistance to the former African areas instead of spending all our resources in the former European areas. We have also taken steps to expand and improve on the marketing facilities. The Government has made large injections of loan capital for production and development, upheld by training and extension services to cover the new fields of science and engineering and commerce.

Evolution in farming is not a matter of a day, or a season. You know that when you plant your seeds you have to weed before you harvest the crop. You have to continue to do this year in and year out before you can claim to be a good or successful or wealthy farmer. This applies equally to national economic plans. But I am able to report to you that our African farmers are already making an impact on the economy of our country, and we are poised now on the brink of a modern agricultural industry, holding out the kind of dignity and reward that will make this attractive as a calling to the coming generation. Our farming is meeting the challenge of technology.

Much of our future prosperity will depend on new strides being made with industrialization, and development of tourism. But a healthy and contented agriculture will represent the backbone of our economic strength and national stability. With so much preparation made now for rural contentment, it is difficult to find noble motives in manufactured outcries and complaints.

This is the time for accelerated nation-building, through the unity of Government and people. And we need to build a modern nation, as the living monument of forward-looking men. What purpose could there be in sweeping the country backwards now into the barren past of power struggles and political intrigue? What progress could there be if men again took to the forest and every family must live in fear? I know that the people have put all this behind them. Only puny and misguided men sneer at years of sacrifice and sow the seeds again of hatred and of strife.

I have warned the country, in the past, about external or underground threats to our national integrity. We have kept up our vigilance in the spirit of creative non-alignment. The Republic today is in no sense in peril. But let me give one warning to those few whose loyalty to Kenya nationalism has proved to be so shallow. I and my Government will never allow real peril to arise, or risk betrayal of the people's trust. We will take such steps as may be needed to prevent the calculated subversion of Kenya to colonialism in any guise, or any subtle and implacable kind. We did not struggle for so long, and at such cost, to see our national dignity defiled again under the ruthless yoke of some foreign ideology.

At present, as I told you earlier, there is no call for alarm. The countrywide reaction to the breakaway of largely minor dissidents has been negative, hardly stronger than indifference. Their following is negligible. Their power is nil.

For many years now the National front in our struggle for the dignity of nationhood and social progress has been our party, KANU. The party now is stronger than it was, relieved of elements of disaffection that formerly sought to undermine it from within. We secured our independence as KANU. We became a Republic as KANU. Our new Parliament drew its mandate from the people as KANU. The party is our platform and the root source of our strength.

When a Member of Parliament is elected he is given a mandate by the people to speak for them. Already many voters have appealed to me saying they did not support the action of their Representative when he resigned. Is it right that voters in any area should be represented by someone they no longer have confidence in? When the majority of the Members of Parliament pass a vote of no confidence in the Government, the Government is forced to resign or Parliament dissolved so that a new Government may be established. In other words the Government must at all times show that it has the confidence of the representatives of the people in Parliament. But what about the Members themselves? Must the people be left at the mercy of irresponsible and reckless Members? This would not be a democracy any longer. It would no longer be a Government of the people, by the people, and for the people, if Members were free to change parties and policies as they would change jackets.

The members of the dissident group claim that they have the support of the voters. We must now ask them to give the voters the chance to express their will. They must go back to the voters and state their case against KANU and my Government. This is fair and democratic.

For these reasons the Government has accepted the resolution of the Parliamentary Group and decided to convene Parliament at once to pass a law that requires all the Members who have resigned from KANU to seek a fresh mandate from the voters. If any of them is returned he will then be able to take his seat as a Member of the Opposition. Thus the people will now have a chance to express their will in a democratic sense and we shall avoid confusion.

I tell you all now that our progress will continue to be rooted in the supremacy of Parliament and the rule of law. The machinery and purpose of Government is something that I myself hold in trust for the people. This trust will only be relinquished when, in a General Election, we shall go back to the people. Until then, my pledge to you all is that my Government will faithfully implement the programme outlined in the KANU Manifesto of 1963. We shall adhere to the lawful provisions of our Republican Constitution, as ratified by the people. We shall base national policies and practices on the approved principles of our African Socialism. And we shall work to achieve the economic objectives of our National Development Plan.

All this is our task and our duty. These are the things that I and my Government have been empowered by the people to do. We will never be diverted from this task by demands from any group that your Government should abandon democracy and betray the people's will. Whether or not all members of the dissident group understand what they have done, this is precisely what was implied by the manner of their betrayal and the explanation for it.

Make no mistake, this has not been the orderly formation of a valid opposition party. There has been no cleavage based on an honourable division in terms of high political principle. Here we have met an endeavour which hoped to make such impact as to destroy national stability and deprive the people of their constitutional rights. It has failed, as all such endeavours will fail. I and my Government will continue to defend these rights in accord with our oath and our duty.

And now let the weak voices of these little men be drowned, in the volume of faith we express in our national motto, *Harambee*.

MADARAKA DAY — 1966

President Kenyatta has sought to commemorate the anniversary of internal self-government — the first instalment of national dignity and consciousness in Kenya — by means of some address to the Nation of significant and suitable weight. On this occasion, June 1, 1966, he dwelt on the strength of national integrity, and the purpose of progress, which were now beyond dispute or meaningful challenge:

*

For all of us in the Republic of Kenya, this is a very happy day. Our minds go back to the moment, three years ago, when Kenya became a self-governing country. On that day I took an oath of office as our country's first Prime Minister. By this act, I promised you all to uphold and defend the national integrity of Kenya with all my strength. I also promised that security of life and property, within our new nation, would be maintained. We have moved since then through important changes. But all the promises I made to you in 1963 are today in the forefront of my mind. We have a nation now in which our people can move in safety. No one is condemned to live in fear. There is no discrimination or privilege; and the strong may not oppress the weak. Men may travel widely to conduct their business, or be separated from their families and homes, and still have peace of mind.

These are the principal elements of national dignity and human respect. They make up the sense of brotherhood which lies at the root of our African Socialism. As the first outcome of Madaraka and Uhuru, we have created equality between men. Men who were in the past poor in body and spirit are marching forward into the forefront of progress and leadership.

Today we remember the take-over of the civil and armed services. Within these ranks my Government has since Madaraka Day, 1963, created the Kenya Air Force and the Kenya Navy. I have been very proud, over these past three years, to watch the growing strength of the Armed Forces and the Police. I wish to pay tribute to all our Security Forces for their loyalty to my Government; and their sense of duty to our nation. The Army and the Police are vastly more mature and competent than on the first Madaraka Day. The morale of these forces is high.

Another tribute today is equally due to the Civil Service, as the executive arm of the Government. I have been heartened and upheld, in my own tasks, by the loyal and able manner in which the Public Service has striven to implement Government policy in every field.

You should all realize that behind these civil and security services must lie considerable organization. It takes a great deal of thought and executive control to man and to operate these elements of Government. But now we have built up both civil and military services, whose directives and operations are entirely in tune with our needs.

All our servicemen, and all our officials, must seek constantly to improve themselves. They must strive to expand their knowledge, to perfect their skills, to equip themselves with new wisdom and human discretion. I have recently formed a new Government, making many new appointments to carry Kenya through a more rapid development phase. As the President of the Republic, I have striven to create the most effective machinery of Government and I expect my Ministers to carry their responsibility. There is no room in my Government for Ministers who see themselves as V.I.P.s, aloof from their fellow men. They must produce results and devote the whole of their experience to the service of the people.

There are some individuals who claim that I should give everything free to the people. This kind of slogan is a cowardly way of trying to win popularity.

Whether in Kiambu or Kakamega, in Kilifi or Kisumu, in Kapsabet or Kirinyaga — all things belong to someone. I have seen farms and *shambas* belonging to somebody, and worked by that man or that family. I have seen trees and crops and cattle, all of which belong to someone. I have seen *dukas* and business premises, and lorries and buses, and workshops and houses, all of which are somebody's property. I ask you, my friends, where are all these free things that can be given away?

Those who speak about getting everything for nothing must mean that I should call out the Army and the Police, to seize by force a lot of land or buildings or livestock or equipment which belongs to some of you. They must mean that I should confiscate the property of one man, just to give it to somebody else. This would mean utter chaos, total injustice, and would lead to the destruction of the State. We believe we must safeguard the personal and property rights of all our people as a vital element of our hard-won freedom. In practice as well, what security or pride could a man feel in being given something free? He would always have to fear that, at the whim of some new master, this would again be taken from him and be given to somebody else.

Even with our massive land reform and resettlement programmes, it was neither ethical nor practical to give free land. To do this, we would have had to be a Government of rascals, providing opportunity for one man by stealing first from another man or group. In fact, since Madaraka, we have settled 170,000 of our people in former European holdings; and we have given them all a new future in ways that involve obligations within their means, so that development is linked with security and self respect.

Nation-building comprises the ability of a country and its people to sustain their independence and national integrity. In our case, it is a matter of keeping faith, with Kenya nationalism and its social commitment through which independence was won.

A year or more ago, we did not have the national strength that we command today. But since then we have laid many needed foundations. Through this Government the African controls and directs land use, commerce and industry, power and communications, finance and employment. If we weaken the Government, we weaken the only major force for African advancement.

This force is expressed through the Government's increasing command of the economy. We have first the widespread activities of the Agricultural Development and Agricultural Finance Corporations. This year will see the setting up or expansion of many projects aided by the Industrial and Commercial Development Corporation, whose work includes design of new industrial estates. There is the Kenya National Trading Corporation, and Parliament recently approved the Act to establish the Tourist Development Corporation. All these are new undertakings; and the Government has of course retained primary interests in the Posts and Telecommunications, the Railways and Harbours and East African Airways.

I should like to mention some further aspects of our intentions. It was made clear when I launched the Seven Forks Hydro-Electric Scheme that the Government will continue to extend its control over the generation and distribution of electric power. This will be done not only to promote economic growth but also to serve administrative centres and amenity schemes, based on the belief that electric power is nowadays a social necessity. And with the co-operation of the people in the various localities, there will be substantial schemes to improve rural water supplies. We intend to put an end to the days when women walked miles to fetch water.

In the principal cities and towns of the Republic, the Government will assume a major interest in the public transport systems. In the financial year which begins in July, a new construction company will be set up to organize African building contractors, and assist them with such matters as tendering, site organization and quantity surveying. The whole Africanization of commerce will be pursued through a number of programmes. We are already engaged in discussions on this matter with major firms and various organizations in industry. At the same time, we are urging businessmen to be more aggressive in their approach to selling in external markets.

The Government has decided that the Worker's Investment Trust must now be urgently established. This will increase the workers' share in the country's developing economy. It will also help to speed up housing schemes and will ensure better retirement benefits for those who participate. A consultant will shortly be engaged to advise the Government on structure and techniques.

For the farmers, we shall be setting up a new statutory board responsible for additional artificial insemination services. I can tell farmers that, as from 1st July, basic fees will be reduced to Sh. 5 in respect of grade cows, and Sh. 2/50 for indigenous cattle. This year as well, there will be at least a modest beginning to an ambitious mechanization programme in support of agriculture. Two units of twenty-five tractors each will be operated by the Government, for field cultivation and for training purposes. And money will be made available through the Agricultural Finance Corporation to enable African farmers to buy tractors under hire-purchase schemes.

Furthermore, I am glad to announce today that work will shortly begin on the Kano Irrigation Scheme. After crops have been harvested next month, the first step will be the opening up of a two thousand-acre pilot project at Ahero.

Following my announcement of free medical services for children and adult out-patients, steps have been taken to reduce delays in treatment by expanding equipment and hospital facilities throughout the country. Training for more doctors and auxiliary staff has also been accelerated. Last week the Government intro-

duced in Parliament yet another major step in the direction of
free medical services; I refer to the Bill to set up the National
Health Scheme. Under this scheme we will at once be able to
introduce a large measure of free hospitalization for most of our
people. Those with higher incomes will in the spirit of African
Socialism contribute towards subsidization of services for the
lower income groups.

I am aware of the great interest our people have in education.
It took the British seventy years to build 141 secondary schools
in Kenya. In the three years since we came to power the number
of secondary schools has increased by 195, making a total of 336.
Such expansion will continue each year. In general, the number
of children in schools has increased from 817,000 in 1963 to
1,027,000 in 1965. In some districts, the attendance is now nearing
90 per cent. The Government will publish a full sessional paper
on education in the next few weeks in which we shall show the
progress being made towards our declared goal of free primary
education.

As far as housing is concerned, the Ministry and the Central
Housing Board will finance the building of more than 1,000 new
houses during the next year. It is intended to start work on the
slum clearance of Pumwani within this year. The City Council
of Nairobi also expects to commence a separate large-scale
housing scheme within the next twelve months.

I have introduced such detail to counter the absurd lie that
the Government has been doing nothing for the people. We know
the problems and the needs. Through all our statutory corporations and active programmes and practical measures, the Government has been working and planning to satisfy all needs in a
co-ordinated way.

Every country in the world, from the oldest to the newest,
knows at least some shortcomings or social injustice. The developing countries in particular are always afflicted by critical social
shortages, in fields of food and employment and education. There
is nothing unusual or unfair in the fact that we in Kenya have
had to meet this challenge.

But the country is geared now for rapid advance, sponsored first
by the modernization of African agriculture. This immediate key
to our progress will be pursued alongside plans for industrial
development and for promotion of the tourist industry. Through
all these forms of economic advance, we shall be able to afford
more liberal social services in fields of education, housing and
health. This is the only road to stable progress. And I will not

insult your intelligence, as the K.P.U. set out to do, by promising to provide you tomorrow with imaginary things that are not available or that cannot be financed.

My friends, three years since Madaraka Day are only a moment of time. Ten years ago we did not even have a single African Elected Member in the Legislative Council. Many of you can remember, twenty years ago, when I returned from Europe to find that the only African political organization had been proscribed. Just one or two of my old friends among you can look back with me to the hopelessness of forty years ago, when we were opposing the forced labour system, and the Crown Lands Ordinance, and seeking education and other basic human rights. Less than five years have elapsed since I returned home to Gatundu from prison and detention. The three years since Madaraka Day is such a little time. But in this time we have built well, ready now to move with confidence and pride into our future.

There are some persons who suggest that our African Socialism is of no account. They would have Kenya surrender to external interests, and put what they call "Scientific Socialism" in its place. Such people are traitors to the cause of Kenya nationalism. And as they parade themselves in all their vanities, let it be remembered that their leaders were purchased with money. These leaders then bought lesser men with lesser sums of money. All the members of this sorry group have simply been bribed, to try and betray our people into the salary of a new colonialism, more grasping and implacable than anything from which we fought free.

Throughout our struggle for Independence one of our greatest obstacles was tribalism, which was played upon by the colonial régime. Right up to the time of Independence there were parties such as KADU and APP which based themselves upon tribalism. These parties merged with KANU in the national interest. Yet now we are witnessing the fostering of disruptive and negative tribalism in a new party.

Every man has the right to take a pride and interest in his tribe — its history, its culture and its customs. We see a healthy expression of positive tribal feeling in football teams, social clubs and welfare societies.

But what we will not permit is the exploitation of tribalism for political ends. Those who try to whip up tribal feelings for political advantage are doing a great disservice to themselves, to their fellows and to the Kenya nation. My Government has allowed tribal social organizations to continue, but some of these have allowed themselves to be used for political purposes. If any society or its

officials engage henceforth in political activities or actions calculated to incite tribal politics, its registration will be cancelled.

The Government has decided to register the KPU but this
decision does not give its leaders licence for subversion or lawlessness. On the contrary, the registration will remain in force only
so long as they are law abiding. Let no man think that he is too
big to be dealt with firmly. We shall never hesitate to take
appropriate measures to ensure the security of the State.

Apart from this, revealing statements have been made already
in the election campaign. After promising free land and education
and jobs for all, dissident spokesmen admitted that they had no
plans for the financial and taxation arrangements that could
support these fairyland policies. They were careful not to say that
their theories could only be based on plans for raising taxes to
impossible levels, and introducing the hated system of communal
labour.

I do not believe that our nation can be built with the bulk of
our people in prison, for failing to pay some impossible taxes.
I am certain that the public would not support the introduction
of compulsory labour. It goes against all our instincts and
traditions to have people herded like cattle into a forced labour
system which we fought so hard to abolish in colonial times.

My Government rejects this whole approach to living. It would
mean misery and oppression for our people. And so long as I
remain your Head of State, no such dreadful system will be
introduced in Kenya.

During last year's Madaraka Day, I warned against external
influences and affirmed our stand on positive non-alignment. Some
nations do not seem to have understood our determination
to manage our own affairs. In these past few months we
have seen positive signs of neo-colonialism when those nations
who tried to flatter us at first resorted to abuse and insult against
our Party and Government. Through their Press and Radio these
nations have supported some individuals who have been rejected
by the people of Kenya. We fought for *Uhuru* so that our people
may be free to have a Government of their own choice. We refuse
to exchange one form of colonialism for a new one. I am sure you
are all with me in this struggle to keep Kenya free.

I wish now to say a word about Rhodesia. Over these recent
months, I have been constantly in touch with the British Government, to exert all possible pressures. I have also worked in
co-operation with other Heads of State representing O.A.U.

member countries, and earlier instructed our Ambassador at the United Nations to press for mandatory sanctions. We will continue to offer all possible assistance to the Republic of Zambia.

It would be wrong to pretend that we in Africa are not bitterly disappointed at the way this rebellion has been allowed to linger on. The responsibility is entirely that of the British Government. There must now be decisive action, in terms of practical politics, and certainly in defence of the moral principles and human dignity that Britain always seeks in argument to pursue and uphold. In our view, no solution can be found in furtive discussions at junior level between the colonial power and delegates of an unlawful régime. Clearly, the African nationalist leaders in Rhodesia must share in the task of negotiating a final settlement. If necessary, this must be brought about by means of compulsion and force. I know that the great majority of my colleagues in the Commonwealth agree very strongly with my view, that the present situation in Rhodesia reduces the whole idea of the Commonwealth to a hollow mockery.

Finally, let me say this. Kenya can be proud of the progress so far made, and of the prospect held out in our unfolding plans. The Republic enjoys national stability and high international standing. The three years that have passed have captured the spirit and drawn up the blueprint of nationhood. The future will call for unremitting energy from all of you. But we can be confident now that fulfilment and contentment lie ahead.

PROGRESS IN NYANZA — 1966

The President at no time distinguished between the various Provinces and Districts of the country: all were part of one nation of Kenya, and he was equally ready to embark on unsparing tours of Ukambani, or Western Kenya, or the Coast. On July 1, 1966, Mzee Kenyatta found a farmer's pleasure — while not forgetting undertones of political advice — in opening an Agricultural Show for the Province of Nyanza:

*

It gives me great pleasure to perform the opening ceremony of this Nyanza Agricultural Show. This Province of the Republic is blessed with suitable conditions for the production of a wide variety of crops, ranging from tea and coffee in the cool Kisii highlands to sugar and cotton, maize, groundnuts and rice, in many parts of Central and South Nyanza.

This Show is a reflection of what surrounding districts can achieve, and of what many individual farmers can do. As you know, for the fulfilment of our development plan, my Government has attached great importance to intensive and efficient agriculture in all high potential areas of Kenya.

Yesterday, I was very glad to launch a pilot project at Ahero for the Kano Plains irrigation scheme. There is already a team, with a project Manager, working in the Yala Swamp area. Altogether in this Province, over a hundred thousand acres of land are available for development by irrigation. And Nyanza has the greatest sugar potential of any part of our Republic.

I mention all these facts in order to underline one very vital point. When the KANU manifesto was published over three years ago, it was made quite clear that our country's future would depend on the hard work of every one of us. In this Province as in others, there is land that can be made fruitful, in terms of crops that flourish and livestock that yield well and multiply. It is up to the farmer to pay heed to the modern scientific advice made available through our extension services. And above all, the farmer must devote all his time and effort to the task of raising productivity.

It is a part of the Government's task to create opportunities for the initiative and success of each producer and farming family. In respect of this Province, I have already mentioned the Government's active concern with large-scale irrigation projects. Planned development of a greatly expanded sugar industry will be supported by considerable investment also in a suitable road network. Food crops such as maize and groundnuts, beans and pulses, will be further developed as part of a smallholder credit programme. Farmers in Nyanza have already been assisted this year, in a campaign to boost maize production, by means of loans, and access to fertilisers, and supplies of seed of hybrid and synthetic maize varieties.

Over the past two seasons in Nyanza, cotton societies have received special loans for cultivation and pest control. Plans for the speeding up of land consolidation and registration will be followed by a new credit scheme to enable better farmers to develop and improve their holdings.

On the livestock side, the Government intends to increase dairy production by encouraging farmers in suitable areas to keep grade cattle. An expanded artificial insemination service, as a major factor in dairy development, will be available to all districts in the Province. Producers should realise that farming is as much of a business as shopkeeping. The raising of native cattle which produce so little milk and meat is today uneconomic, and farmers should dispose of such cattle in favour of grade stock.

Funds are being sought for Tsetse eradication in parts of South and Central Nyanza, so that more land can be made available for production of livestock and crops.

At this point, I must draw your attention to two serious matters. In respect of many cotton co-operative societies, I am informed that the loan repayment position has been poor. This has been disappointing, and has created many difficulties for the Government in its effort to help farmers. The Societies concerned must ensure repayment of their oustanding loans before any further funds can be made available to them. Anybody who expects that a loan advanced by the Government can suddenly become a free gift had better think again. The Government will not hesitate in future to use legal methods to recover these loans.

The second matter arousing concern is that of coffee quality. The quality of coffee has gone down in recent years to a very serious degree. An investigation is being carried out, and firm measures will be taken to rectify this situation. Such measures may seem to hurt a few people, but they will be designed for the benefit of all coffee producers. In the meantime, coffee farmers in Nyanza are urged to listen to advice from extension staff, and to carry out all recommendations.

To assist in overhauling the coffee industry, finance will be made available as loans to coffee growers' co-operative societies. This will permit expansion or new construction of factories, to ensure quality processing of the crop. The extension services will also be intensified, to improve the quality of coffee in cherry and parchment form.

These are all vital matters, affecting the daily livelihood and future prospect of all our families who live on and by the land. I tell you all now that representation in Nairobi may be a question arousing emotions, or can be the subject of intrigue. But what is really important to the people is national unity, a sense of national integrity and purpose, and well-planned economic development undertaken in the true spirit of Harambee. We are one country, and the soil is enduring. The Republic is the people. And it is the future of all the people that my Government still holds in trust.

There is no room in our Republic for idlers. We cannot give any sympathy or encouragement to laziness, or to men who think the country should somehow give them everything while they give nothing in return. We live in a harsh economic world. By the full development of our own human and natural resources, we may through our own efforts banish the miseries of the past and move into a new future of social justice. But this requires from every citizen dedication to Kenya, understanding of the Government's policies and programmes, and personal efforts which in total become national well-being.

And now I wish to congratulate all those who have been concerned with arrangements for this most commendable Show, and I have pleasure in declaring the Nyanza Agricultural Show of 1966 officially open.

THE CENTRAL BANK — 1966

Mzee Jomo Kenyatta presided at the opening of the Central Bank of Kenya on September 14, 1966. The ceremony marked a significant stage in what — on another Presidential occasion — was described as the financial independence of the Republic:

*

This ceremony which we are now attending marks an important milestone in Kenya's history. From now onwards, we have money of our own to be issued by our Central Bank, and I am happy to take part in this ceremony.

The chain of events and circumstances which led to the break-up of East African Currency are well known and have been discussed on many occasions. The idea of having a common currency issued by a common Central Bank for three African countries was carefully scrutinised and found considerable favour. However, practical difficulties soon overshadowed the theoretical advantages. It was repeatedly stressed that, in the absence of a centrally directed and unified economic policy carried out on behalf of all three East African countries, a single Central Bank would soon be condemned to inaction or exposed to the danger of the lack of cohesive policies in the monetary field. There was no other way but to proceed with the creation of a separate bank for Kenya.

However, the idea of a common monetary area as a counterpart to the common markets has not been abandoned. Agreement has been reached between the three Central Banks to co-operate in order to make payments between the East African countries as smooth as they have been so far, and ensure an easy method of exchange should banknotes of one country have found their way, in the course of business, to another one. It is also contemplated that periodical meetings of the Governors of the three Central Banks should be held in order to find out areas of activity in which a common policy of the three banks could be established.

Once the monetary reform has been completed the East African Currency Board will have discharged its responsibility — so well carried out over many years — for providing currency for East Africa, and it will eventually proceed into liquidation. It is my pleasant duty to thank the members of the Currency Board and its staff for their close and loyal co-operation in putting into action the currency reform.

The Central Bank of Kenya is constituted as a part of the National machinery, an institution created and commissioned by law for taking care of all monetary and credit matters. It is responsible for the sound position of the currency and its orderly issue according to legitimate needs. I am sure that the Central Bank, its board, management and staff are aware of their duties in this respect and that they will discharge them with zeal and devotion.

In times back in history the issue of money was for long ages a privilege of the ruler of a country, whoever he was. A ruler was regarded by his subjects, and by history, as a good one when he ensured for his people law, order, justice and good money. Now, Emperors, King and Princes have mostly disappeared into the shadow of the past, but the principle still stands: a Government is good if it offers to the citizens law and justice, order and security, and good money: money that everyone is glad to keep in his pocket, his wallet, or in his savings book without the apprehension that tomorrow it may be worth a little bit less than today. The policy of the Government carried out through the Central Bank of Kenya will certainly be to strive to this end.

However, one thing cannot be forgotten: currency issue and management is a real business, and no magic. The bank cannot make something out of nothing and the Government cannot by order, or "fiat", grant to a printed piece of paper a value independent of the backing which it possesses. Such backing is provided by foreign exchange, into which the Kenya Currency will be convertible at its established par value. I am glad to say that the ratio of the foreign exchange cover is high and will remain so.

But ultimately the value of the currency is determined by something still more real and durable. When we look upon the banknotes which in a short time will officially go into circulation, we see several pictures showing Kenya's natural riches and the people working on them. This is indeed an indication of where the country's economy, and the country's money as well, takes its strength from. It is ultimately the productive work done by the people on which growth and the balance of the national economy depends. With hard and well organized work there should be enough goods to consume, enough goods to be exported in order to maintain the balance of trade and the currency reserves. With everyone contributing to the rise of the real national product, the task of the bank to provide the country with sound money will be possible and easy to achieve.

Having a firm belief that this will be done, I declare the Central Bank of Kenya open.

KENYA YOUTH FESTIVAL — 1966

A major Festival of Youth was staged in Jamhuri Park, Nairobi, on October 16, 1966. On occasions of this kind — as at ceremonial parades of any of the Armed Services — Mzee Kenyatta always felt and managed to impart a particular sense of national pride. Addressing the ranks of young men, and women now, the President said:

*

This great assembly of the united youth of Kenya inspires a warm surge of confidence in the future of our country. In our old communities youth has always fulfilled an important role: as the custodians of our security; and as the carriers of the best traditions. You have the same role today in the larger community of the Republic.

Throughout the long struggle for freedom, the burning faith which sustained me and my brothers was that the youth of this country would be free to give their love, loyalty and readiness for personal sacrifice, to the development and welfare of all our peoples. We should today dedicate and pledge ourselves to the realization of this faith in the life of our country.

Accepting this trust means a life of hard work and even danger, in the development and defence of our country. But youth has never feared either work or danger. There will be pressures and temptations to put personal or tribal interests before the interests of our country. You must resist these temptations. But there will also be reward or excitement, adventure and all the satisfaction of building a great future.

I am satisfied that we have made a good start, though there are those who have not yet met the challenge of moving from tribal to national consciousness. Their eyes have not been opened to the harsh realities of the world. They do not understand that to earn our fair share of the fruits of the modern world we must be strong. To be strong we must be united. To be united we must treat our neighbour as our brother.

All of our people must take part in our forward march. As we progress, my Government aims to reduce the inequalities which exist among our people, whether these derive from past or present circumstances. It is these inequalities of opportunity and of well-being which create the greatest obstacles to our national unity. This means sacrifice by some sections of the community in the interests of others. It is one of the obligations of nationhood and of our traditional African Socialism.

This festival of youth is symbolic of that unity to which my Government is dedicated, and I am glad to pay tribute to the work of the Youth Council of Kenya which made it possible. The dedicated voluntary service of that Council, and of all the groups represented here, is greatly appreciated by my Government.

"Youth with a purpose" is a theme with a stirring challenge. The presence of so many of our youth here today, strong upright and confident, gives comforting evidence that the challenge is accepted.

The Republic of Kenya represents a coming together of our family and should mean an end to the dissensions which have weakened us in the past. It is good to be together; but to be together for a purpose is even better. Our national purpose is to develop the resources of our land so that our nation is strong and quick to defend its rights, and so that all our people may lead a happier life. My Government is planning to ensure that opportunities are available for every citizen of this country to develop and use his talents to the limit of his capabilities.

Not so long ago the majority of young people of this country were regarded as a future source of manual labour; hewers of wood and drawers of water. But now we can feel proud that among you are future leaders, doctors, engineers, lawyers, soldiers, policemen and farmers. It is an exciting prospect and I am confident that you will seize every opportunity in the spirit of service to our nation to advance and improve yourselves.

Not everybody can reach the top of the profession of his choice. But the service of all is equally important in the life and development of our nation. The farmer who improves the productivity of his land may be making a greater contribution to the national progress than a learned scientist. There is work in Kenya for all, but you must go out and seek it. For the great majority of our people the work will be on the land —our greatest national asset. I expect our young people to play a vital part in the development of our agricultural potential. Here is a challenge and a purpose for youth which holds out the attractions of adventure, education and profit. If we are to meet it we must be willing and able to bring new knowledge to supplement our traditional experience in farming. We look to you, the Youth of Kenya, to modernize our agriculture.

The vigour and vitality of a nation depends on its capacity to renew itself in each generation. This great festival holds bright promise of such renewal. I pray that when you return to your homes you will preserve within you the spirit of national unity by which the festival was created. Carry it with you into your daily lives as an essential part of the new thinking in Kenya. Begin each new day with the determination that you will make a personal contribution to the elimination of barriers to understanding and unity among our people, and to further our already great progress. If these are the purposes which youth elects to serve, then my generation can rest content that the national integrity of Kenya which we strive to maintain and protect is secure.

The future is bright with promise and it is in your determination that the greatness and prosperity of Kenya lies.

And now my friends, from the roots of the past and looking to your boundless future, I salute you.

UNIVERSITY CONGREGATION — 1966

Speaking in his formal capacity as Visitor, President Kenyatta attended a Congregation at the University College in Nairobi on October 19, 1966. He was concerned with inspiring graduates, and all who listened to his words, towards the urgent and unrelenting tasks of nation building in a modern world society:

*

Today it has been my pleasant duty to confer degrees and to present certificates to students who have successfully completed their studies here. These awards recognize a measure of achievement in academic studies. These students who have graduated today are a welcome addition to our high-level manpower.

We expect our educated people to get things done. The degrees and certificates which you have earned should not therefore be regarded as passports to privilege but as contracts of service. Their value depends on the ability of university graduates to demonstrate that they can apply their knowledge to getting things done. The cap and gown which you are wearing today will not automatically open the doors to success in your profession.

In the world of action the competition is already keen and will become more so. The university graduate who thinks that his degree can carry him forward without further effort to improve his knowledge will soon fall behind in the race. I hope and trust there will be few such failures. For it is they who will devalue the degrees and certificates which I have today awarded. In a very real sense the graduates of the university are the trustees of its reputation. It is on their performance in contributing to the development of our country that my Government and the people of Kenya will judge the value of our investment in this institution.

We live in a period of far-reaching social and economic changes. We seek to use our independence to improve the living standards and social security of our people. To achieve this we need to apply the most modern technology to the development of our resources.

We need to adopt the scientific approach in every field of our national endeavour — in farming, in education, in medicine, in industry and in commerce. It is to the universities that we look for the man and for the woman who will lead the nation to the frontiers of knowledge and achievement. To be a leader in any field of activity you must have followers who have confidence in your skills and your judgements.

I know that this college is facing difficulties in finance, accommodation and staffing. But in spite of all this, the student numbers are substantially larger than was originally envisaged, the staff more numerous and the facilities more diverse. I particularly welcome the creation of the Institute for Development Studies, which is working closely with our planning agencies. I welcome too the new Department of Education and look forward to its adequate assistance in our education programmes. Next year a Medical School will be established to add its contribution to our fight against disease.

The magnitude of our problems and the limitation in our financial resources indicate that for some years to come this University College will have to concentrate on our immediate needs. In the light of this role the traditional University patterns and timetables may require replanning, if we are to meet our targets. These are tasks which must be left to the University authorities and we are happy to do so, in the knowledge that there is no conflict between the aims of the University and the needs of the country. The past record of this College justifies our confidence in the ability of the Principal and his staff to meet this challenge.

We are all engaged in the common task of nation building. Let us all therefore pull together in the spirit of Harambee so that the strong, united and prosperous Kenya we all desire will be maintained.

To those who leave the College today, I wish you good luck in your future careers. During your years of study you should have learned to think straight, to work hard and act courageously. Do not forget the College which gave you this teaching. May your service to the Nation enhance its name and provide inspiration for future students.

UHURU/JAMHURI DAY — 1966

In a message to the people on December 12, 1966, the third anniversary of Kenya's full independence — and after two years as a Republic — Mzee Jomo Kenyatta devoted his Presidential theme to an appreciation of all those factors and ingredients which had brought the country to nationhood. He spoke not only as a world statesman, but as a richly endowed observer of the human scene:

*

Three years have passed since the ceremonies which marked the independence of our country and the birth of the Kenya nation. Each time I come to speak on these anniversary occasions, I feel closer to you all. We are bound together by the problems we have overcome, and by the outlook we share, and the future we are jointly building.

We have experienced together the triumph of Uhuru and the deeper satisfaction of Jamhuri. Any determined community can break through the walls of oppression and colonial domination. But unless there is more solid purpose, served by human endurance and effective organization, this by itself cannot lead to mature nationhood. And my message today, delivered with pride and as a tribute to you all, is that Kenya has truly become a nation.

These three years have been enought to show that Kenya has won the battle of consolidation. We can go forward, from today, with greater confidence, for all the attitudes and the achievements that we see around us have given practical meaning to our independence.

I have spent nearly half a century in public life and in the service of the people. During this long time I have come to recognize the symbols of real stability and progress and contentment. Within our Republic we have learnt to become self-reliant. We have adapted ourselves to the workings and needs of modern life. Nevertheless, the traditional spirit on which our culture must be built has endured. During my visit to the countryside, I find a re-awakening of the arts and the expressions of our culture. The people are alive and proud of their heritage.

In the eyes of the world we have also demonstrated that people of many origins can live happily together in an African country. We believe that the majority must govern and that the rights of a minority can only be protected by the majority. That is why we condemn the white minority regimes in Rhodesia, South Africa, Angola and Mozambique and we are determined, together with our friends, to continue to honour our commitment to emancipate the African peoples in these countries.

In these intervening years, working together, we have built a country with identity and character. There has been greater understanding, as well, of the functions and the place of a Government within the nation. Three years ago there was a tendency to look to the Government not only for national leadership, but also for direct solution of every kind of problem and satisfaction of every individual need. Today there is a more mature recognition. The people realize now the primary tasks of the Government as stated in our Manifesto of African Socialism: the Government aims to achieve high incomes, so that all our people are free from want, disease and exploitation. It is our task to ensure political equality, social justice, human dignity and equal opportunity, so that every man and woman can enjoy the fruits of initiative and self-respect.

Here again, wherever I go, I find assurances of nationhood. These can be found in *Harambee* schools, nursery schools, hospitals and in community development projects of every kind. In all walks of life personal and group initiative and a spirit of social responsibility have become dedicated to the task of nation building.

I want to emphasize that the real foundations of our future could only be national integrity and hard work. Now productivity is everywhere increasing as the principal key to our economic progress; but beyond this, we have enormously expanded the facilities for education. In new industries and services there is outlet for talent and ambition. And in every field of duty and responsibility, we see the Africanization of opportunity and effort.

Let me say that Africanization has been one of the greatest elements of our national maturity. The needs of our people have been met in such a way that standards have been maintained and productivity has risen.

You already know that as Commander-in-Chief of the Kenya Armed Forces, I have appointed Brigadier Joseph Musyimi Lele

Ndolo to be the new Commander of the Kenya Army. This is important in respect of our whole approach to defence and to the operations against outlaws and bandits in the North-Eastern Province. There, we are seeking to crush the shifta and to win a moral victory to show that nationalism rooted in social justice can and must triumph over evil and intrigue.

Independence opens many doors to social conscience and human ambition. But modern nations can only sustain independence through planning. Material and human resources have to be measured so that priorities can be determined. Areas or projects earlier neglected must be brought into focus. And whole patterns of social injustice must then be put right. This planning is not easy. It must take account of practical realities. And rejection of the past must be set alongside many world-wide problems. We are ahead of our hopes and our targets in many different fields of our Development Plan. Increasingly now, the plan is being translated to bring all our national capacities into play, and to ensure social advancement for every family. We have always been inspired by this human purpose as stated in our KANU Manifesto.

In my visits round the country I see people living in better homes, with piped water in towns and villages, and people taking advantage of adult literacy programmes. Everyone can think back to even a few years ago when African ownership of motor-cars, radio sets, or sewing machines was rare. Both in urban centres and in rural districts these things are commonplace today.

Of course, just within these three years of creating national identity and making early progress, all our problems have not been resolved. Many of our people continue to live in want. But on the solid foundation of what we have achieved, the future is boundless. I will not reveal details today, but within the next few weeks it will be my task to preside again at the State Opening of Parliament. On that occasion, I will be outlining the Government's full programme for the forthcoming period.

I would like to add one further word about a movement now known as "Back to the Land". This is not just a question of a young man in search of work moving from the town streets. Our land is not only the greatest asset we have, but it has made us what we are.

Through the impact of modern machinery and equipment and scientific techniques, our land offers a challenge to the imagination and skills of young people. Besides a successful rice scheme in Mwea, we are also opening new tracts of land by irrigation on

Tana River in the Coast, Ahero in Nyanza, Bunyala in the Western Province.

I am happy for the warm response which old and young people have given to the call of "Back to the Land". I have been encouraged to learn that the Masai have now realized the value of land cultivation. They have shown increased demand for better breeds of cattle and tractors for development of wheat schemes. "Forward on the Land" is a faith in the whole future of our nation.

Hope and trust, determination and hard work have marked the last three years of our independence. To advance further along. I am asking you to intensify these attitude and efforts in future.

But I know that amongst us there are lazy and disgruntled individuals who regard work as undignified. These persons sit down all 24 hours of the day imagining how the world could be put right by the labour and sweat of others. Some start by begging for tea and free drinks in restaurants and beer-halls and turn into thieves and robbers if these things are denied them. Their wives and family are made beasts of burden and slaves for their leisure and convenience. When placed in positions of authority, they misuse it and invite bribes and corruption by every device. Altogether they are a public nuisance and live like parasites at the expense of the nation.

These kind of men would not have deserved mention if they had not found a handful of salesmen and promoters for their ideas at public meetings and even in Parliament. To carry out their idle designs and personal ambitions, they go about begging money from foreigners. I want to say today that Kenya is built on the solid foundation of Kenya nationalism, by the love and loyalty of its own people, who will never agree to be bought by money or false promises.

Before independence, KANU encouraged contacts with all friendly countries overseas and the Government has forged ahead with the development of brotherly relations with all countries. Through the United Nations, the Organization of African Unity and the Commonwealth, we have made our contribution towards the maintenance of peace and security throughout the world on the basis of respect for sovereign independence of all member States and we are always guided by the principles of non-alignment. All we ask from other nations is to reciprocate the spirit of respect for national integrity and independence. I have unshakable faith and trust in the character and judgement of our people. I am certain the Government is assured of full support in stamping out traitors and anyone who dares to threaten or insult the respect and dignity of our nation.

My Ministers and myself share with you the success, the joys and sorrows of our nation. We are happy to work for each child to get good education, good health and good food. Our youth everywhere are an inspiration in sports and traditional dances; we are all proud of the achievement of the National Youth Service in constructing new roads to Garissa and Moyale and other areas. The Armed Forces, the Police and Civil Servants have upheld the high standards of efficiency and loyalty. There is no other way of building a nation.

Confidence and hard work have led us to this day. The loyalty and effort of the people have done honour to the past and will continue to inspire Kenya's future. We move now into the forth year of our destiny, away from the dark hours of colonial domination into the light of the future.

HARAMBEE.

STATE OPENING OF PARLIAMENT — 1967

Mzee Kenyatta performed the State Opening of the new Parliament on February 15, 1967, outlining the scope and content of the Government's nation-building programme during his Presidential Address. The occasion was of particular significance in that, following further and agreed constitutional adjustment, the former Senate and the House of Representatives had now come together as a single National Assembly:

*

It is with deep satisfaction that I address today a National Assembly that has unified itself into one single chamber. Unity is the desire of our people; it is the hope for our nation.

I rejoice that we now have one House of Parliament which is sovereign for all Kenya. We have demolished many strongholds, and in their place we have built a fortress of unity in this new National Assembly.

To the honourable Members of this Parliament, here assembled on this momentous day, the thanks of the nation are due. In the three years since *Uhuru* you have used your powers to create unity out of disunity. You have been faithful to our people, and to our traditions. By this last act of unification, you have completed a chapter of historic achievement.

The lasting gratitude of the nation should go to the Members of the former Senate, who held in their hands the power to resist the centralization and unification of our institutions of government, but who put the cause of national unity before less worthy ambitions.

The unification of this Parliament is the culmination of our constitutional struggle. We are now equipped for more rapid advance, and my Government is determined that the pace of nation-building shall now be accelerated. The policies and programmes of the Government, about which I shall be speaking, are conceived in that spirit.

The success of our endeavours will demand strength and determination from the Government, mature judgements and loyalty from this Parliament, and above all, hard work from all our people. Let this historic day therefore be, for each one of us, the day on which we rededicate ourselves to the service of the nation.

In the three years since *Uhuru* we have been fashioning a constitution for the Republic of Kenya which embodies our traditions and reflects our aspirations. It is our pride, and evidence of our strength, that the radical changes we have made to the Independence Constitution have all been made by Parliament in the manner provided by the law. Under my instructions the Attorney-General will bring these constitutional labours to full fruition by presenting to this House for approval a revised edition of the Constitution.

The expansion of the economy in 1966 has been encouraging. It has now been calculated that in 1966 the national income rose by approximately 8 per cent. This means that the nation has more than recovered the ground which was lost earlier, due to the drought and to a fall in world prices. This expansion will mean that the Government will have a larger revenue at the existing rates of taxation.

In the new phase of nation-building that is about to begin, the Government will take active measures to ensure more rapid Africanization throughout the whole economy. In the commercial and industrial fields those measures will apply to ownership, and to employment and training at all levels.

In the working towards African ownership in industry the Government and the country have to face certain harsh realities. The level of local savings will, for some time to come, lag behind the country's need for development capital. Industrial success, in a world of competition, requires technical and administrative experience, which sufficient numbers of our people have not yet acquired.

For these reasons, we shall continue to attract the foreign investment needed to supplement our domestic savings and to expand the economy in accordance with the Development Plan. Nevertheless, the Government has decided that the Industrial and Commercial Development Corporation must play a substantial part in future industrial progress. This body will be given additional finance, which will enable it to participate in new industrial ven-

23 Kenyatta, Nation

tures, to assist African enterprises, and also to hold industrial shares until the individual African is in a position to become an investor.

An industrial planning scheme for Kenya is now being prepared. This scheme will be based on a new survey of resources and of the pattern of demand, and it will aim to decentralize future industrial development. Feasibility studies are also being undertaken, with the purpose of promoting more industries, and of attracting the participation of foreign investors in selected projects.

There will be a new emphasis on industrial and commercial expansion. Since *Uhuru* our efforts have been largely concentrated on our agriculture, as it is the backbone of Kenya's economy. This effort will not be slackened, but the time has now come when we can devote considerable planning and material resources to other forms of enterprise. Economic and social advancement cannot be achieved at a sufficient pace in a developing country without the growth of industry.

The Government is giving special attention to our power supplies and communications. It is the duty of the Government to ensure, by far-sighted planning, that industrial and social progress is not retarded by a lack of these basic services. Accordingly, the Government has been working on a 20-year nation-wide development plan for electricity. This plan will shortly be completed. Within that plan, the Kindaruma Dam, which is the first phase of the Seven Forks Projects, should be completed towards the end of this year.

The Government is at the same time pressing ahead with plans for extending the supply of domestic electricity. For example, in this year 1967 it is planned to extend the supply of electricity to Homa Bay, Kwale, Kapsabet, Molo and Turi, and work will begin at Lamu and other places. There are other plans for the extension of supplies to villages, trading centres, irrigation projects, farms and small industrial undertakings, in all parts of Kenya.

The Government is also pressing ahead with road construction. About 70 per cent of the Nairobi-Mombasa road has already been completed to bitumen standard. Within the coming financial year the construction is expected to begin on new tarmac roads between Eldoret and Tororo, and between Athi River and Namanga. In the present financial year, over one and one-quarter million pounds is being spent on general trunk road development, and there is another programme for minor roads in rural areas. In addition, more than a million pounds has been allocated for road networks in tea-growing and sugar-growing districts.

The three East African Governments have guaranteed a United Nations loan of thirteen and one-half million pounds for the modernization of the railways and harbours. The expansion of the Nairobi and Mombasa airports is now being studied.

Our tourist industry is exceeding our expectations. The number of tourists visiting Kenya already greatly exceeds the target in our current Development Plan. This industry is expanding more rapidly than any other. It will soon become our greatest single source of foreign exchange. We look to this industry to provide considerable increased employment and to stimulate the provision of other goods and services.

As envisaged in the Development Plan, new national parks will be established in the coming year, and some existing national parks will be enlarged. The Narok County Council has decided to extend the magnificent Masai Mara Game Reserve. Particular attention is being given to plans for opening up areas of western and northern Kenya for tourists.

The Government is actively developing our fishing industry. Good progress is being made on the coast, especially in the Lamu Area, and at Lake Baringo. Spectacular advances are expected this year on Lake Rudolf. A plan is now being completed for the advancement of the fishing industry in the whole of Nyanza.

The exploitation of our timber resources is gathering momentum. Nation-wide afforestation schemes are in progress. A further 2,000 acres of trees will be planted in the Timboroa Area, for the proposed pulp and paper industry at Broderick Falls. Three new sawmills, one at Nakuru, one in the Nyeri Area and one in the Londiani Area, will come into operation shortly.

Many schemes for new or improved water supplies will be begun, and some will be completed, in this coming year.

While the Government is now placing increasing emphasis on industrial development, we must not forget that agriculture is still the backbone of our country. There will be no relaxation of our efforts to develop our land to increase our crops and to improve the skill of our farmers.

There are clear signs today that unemployment among wage-earners has decreased. Large building and construction programmes are being understaken in our towns. This is a reliable indication of economic expansion. But it only represents the efforts of the Government and large private enterprises in undertaking capital development. The solution of the unemployment problem depends equally on the efforts of the many thousands of our countrymen whose livelihood comes from the land.

I urge all our farmers and stockmen to stick to their task of developing the land to its greatest capacity. They will be helping themselves by increasing their earnings. They will be helping their less fortunate countrymen by creating more employment in agriculture and in other industries associated with agriculture.

The land is the place where the ordinary man and woman can do most to build the nation. When one farmer increases his cultivations and improves his farm by harder work, it is a personal achievement. When ten thousand farmers follow his example, it becomes a national achievement.

For this reason the agricultural policy of the Government will be directed increasingly to the encouragement of personal effort and to the creation of incentives.

I recall at the time of Jamhuri reminding the National Assembly that the Republic is the people. While the Government and this Parliament must be dedicated to the service of the people, we must remember that the people of Kenya are individual men and women who need opportunities for the exercise of their personal initiative and for the fulfilment of their individual ambitions. That is why in this year 1967 the key note of Government policy will be the creation of opportunities for the ordinary citizen, in industry, in trade, and on the land, to improve himself, and to play his full part in the progress of the community. This is the foundation on which we shall build our nation.

Out of the increasing wealth of Kenya we must find the means to expand the social services, and in particular, education and health. The expansion of these services is essential to our plans for sustained economic development. My Government will continue to give the highest priority to education. Education in all developing countries has a vital role to play both in facilitating the fulfilment of the required manpower needs as well as in assisting to raise the standard of living to enable the people to enjoy the good life and to become good citizens. My Government is preparing a broad statement of policy on education which will be based on the recommendations of the Kenya Education Commission Report otherwise known as the Ominde Report. It will be necessary to bring these aspects up to date. Any other necessary changes particularly in the areas of the organization, content and practices of education, will be effected at the existing different levels of educational institutions.

My Government attaches great importance to the extension of the health services. Work is proceeding rapidly to extend a number of hospitals throughout Kenya, and to construct larger out-patient departments.

In a spirit of self help, many people and communities are actively building health centres, as well as collecting money for hospital wards and maternity units. The Ministry of Health will continue to assist and guide these efforts. The Government looks forward to the opening of the new Medical School in Nairobi in July of this year.

The Ministry of Housing has been charged with the task of organizing and financing a programme to ensure decent living accommodation for our people, at rents they can afford. Work to improve the standards of rural housing will also be intensified in the coming year.

The reconstruction and development of the co-operative movement will be pursued with vigour. Under the new Co-operatives Act, the movement will be reconstructed and revitalized. The Government will encourage the establishment of district co-operative unions, with primary societies at village and locational levels. A massive educational programme for officials and members of the co-operative movement has been launched.

That is just an outline of the Government's policies, plans and programmes for the more rapid development of our country. I must now address myself to our relations with our neighbours in Africa.

The progress made so far in our negotiations with our East African brothers in Tanzania and Uganda for the creation of an East African Common Market have been encouraging. We look forward with confidence to the satisfactory conclusion of these negotiations, which should bring immense benefit to East Africa.

When we look in some other directions, however, we have no cause for satisfaction at the present time.

In the North-Eastern Province and neighbouring areas of Kenya, shifta gangs still pursue the cruel and senseless destruction of life and property.

Since Madaraka Day in 1963, many shifta have been killed and many local inhabitants have been murdered by shifta. Nearly two thousand lives have been needlessly sacrified. Casualties in our Security Forces have fortunately been very light. It is the shifta who have suffered, and the local inhabitants whom the shifta have murdered.

The Government will not rest until the last shifta has been
eliminated, and conditions of peace and prosperity have been fully
restored in these areas. The officers and men of our Armed Forces
are experienced and well-equipped, and their resolution is un-
shakeable. I know that this House and the whole nation will wish
me to express our appreciation for the heroic work being done
by these brave men.

Kenya wishes to live in harmony with all her neighbours. We
covet no inch of their territory. We will yield no inch of ours. We
stand loyal to the Organization for African Unity and to its
solemn decision that all African States shall adhere to the
boundaries inherited at independence.

We pray that the day is not far distant when all African States
will see the wisdom of honouring to the full that decision of the
Organization.

All that Kenya wants is an end to bloodshed, misery and
waste, so that our people in the north-eastern areas may play a
full part in our Government's plans for development, and so that
they may enjoy peace in the area and share in full the benefits
of our national prosperity.

My Government remains deeply disturbed by the course of
events in Rhodesia. We will not be satisfied with lip-service to the
principles of human equality and human dignity. We cannot tolerate
the racial oppression of Africans on their own soil. All racial
discrimination is repugnant. We will not rest until this rebellion
has been crushed.

A gang of disloyal settlers has imposed a Police State on the
Rhodesians, black and white alike. They are desperate men. There
may be no limit to the misfortunes they would bring down upon
the Rhodesians rather than surrender. They must be made to
surrender. If one method fails, another more effective method
must be used. We look to those who proclaim their friendship for
Africa, and their belief in justice, to give convincing proof of their
sincerity.

When lawful Government is restored in Rhodesia, it will be the
responsibility of the United Kingdom Government to invite
representatives of all political parties to the conference table, and
to foster reconciliation and the search for constitutional solutions.
There will be no lack of goodwill in Kenya.

The burning issue of Rhodesia has never for a moment made
us forget the plight of our brothers in Angola, Mozambique and

South Africa. They are assured of determined support from the Republic of Kenya in their struggle against cruelty and oppression. During this year we shall look forward to the implementation of the United Nations Resolution on South West Africa. We have noted the growing extremism of the South African Government and the increase of their armaments. But let these last apostles of apartheid remember that no one in history has prevailed for long against the determined demand of the human spirit for freedom and justice.

Kenya seeks to earn the respect of the world. In Kenya we strive for political stability, justice and equality under the law, and material progress. The full riches of our land will be ours if we guard our national unity, plan our resources carefully, and work hard.

The Kenya Government, with the loyal support of this Parliament, may now place before the people the promise of more rapid economic and social advances, bringing more widespread benefit. But to fulfil our promise we must demand from all our people, renewed effort in their work. Our future depends on the faith loyalty and enterprise of our people. This is part of the call I still make to everyone in Kenya: *Harambee!*

KENYATTA DAY — 1967

This whole work may be concluded, not with a set speech from formal script, but virtually with a conversation piece: the address by Mzee Jomo Kenyatta to his people, at a mass rally in Nairobi, on October 20, 1967. The President spoke informally, and in Swahili. There can be no precise reproduction of the substance and style of his words, in any other language: the sincerity, the joviality, the strictures, the overall command. But what follows is a representation — no more — in English of Mzee's views and advice and remarks:

*

I am very happy today that we are all at Kamukunji again, to celebrate this occasion. On this day back in 1952, the whole country was sad. I myself was arrested at night, and was put into an aircraft not knowing where I was going. Around this time (fifteen years ago) I was sitting all alone, trying to make out exactly where I was, as I had never seen that place before...I was not the only one (to suffer). Hundreds of freedom fighters were taken off to different places, without any knowledge of what would happen to them. That indeed was a sad day. I remember how, in the early hours, somebody came to my house — representing the people who wanted me to escape, saying: "We are now ready to help you to escape. You are due to be arrested later today. If you are arrested you will be put in an aeroplane, and then while this is flying the colonialists will drop you through the window. If you are dropped out, nobody will ever know where." My answer then was: "Never mind." But as I had known this informant to be a reliable person, I half expected at any time throughout the flight to be dropped through a window . . . That was a sad time, but through God's will we have come to this day, and to a time for celebration. Brothers, you all know that this day is one of great inspiration. It is very important, because without (the events sparked off by) October 20, 1952, we would still be chained and handcuffed by the colonialists.

Those who do not realise these are foolish men .... Brothers, before I continue with this speech, it would be fitting for us to stand in silence for one minute, in remembrance of thousands of our people who were shot dead, and those who died of diseases, and those who were persecuted by the colonialists ....(Pause) .... My brothers, the minute is over, and I think everyone was recalling the victims and the hardship of those times .... I am telling you now that what we want in this country (today) is UNITY and PEACE. Brothers, there are those who ask: "What is the Government doing?" And there are those who say: "The Government has done nothing as yet." But I am telling you that, even if we had done nothing, I think every citizen should be proud of being free. Each man is free, and is no longer anybody's slave. For a man to say that he is free, and that he is governing himself, is a very important thing. It is likely that many of you (now) do not fully realise what being free means. But I — and some others — know (the significance of) this. I remember one day when we were called out at Lokitaung prison. I myself was ordered: "J.2 come here!" We did not even have names, and had even been told that: "As from today, you should know that you have no names, but numbers." Mine was J.2: the number J.1 had been given to Kungu Karumba. All this has passed into history, but is still saddening. After we were told that we had no names, but only numbers, I went forward (to protest) but was ordered: "Kenyatta, sit down!" ... (Mzee then demonstrated the difficulty of complying with this, due to the manner in which the prisoners were chained) . . . You will realise that if a man wanted to go to the toilet, he had to pull down his trousers. So when we say that we broke the colonialists' chains, don't think that we are just talking (metaphorically) .... Many of us were heavily chained in detention camps and prisons. Try and imagine some of my colleagues having to draw water (from) about two miles away; carrying it in tins on their heads ... (Mzee again demonstrated in mime how this was done) .... Of course some (people) were fortunate and did not experience these things. I do not want to say much today (about it all), but I am just letting you know that people were chained, and that in time all those chains were broken ... Whoever dares say (now) that the Government and the citizens have done nothing must realise that he is an enemy of our country ... I want to tell you, countrymen, that (today) we should never discriminate. Sometimes I hear of freedom fighters described as those who brought Uhuru. But I want to emphasize that freedom could not have been brought by one person, or by a single group of people.

Freedom came (to us) through AFRICAN UNITY. It was all of us being united: those in prisons and detention camps, in the

towns and in the country. We were all seeking freedom (together).
and therefore it is not right to discriminate, saying that one man
served to bring freedom while another man did something else.
All we Africans were in a state of slavery and all of us (together)
brought our freedom. We must, therefore, always remember
that ... Another thing is that Kenyatta Day is not 'Kenyatta's Day".
It was so named because I was the leader, and was (even) called
the "Mau Mau Chief". I remember how during our trial at
Kapenguria, I was told that there were two charges against me.
I was charged first with "leading Mau Mau", for which I was
sentenced to seven years imprisonment and (then) secondly — for
"being a member of Mau Mau" — I was sentenced to three years:
altogether ten years of imprisonment to run concurrently. And
so, brothers, Kenyatta Day is not Kenyatta's (alone) but a day
for all our citizens. It is and should be a day to be remembered
by us all ... While we are all united like this, it will be our duty
to defend our Uhuru, for there are many who want to spoil our
Uhuru, and others who want to ruin our country .... I am saying
(now) that we managed to fight the colonialists, and —as I said
some time ago — we had no guns, although some people used to
steal one here and there.

The people had no guns, but they were all united. I was
(regarded as) the leader, because I used to teach people to know
that they were human beings just like other people, that the
Europeans were not born with different brains, that the Asians
did not come into the world with different brains. We know that
this is true, because in our present schools we succeeded in defeating
them. But because (in the old days) they understood that they
had weak brains, they did not want us to know it. They did not
want us all to go to school together, lest we discover their secret.
But I knew (and had found out) the secret in their own country,
for I used to defeat many of them and discovered that their
theories were baseless .... When they used to say that Kenyatta
was a danger, what did I have? I had no gun. I did not (even) buy
a gun, and if you look at me today I (still) have no gun. But I was
possessed of one thing which they feared: knowledge. Often it is
dangerous to know. They said (to themselves): "This man is
dangerous. He will tell his people all our secrets, and if they know
our secrets, where shall we be?" You remember a Kiswahili saying:
"When an ignorant person becomes enlightened, where will the
clever one (then) go? He will be in trouble." So I became
dangerous, although I had no guns, no atom bombs (or anything).

They themselves had all these things ... What I am saying to
you now is: let us be united. We won our Uhuru, and gained it
because we had unity, and in taking the oath (of office) we
pledged ourselves to work together. People were united (in the

old days), and when it was necessary to use the weapon of UNITY, the people said: "We have no firearms. What shall we do?" They turned to pangas, and through pangas they obtained some guns. We must sometimes chat a little about the past, so that we all can know what took place then .... There are some who roam about in this country saying: "Kenyatta, you have forgotten the freedom fighters." I myself would like to see any freedom fighters who claim that only they themselves — and not everybody in Kenya — brought Uhuru. There is no such thing as being forgotten, for we (were and) are all freedom fighters.

We all fought for Uhuru, and it is only the cowards who used to hide under beds while others were struggling who go about talking of "freedom fighters". Those are the kind of people, loitering about the place, who say that freedom fighters have been forgotten. Suppose we were to ask such a person directly: "Where did you fight? How many weapons did you use? How many guns?" He would be ashamed, because he never really played any part .... All this is true, and when I say these things I shall have to do some denouncing of the KPU (Kenya People's Union). You all know the KPU. Who are the KPU leaders? You all know them as well. Ask them where (and how) they were fighting for Uhuru. Ask them openly — apart from Achieng who was with us at Lokitaung, and maybe Kaggia — and if they come here I would like them to tell us. But in terms of actual struggling (for freedom) who did what and where: what did they do? Nothing! They only go about cheating people (by saying) that freedom fighters have been forgotten. And even if we had forgotten them, what have these other people done for them? We have in fact given (to many freedom fighters) shambas and other things. What have the KPU ever done for anybody? I am telling you that these (KPU leaders) were once my friends. I taught most of them politics. Now I am calling upon them to change their minds and return to KANU before it is too late, or else the door will be closed, and when we close the door (it is final) ... I am telling you now — and I want you to listen attentively, as I don't talk nonsense — that if you see a KPU man, and some of them are here, know then that you have seen a snake hiding in the grass. He dare not come out (into the open). What do you do when you see a snake? ... (Answer: we kill it!') ... I do not want to see people spoiling our Uhuru. So as from today, KPU are to be regarded as snakes (in the grass). I repeat that as from today they are snakes. We shall call them so because — although I sympathise with some who were my friends before they ran away — perhaps their brains were not working properly. Let them try and re-examine their minds and return to KANU. If they do not do so, KPU should beware! The fighting for our Uhuru is on. Whoever has ears to hear, let him heed this. We say we are ready to fight for our Uhuru.

We do not want these people who have nothing good to do (or to contribute), but seek only to spoil our country, to deceive the citizens. I am (deliberately) stressing this, my brothers, and I am telling those KPU (members) who are present to mark what we are saying, so they can go and tell their friends that, as from today, we call them snakes. And if any of them dare to bring their nonsense here, we shall crush them like snakes .... I myself have no more mercy (left), although I have always been very merciful. Such people are (similar to) the ones who cause trouble in countries like Nigeria and elsewhere. Who did you think ruined countries like that? Such people should flee. Let me tell you why I am saying that such people are snakes: because there was a group of people who wanted to spoil East Africa through bribery. Some of their friends who were in East Africa have already fled. I do not want to interfere in other people's affairs, but there are some people who have already run away because things were serious in their own countries. I want all such people in our country — if they do not want to co-operate with us — to do the same: (that is) to go to the countries from whence they are being bribed and live there (instead). They themselves know what I am talking about, for they had their own secret organisaton, but I have discovered their secret. What did they want to do? They wanted to bring a revolution to the whole of East Africa, but through God's will we found them out.

This is why now — on Kenyatta Day — I am telling these people that we have already discovered their plans. We know their associates, with whom they have been consulting. I am telling them that they are too late, and I am declaring these people snakes: from today we shall all know the work of snakes. Brothers, I am saying that if we have such enemies amongst us, then they should know that a thief has only forty days and no more ... So, my countrymen, we want PEACE in our country, because we want prosperity, and that comes through capital. If we have (and attract) capital, we shall have more business opportunities and employment in the country for our people. So, my brothers, let us be patient. You have already witnessed the reconstruction of Kariokor. Our next project is to rebuild Majengo in the Pumwani area, so that (more of) our people can live better. Everywhere we are building houses for the people, and providing them with shambas. You heard recently that I went to the Coast to distribute some shambas to citizens there who want to farm. I am soon going to (visit) Nyandarua to provide land to those who live in villages. We have also made arrangements to provide people who live in Kiambu — and who are still in villages — with better settlements. So what other magic do you want us to apply? We are doing all we can.

Up-country as well, we are proceeding to settle the Nandi and others. Yet there are still people who say we are doing nothing. What (in fact) do they want us to do? To go and cultivate their shambas in their home areas for them? That we cannot do, but we are pushing ahead (with policy and planning) ... Brothers, I am advising you that if you have any shamba — even if it is a small one — cultivate it. I know that there are some of you here who prefer the city life, leaving your fathers and mothers, brothers and sisters, behind at home struggling in the shambas while you are in town, and in some cases gambling. There are men in this City — and here I am going to reveal something else — who are worse than the prostitutes, because they also engage themselves in prostitution. They go and collect young girls from their homes and bring them into town, and start roaming about from hotel to hotel asking foreigners: "Do you want a woman?" What kind of men are these, who (would) sell their sisters to foreigners? Such people will be cursed by God for their filthy deeds, yet they call themselves men. I have heard also that some of them go out and sell themselves, and perhaps some of that type are right here (today). They act like women, and yet you see them loitering about in trousers ... Now listen, my brothers. I am telling you that your Government cares for the citizens. I have decided to reduce Graduated Personal Tax for those who used to pay Shs. 48/- to Shs. 24/- only ... (Applause) ... That is the work of KANU, to care for its people. But what is the KPU doing? ... In addition — last year — I launched the "Jomo Kenyatta Foundation." This is in effect a collection of funds to help the citizens. In January 1968, we shall give scholarships to 100 students for four-year Secondary School education. I shall make sure (in this) that every Province will be represented. I have set aside Shs. 40,000/- to educate these 100 students in Secondary Schools — and more funds will be collected to increase this amount — so that they may complete four years without paying a single cent. Later on, we will be able to educate more children by offering scholarships to those who would not otherwise have gone to Secondary Schools, due to lack of ability to pay the fees. This is action, and not mere words. This is (an example of) what we want to achieve for the citizens ... Countrymen, let us consider now our relationship with the Somalis. We want to try peaceful means to solve this problem.

This endeavour started in Kinshasa, where I sent Mr. Moi to represent me. He conferred with others, and President Kaunda

was made the Chairman (of a mediating group or committee).
At the end of this month we shall be meeting at Arusha, and I
shall lead the Kenya delegation for discussions with President
Kaunda and the Prime Minister of Somalia, in an effort to find
means of ending this problem of misunderstanding. Now, brothers,
on your behalf today — because this is Kenyatta Day — I shall
offer an amnesty to the shifta lasting for one month until November
20. All those shifta, including those in high command inside
Somalia, who will surrender themselves and their arms, will be
forgiven, regardless of their past crimes.

All those who are now listening should therefore inform and
advise the shifta to surrender. We are doing this as a sign of
goodwill, in preparation for the talks, so that when we arrive for
the discussions they will know that we mean good neighbourliness.
I am conveying on your behalf to the shifta the message that
we will forgiven them ... Now, countrymen, there are a few other
things that I would like to tell. We cannot end Kenyatta Day
without remembering our brothers in South Africa, Mozambique,
Angola, and those even nearer to us in Rhodesia. If we are free
while they are not, our freedom is meaningless.

We pledge (ourselves) to help them in any way possible, to
set them free from colonial slavery. It is a duty of every citizen
to help, and to remember our brothers who are in such a state ...
Brothers, after ending this rally, I want all of us to go home
and live peacefully, remembering that we attained our Uhuru
through blood and sweat ... Although I ask you to forgive those
who have (in the past) offended us, there is a section among the
Europeans and Asians who are still proud ... (arrogant) ... and
who regard the Africans as their slaves instead of as fellow human
beings. I am warning these people. They know our record, and
they know that we are not weak. I do not want such a group to
humiliate our people. But I am telling you as well that many
of you allow yourselves to be insulted.

Many of you are abused like children, and just say: "Never
mind, I'll go and tell Kenyatta". But if someone abuses you, he is
a man just like yourself, so give him a blow ... (i.e. give him as
good as you get) ... What is the point of coming to tell me that
you have been abused? Why let yourself be abused in the first
place: do you not have two hands? I do not want you to cause
trouble. I want us all to live in peace. But if a man insults you
for nothing (it is different), and even I cannot tolerate this. I would
deal with him accordingly. You should know, therefore, that you
are the boss in this country. But some of you still have the
colonial mentality. If you see a person of another colour, you say:
"This is a European, or an Asian".

But today you should realise — and telling you this was why I was called dangerous — that you are men and women like any other people. Do not let anybody look down on you. Be proud, knowing that you are the rulers of this country. Are you not the rulers of this country? Do you think it is Kenyatta alone? This is not so. I am not ruling: it is you. Let other people know that you are not weak, for this is what makes them despise you. Some of you cannot even talk to another person, or — when you speak — you cannot look straight into his eyes, so that your eyes look down like a woman being seduced.

I want every one of you to know and to appreciate that this is our country, and our soil, irrespective of how rich any other person may be. (The act of) self-governing is more important than wealth ... Brothers, I want you all to be good Kenya citizens, to obey the laws of your Government, and all of you to understand (both) that there is a Government and that the Government is yours. Who elected me? ... (Answer: "We did") ... In that case you are important to me, because if you do not use your votes, whom shall I govern? ... When you are electing a representative, try to elect somebody who will be able to represent you properly, somebody who understands and appreciates your problems.

Do not pick on a person just because he speaks English. The English language is nothing, and cannot do anything for you. What matters is trustworthiness, integrity, and helping the citizens. I am telling you that if an M.P. or a Minister does not work for you properly, tell him: "We elected you to work for us, and not just to live in Nairobi" ... I myself work in Nairobi, and I have a nice house called 'State House' to work in. You gave me this house, but I have never slept in that house even for a single night, because it is full of colonial ghosts.

I work during the day, and then after work I go home to my shamba and have a look at my bananas, potatoes, poultry and other things. If you elect somebody who spends all his time in Nairobi doing nothing: what good is that? What does such a person — whether an M.P. or a City Councillor or a KANU official — show us he is doing back at his home and in his shamba, where his parents are? Of what use is it roaming about in Nairobi in bars and hotels? This only brings poverty and prostitution in this country. Many of you write letters blaming the women, saying that these women prostitutes are spoiling Nairobi, but you do not tell the truth. It is the men who are prostitutes.

If a man did not go to a woman, what would that woman do? ... Brothers, I would like to end our rally now, because we have another function at State House to honour many of our

Ministers who are present here: because they have done a good job, and also to encourage them to go on working well. This (ceremony) will also include some of our brave men in the Army and Police, acknowledging their good work in the North Eastern Province and elsewhere. I hope you will think of us during this function, which some of you will attend... I wish to thank you all very much for having come here in such large numbers. We want the KPU to tell us: who are these citizens on whose behalf they claim to speak? Where are they? Can the KPU show us such a large gathering of citizens as this?... Before we end, let us cry out HARAMBEE three times. But first, those of you who want us to do away with KPU, put up your hands... (Vociferous demonstration)... Thank you very much. Now those of you who have faith in KANU and its Government, put up your hands... (Tumultuous demonstration)... Thank you all very much again... HARAMBEE!

Published by the East African Publishing House, Uniafric House, Koinange Street, P.O. Box 30571, Nairobi, Kenya, and printed in letterpress by afropress ltd., P.O. Box 30502, Saldanha Lane, Nairobi.